Effective Communication for Modern Business

Phil Baguley

McGRAW-HILL BOOK COMPANY

London · New York · St Louis · San Francisco · Auckland
Bogotá · Caracas · Lisbon · Madrid · Mexico
Milan · Montreal · New Delhi · Panama · Paris · San Juan
São Paulo · Singapore · Sydney · Tokyo · Toronto

Published by
McGRAW-HILL Book Company Europe
Shoppenhangers Road, Maidenhead, Berkshire, SL6 2QL, England
Telephone 0628 23432
Fax 0628 770224

British Library Cataloguing in Publication Data

Baguley, Phil
Effective Communication for Modern Business
I. Title
651.7

ISBN 0-07-707827-6

Library of Congress Cataloguing-in-Publication Data

Baguley, Phil.
Effective communication for modern business / Phil Baguley.
 p. cm.
Includes bibliographical references and index.
ISBN 0-07-707827-6
1. Communication in organizations. 2. Communication in management.
3. Business communication. 4. Interpersonal communication.
5. Communication in organizations—Problems, exercises, etc. I. Title.
HD30.3.B338 1994   93-37967
658.4′5--dc20   CIP

12345 CUP 97654

Typeset by Computape (Pickering) Ltd., Pickering, North Yorkshire
and printed and bound in Great Britain at the University Press, Cambridge.

CONTENTS

PREFACE

We are all, whether we realize it or not, in the communications business. Our involvement starts at our mother's breast and continues to (and it is believed by some beyond) the grave. For some of us, this involvement becomes the core issue of our working lives and involves us in reaching others through the printed word and pictures or through images on large or small screens. For others of us, the challenges of communicating with others are those which we meet on a less public and day-to-day basis, but in just as effective and valuable ways.

The need to communicate with others appears to be of one of those basic needs which is common to all of the family of humankind, whatever their race, gender, religion or social grouping.

This process of communication is inextricably interwoven in the 'warp and weft' of all our lives and the integrity of our individual actions in carrying out that process can significantly influence the quality of our lives. The probity of our communications affects, limits and enhances our choices and potentials in love, war and work. It is, as Carl Rogers[1] so eloquently reminds us, a key element in that process of 'becoming a person'.

This book focuses upon those aspects of communication that are particular, though not uniquely so, to the process of managing.

Managers work in organizations, and these organizations are, as Gareth Morgan[2] vividly illustrates 'generally complex, ambiguous and paradoxical'. These organizations are also diverse in terms of history, size, structure, culture, technology, geographical location and evolutionary stage, but they are all, as H. Igor Ansoff[3] describes, 'purposive organizations whose behaviour is directed towards identifiable end purposes or objectives'. While the nature of these end purposes or objectives may differ from organization to organization, their use of and dependence upon the skills and abilities of people in the achievement of those objectives will not. In reality, this dependence upon human beings is more deeply rooted than the organization's dependence upon money or raw materials or other resources. These people do not, as Pugh and Hickson[4] point out, only work for the organization – *they are that organization*. It is in the management of this human resource that those aspects which are common to all managerial roles are contained. The value and contribution of consistent, effective communication to that process of managing people is considerable. Indeed, it can be argued that without effective, open and truly interactive communication, the process of management becomes a habit-based routine which does little to inspire or empower those who are managed.

Throughout its design and creation this book has been envisaged as a working text or examination preparation book for management courses. As such it will be of value to:

- Undergraduate business studies courses, such as BA or BSc in Business Studies or Business Administration.

- Graduate and post-experience students on business and management programmes, such as entry-level MBA, Diploma in Management, Certificate in Management, IPM.
- Professional and technical courses whose contents include a module or section on what is often called 'interpersonal skills'.

While written as a textbook, it will also be valuable to practising managers as well as those professionals such as lawyers, accountants, nurses, doctors, builders and engineers who, while they may not carry the title of manager, are responsible for the work of others.

The book is built around the idea that communication is a dynamic, interactive, lively, fruitful and, if we allow it to be, often enjoyable process. This process, if executed well, can be used to convey facts, ideas and feelings powerfully and effectively, and in so doing exert considerable influence on the behaviour, motivation and performance of others. However, the intention is not that readers should consume this book at one reading but that they should dip into and browse through it. It is also intended that they should continue to use and refer to it as their experience and skills grow. The content of the book combines theory and practice, with the text strongly based on theoretical concepts, but with useful ideas and pointers to appropriate methods and helpful tools.

For communication to be effective it needs to be prepared, planned and undertaken with care and thought. This book is aimed to encourage students of business and management, as well as practising managers, to start and continue that process with hope, confidence and enthusiasm.

The book has four parts. Part One provides an introduction and background to the theory (Chapter 1) and context (Chapter 2) of the communication process. Part Two is concerned with those aspects of communication which involve the use of the spoken word and examines the processes of listening (Chapter 3), interviewing (Chapter 4), negotiating (Chapter 5), working in teams and groups (Chapter 6) and presenting (Chapter 7). The written word is examined in Part Three, with Chapter 8 examining the process of generating text and Chapter 9 dealing with the use of that text in generating a wide range of business documents.

Part Four examines the relevance and contribution to the communication process of what is often called 'body language' in Chapter 10, style and other issues in Chapter 11 and images, icons and information in Chapter 12. There follows a list of further recommended reading material.

Each of the chapters contains exercises for group or individual use and many of them also contain, as appendices, self-assessment questionnaires which will help readers to apply the concepts and theories described in that chapter. These self-assessment questionnaires are not intended as formal or rigorous tests, but as mechanisms to help readers to identify and achieve their own learning goals.

In a number of the examples given throughout the book, the names of people and organizations have been used to add to the verisimilitude of the material. These names and addresses of firms, organizations and individuals are all fictitious and any resemblance to the name or address of an existing firm, organization or individual is coincidental.

Acknowledgement is made of the early vision and confidence shown by Brendan Lambon of McGraw-Hill who saw the future shape and potential of this book, and the patience and understanding shown by my production editor, Lavinia Porter. Also for the early support and help given by John McCullough, who, as a colleague and friend, was there at the beginning when he was needed. Finally, my special thanks to Linda, who became my wife during the writing of this book and who gave her counsel and support so generously and unconditionally during that process.

REFERENCES

1. Rogers, C., *A Way of Being*, Houghton Mifflin Company, Boston, 1980.
2. Morgan, G., *Images of Organisations*, Sage, London, 1986.
3. Ansoff, H. I., *Corporate Strategy*, Penguin, London, 1968.
4. Pugh, D. S. and Hickson, D. J., *Writers on Organisations*, Penguin, London, 1989.

THE OVERALL PICTURE

'Communication, to be effective, cannot be a haphazard process.'
John Adair

ONE

COMMUNICATION – WHAT'S IT ALL ABOUT?

'Good communication is as stimulating as black coffee – and just as hard to sleep after.'
Anne Morrow Lindebergh

INTRODUCTION

There can be little doubt that, for most of us, the ability to communicate is important – indeed vital – to our lives, whether at work or at play. However, this core skill or competence is not something for which we are formally trained or educated. Most of the training or education that we undertake or expose ourselves to is aimed at acquiring the specialized knowledge that we need to do our jobs and to be, for example, good accountants, social workers or engineers.

And yet accountants, social workers, engineers, doctors, teachers, nurses, salespersons and managers are just a few examples of roles in which effective communication is important. Ellis and Whittington[1] state that while there are very few jobs which are devoid of interaction with others, there are some jobs which 'have skilled interaction as a primary focus'. For example, reviews[2] of management consulting practices suggest that 70 per cent of assignment time is spent communicating with others, with the remaining 30 per cent being spent on problem analysis and related matters.

It is also evident that the job of a manager is one of those jobs whose focal point is skilled interaction and that managers spend a considerable portion of their working lives in communication with others. McCall *et al.*[3] report that managers spend up to 90 per cent of their time talking to others, and Stewart[4] found that almost a third of a manager's time is spent in one-to-one meetings. Peters[5] writes about the need for managers both to express the empowering vision *and* to stay in touch with the needs of the real world in which that vision is being implemented. Many of the professional roles mentioned above are also increasingly involved in areas of activity outside their specialism and associated with decisions about the use of resources and people, i.e. the process of managing. This shift demands the use of more generalized communication skills, as distinct from the knowledge-based and technical skills associated with their profession.

So communicating is something that all managers, whatever their job title might be, are involved in, all of the time.

Yet communicating appears to be a process to which these managers give little attention and often take for granted!

Horn and Lupton[6] found that managers are consistent in their underestimation of the amount of time they spend in one-to-one communication and Handy[7] states that organizational communications are typically poor, with examples of information retention levels lying in the range 20–50 per cent. As communication pervades all that managers do, even small improvements in that process will benefit their working lives enormously. Smithson[8] states that success in management depends upon being a good communicator. However, the development of this communicative skill and ability is not something that happens overnight. It is a part of the process of growth and development that everyone experiences. For example, children quickly learn to use language as a way of communicating. Lovell[9] reports that an average child's active vocabulary grows from three words at twelve months of age to over 2000 words at five years of age. Morris[10] describes this rate of language acquisition as being unique to our species, and states that it is related to the pressing need for 'more precise and helpful communication'. The patterns of this communication change as the child grows, experiences the upheavals of adolescence and moves into adult life. By then the common skills or core competences are seen[11] to be:

- The ability to receive and respond to a variety of information.
- The ability to present information in visual forms.
- The ability to communicate in writing.
- The ability to participate in oral and non-verbal communication.

The effectiveness with which managers demonstrate and use these abilities can make a considerable difference to their performance. In their initial management roles, managers will be expected[12] to be able to write reports, undertake presentations and to motivate their staff. As experience and role responsibilities grow these abilities will also extend to include those associated with interviewing, negotiating, appraising and counselling. Skilled and experienced managers will also be able to use a range of verbal and non-verbal skills that result in people feeling valued and being given feedback.

All of this communication takes place within a social environment, and as such is often described as a social skill. But it is, nevertheless, a skill or group of skills that some managers are better at than others.

This book is about communication between people in the social environment of work and those interactions in which managers, whatever their job title, are involved on a day by day basis. There can be little doubt about the importance of this process. Whether managers' communications are primarily one-to-one or within a group or team it is essential that they manage the process of communication effectively. Failure to do so in the workplace will not only limit the managers' effectiveness but also the effectiveness of those with whom they communicate.

Managers communicate with a very wide range of people during their working day. Examples of these people and the groups that they fall into might, for example, include:

- Their boss.
- Fellow managers.
- Staff and team members.
- Staff from other departments.
- Customers, clients, patients.
- Union representatives.
- Suppliers of goods and services.
- Competitors.
- Who knows who else!

The list could be almost endless – and all of them are also trying to communicate with their managers. Managers may also need to be aware of, and able to influence, the communications flowing between other members of the teams or groups in or with which they work. Peters and

Waterman[13] state that innovation is fostered within such teams when organizational communication systems:

- are informal
- display 'extraordinary' intensity
- are given physical supports
- act as 'forcing devices'
- act as tight control systems

It is argued by many writers that the importance of communicative ability will increase in the future. Makridakis[14] in attempting to predict the type of manager most likely to emerge in the 21st century states that 'dealing with people will always remain a critical management task'. However, the nature of that task is seen as changing to one that involves the management of smaller numbers of people who are in more creative roles. Pedler *et al.,*[15] in describing the 'Learning Company' of the future, identify 'Internal Exchange' as one of eleven characteristics of such an organization and identify the need for managers to 'facilitate communication, negotiation and contracting rather than exerting top-down control' as a part of that characteristic. A Massachusetts Institute of Technology review of American industrial performance,[16] conducted at the end of the 1980s, observed that communications in many US companies were restrained by 'steep hierarchical ladders and organizational walls'. This study also identified the need for greater employee involvement so that the employee becomes a 'full participant in the enterprise – with obvious communication implications. Bartlett and Ghoshal[17] report that organizations that are able to change their structure successfully have done so by the creation and communication of a 'corporate vision'.

So, given that communication is important and, indeed, unavoidable, for managers, the first step will be to define what is meant when we use the word 'communication'.

COMMUNICATION – MEANINGS AND DEFINITIONS

A typical dictionary definition for the process of communication identifies that it involves the actions of imparting, bestowing, revealing and sharing with others. A typical thesaurus also suggests meanings of interaction and conversation. Further probing will reveal synonyms of intercourse, transmission, contact, connection and touch. A more formal, though restricted, view of this process is taken by the definition[18] which sees communication as:

The process by which information is passed between individuals and/or organisations by means of previously agreed symbols

However, our own experience tells us that communication in the workplace can be concerned with any aspect of our interactions with others. It can be, for example, not only concerned with passing information but also expressing praise or displeasure or opinions. It can also be about maintaining or initiating social relationships by, for example, merely passing the time of day. Kakabadse *et al.*[19] report that communications are about

- facts
- feelings
- values
- opinions

Hargie[20] suggests that skill in communication is a social skill by means of which the individual is able to 'interact effectively' with others.

From these comments about communication it is evident that this process occurs when ideas, information and feelings are conveyed from individual to individual. However, communication is not restricted to one-to-one situations. It can also take place when an individual addresses a group, crowd or audience of people or when one group interacts with another group or within a group itself, with several people involved in the process. This process of communication is one which is capable of use in a wide range of circumstances and for a wide variety of purposes. The definition that will be used in this book is that:

Communication is the process that occurs when ideas, information and feelings are conveyed between individuals or groups of individuals for deliberate purposes.

The process of communication is not limited to conveying information *or* ideas *or* feelings at the same time. All of these can be conveyed or transmitted simultaneously. When individuals communicate with others they are often conveying, at the same time, not just ideas or information, but also feelings. For example, someone may tell their manager that the report that they are writing will be a week later than had been promised. The manager may tell the person that he or she is not happy with that and ask for that completion date to be improved on. But the content of the message that the manager sends is not limited to the words spoken. When the manager speaks then the tone of voice will be part of the message that is sent. If those involved in this interaction can see each other, then gesture, use of space, body contact and facial expression will also be a part of the message that is sent.

One way of differentiating between the different parts of the message in this example is shown in Fig. 1.1. This figure indicates that communication can be classified initially on the basis of whether it is:

● *Linguistic* in nature, i.e. based on language. This will include all aspects of the use of language in speech and writing.

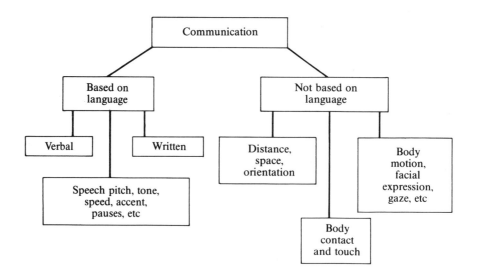

Figure 1.1 Classifications of communication.

- *Non-linguistic* in nature, i.e. not based on language. This will encompass all bodily communication.

Language-based or *linguistic* communication covers all aspects of language use, including:

- The words used and their verbal or written content and meaning.
- The tone, speed, volume, pitch and accent of speech, i.e. the paralingual content.

Non-linguistic communication is divided into:

- Body contact and touch (tacesics).
- Interpersonal distance and territory (proxemics).
- Facial expression, head movements, posture, gestures, gaze, etc. (kinesics).

As we saw in the earlier example, communication is often thought of as a one-way process, as in telling someone something. But communication is not a one-way process. All communication is a two-way process – however it is undertaken. Even when the communication is primarily concerned with issuing instructions about what to do or where to go, the listener is providing the speaker with feedback. This feedback does not have to be linguistic – it can be concerned with the expression on the listener's face, whether the listener is looking at the speaker and what his or her body posture is. All of these provide the speaker with feedback as to whether the message has been heard and understood and what the listener feels about that message or the speaker.

One of the earliest models for the process of communication was produced by Shannon and Weaver[21] as a result of their work in the Bell Telephone Company Laboratories. However, this model, perhaps because of the influence of what was then the developing field of information theory, viewed communication as a one-way linear or sequential process in which Transmitter and Receiver alternated, i.e. one person speaks and then the other speaks. An example of a simple sequential communication process is illustrated in Fig. 1.2, where Tx and Rx are the Transmitter and Receiver, respectively. However, experience tells us that communication can flow in both directions at the same time: for example, when someone smiles at you *as*, rather than *after*, you speak to them. The linear or sequential nature of the process portrayed in this early model can also be challenged by more recent neurobiological evidence,[22] which suggests that this aspect of the operation of our brains involves a series of interacting and parallel operating 'structures'.

The manager who is aware of the need for and value of effective communication would have, in preparing the message, taken into account a number of factors about the intended receiver. These, among other things, would have included the receiver's language, proximity and availability. The manager's message would have used appropriate language in the verbal or written

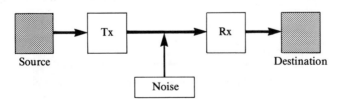

Figure 1.2 Simple model of the communication process.

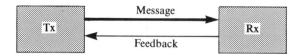

Figure 1.3 Communication with feedback.

medium and a transmission channel, i.e. telephone, face-to-face, letter, etc., which would have given the manager a reasonable expectation that the message would be received and understood.

However, the manager needs feedback to gauge whether and how the message had been received. Figure 1.3 indicates how this feedback, which may be limited to a nod or a grunt, operates, and shows the receiver sending a comment or reaction (feedback) back.

Some views of communications called this type of interchange 'partial communication', because the Transmitter is still the chief communicator – the Receiver, in this instance, is only communicating information indicating the receipt of the Transmitter's communication. But, it is, nevertheless, an example of two-way communication, and merits being viewed as such. Despite the fact that the feedback is non-linguistic, it can be just as meaningful and valid as the original message. In many face-to-face situations, this level of feedback is acceptable. For example, the manager may have given an instruction to someone to work overtime, and only needs an acknowledgement that the person has heard what the manager has said.

But this can and does change when the content of the feedback contains more than an acknowledgement of the message. For example, the employee might respond to the manager's instruction by saying '*OK – but can I ring George first?*'. When the feedback contains as much information (from the Receiver) as the original message, then the picture changes to that shown in Fig. 1.4.

In this interchange the Transmitter and the Receiver are roles which can alternate and overlap. Both of them can fully convey information, ideas and feelings. This process is sometimes called full communication. Examples might include:

● Conversations with high levels of openness and intimacy, e.g. between close friends.
● Conversations between individuals with shared concerns or objectives, e.g. colleagues or team members.
● Some appraisal interviews.
● Some but not all team or project meetings.
● Letters between close friends.

This process gives managers feedback about their own message *and* a message back in return.

The full detail of the communications process is illustrated in Fig. 1.5, where:

● *Encoding* will involve choosing the appropriate 'code' or language to use. This will need to be appropriate for Receivers and their skills, language and abilities and also appropriate to the

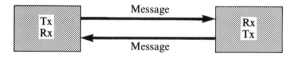

Figure 1.4 Messages.

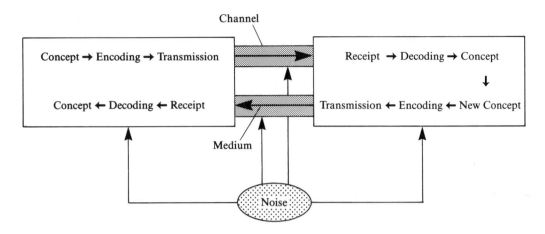

Figure 1.5 The communication process.

channel and medium used. Examples of inappropriate 'coding' might include the use of technical jargon, which could confuse the Receiver, or the use of very formal language at an informal social event.

- *Decoding* means interpreting the information sent, and can mean translating to another language or understanding what a nod or a wink means. Neisser[23] says that this is a part of a larger process, for which he uses the term 'cognition' and which he describes as 'all the processes by which the sensory input is transformed, reduced, elaborated, stored, recovered and used'. Hargie and Marshall[24] state that individuals skilled in this process are able to 'size up' people and situations.

- *Noise* means any form of interference with the message, which has the result of reducing the quality or strength of the message 'signal' or generating spurious, distracting or inaccurate information. This can be external (traffic noise, bad telephone line, a bad fax copy, a misspelled or incorrectly used word) or internal (preoccupation with other messages, a headache, strong negative feelings about the Transmitter).

- *Channel and medium* These are often used interchangeably or confused. This book will use *medium* as the means of communication, e.g. the spoken word or written word and *channel* as the conduit through which the message passes, e.g. a book, note, telephone call, film, etc.

REASONS FOR COMMUNICATION

Communication was defined earlier in this chapter as that process which occurs when ideas, information and feelings are conveyed from individual to individual or group to group. So communication is about transmitting and receiving ideas, facts or feelings. We have already noted that communication is an example of social skilled behaviour. As such it does not occur without cause or reason or in a disordered manner. In common with all social acts, communication will be subject to the rules or norms for social behaviour. If it is to be effective, the nature of the communication must be such that it is perceived by others to be appropriate to the situation. Communication is also generally undertaken with an objective or outcome in mind. So what are these outcomes?

Obviously, we communicate for a wide range of reasons, but generally because we want to influence other people and their attitudes and perceptions, and ultimately their behaviour. That is, we want to affect the way that they:

● think and feel about things

and/or

● do things

In order to achieve these objectives, managers need to ensure that:

● both they and the receiver(s) have a full understanding of the message.
● the receiver or receivers respond in the required manner.

Managers are involved in communication, the main purposes of which can be classified as follows:

Instructing

The purpose of instructing is to change the ways in which people act or behave. Examples are:

● *'The nut A is now placed on the top of screw D.'*
● *'I am writing to instruct you to ensure the completion of this project on time and to budget.'*
● *'Write to me when you return.'*

Influencing

When managers influence people then they are motivating (in a negative or positive way), persuading or encouraging. The outcome should be a clear and identifiable change in behaviour. However, the difference between influencing and instructing is that influencing is:

● less explicit
● can be:
  — encouraging
  — suggesting

An example might be:

> *'If we attain our monthly sales target, it would mean that you all share, under the new incentive scheme, in the benefits of this achievement.'*

Exchanging Information

This involves:

● *Giving information,* i.e. informing people. The receiver may need this information in order to, for example, make a better decision or to be better able to inform someone else, e.g. a customer. The information given might include:

— Facts: '*Turnover was up by 10 per cent last month*'.
— Ideas: '*Why don't we do it this way?*'.
— Interpretations based on facts: '*She persists in not reacting to falling sales*'.
— Feelings about all of the above: '*I believe that, based on the evidence available, it is time for us to move into a new marketing strategy.*'

● *Seeking information*
This is the opposite of giving information, and can be achieved by:
— Asking questions: '*How do you do that?*'.
— Giving information about needs: '*I'd like to know more about that*'.
— Showing openness to receive information: '*Yes, I would like to hear about your holiday.*'

Managers can, of course, combine all of the above types of communication. However, they will have to decide what is the main purpose of that communication.

WAYS OF COMMUNICATING

As shown in Fig. 1.1, we communicate through a variety of media with an initial distinction being made between the use (linguistic based) or non-use (non-linguistic based) of words. The purpose of the communication will also influence both the medium and the channel used.

The factors that influence the 'how' of communications are:

● *Objective* Managers need to be clear about whether they are persuading, informing, questioning or instructing, because all of these objectives will influence the choice of both the medium and the channel used. For example, disciplinary processes will generally need to be recorded in writing, with the use of clear unambiguous language, because of the need to have a record and to make sure that the recipient understands. However, before deciding which make of computer to buy for their department, managers may choose to explore options or choices before taking a formally recorded decision and to do so verbally and face to face (rather than over the telephone) with individual colleagues.
● *Needs* The nature of the message (formal, informal, confidential, etc.), who is receiving it (boss, the project team, the machine shop, etc.), the channels available and their cost (meetings, letters, telephone calls, faxes, conference calls), the need to record the content and/or the feedback, the need to ensure consistency of message – all of these, and others, significantly influence the 'how' of communications.

Samples of management communication are shown in Table 1.1, together with comment about the media and channels used and receiver and message needs. In general, the factors that the manager needs to be aware of are:

● *The spoken word*
— is the most direct form of communication.
— can be done formally (interviews) or informally (discussions).
— can be done briefly or at length.
— can be recorded but requires additional equipment to do so.
— can be an expression of personal style.
— can be done with individuals or groups.
— can be face-to-face or remote (telephone).

Table 1.1   Samples of management communication

Example	Channel	Medium	Message requirement for effective communication	Receiver requirement for effective communication
Change in company logo.	Notice on noticeboard.	Language: • written	• Concise • Clear	Able and willing to read and understand.
Sanction of new manufacturing equipment.	Note to managers.	Language: • written	• Concise • Clear	Able and willing to read and understand.
	Briefing of staff by managers.	Language and non-language: • verbal • partial communication	• Concise • Clear • Lack of jargon • Responsive to questions	Able and willing to listen and understand.
Company annual results.	• Video • Company written results	Language and non-language: • written • verbal	• Concise • Clear • Lack of jargon	Able and willing to listen and understand.
Team's weekly performance review.	Meeting of all team members.	Language and non-language: • full communication • verbal	• Concise • Clear • Lack of jargon • Open to questions and feedback	Able and willing to listen, discuss respond and understand.

    — makes people feel that they have been consulted or involved.
    — can lead to interchange of feelings as well as facts or ideas.
    — provides a means for those involved to share and compare.
    — facilitates non-verbal communication and immediate feedback when face-to-face.
    — can be influenced by rules or norms about style and content.
  • *The written word*
    — is indirect in nature.
    — can be done formally or informally.
    — can be done briefly or at length.
    — can, for the experienced writer, reflect an individual style.
    — is often, in organizations, subject to 'rules' about style and presentation.
    — enables more thought to be put into the choice of words through the process of generation.
    — can be reshaped until writer is satisfied.
    — enables writer to express his or her own ideas and feelings without having to respond to others' reactions and responses.
    — can be easily copied and so provides physical evidence of transmission and content.
    — can be sent to a number of people at the same time.

- *Non-linguistic communication*
  — is often described as 'body language'.
  — requires direct contact between Transmitter and Receiver.
  — operates in parallel with the verbal process.
  — can reinforce, contradict or neutralize the spoken word.
  — is often more effective at communicating feelings.
  — is often not consciously used or perceived.
  — can, if used well, make significant differences to the effectiveness of communication.
  — may lead to guesses not just about what others are thinking or feeling at the time but, more basically, about what kind of person the other is.

COMMUNICATION DIFFICULTIES

Communication is not always successful. The reasons for this can be as varied as the messages sent, but examples might include illegibly written or printed letters, wrongly addressed letters, whispered comments that are misheard and misunderstood, shouted expressions of affection and messages with a warm content that are said without a smile. These and many others are examples of our inability to communicate effectively.

So why does it happen?

There are a number of reasons that can prevent people from exchanging ideas and feelings as effectively as they might, and these can be classified as follows:

- *Lack of clear objectives* This leads to uncertainty of message (i.e. the Transmitter cannot decide what to say) and may be due to not knowing what or how the Receiver needs to be told, or not wishing to offend, upset or shock them.
- *Faulty transmission* means that while the Transmitter knows what he or she wants to say, the message is sent by the wrong medium or channel. An example might be sending a personal message in writing when a telephone call or a visit would have been more appropriate, tactful or understanding. Other examples might be that we speak too quietly or slowly, or use jargon or inappropriate language. The Transmitter may also expect the Receiver to absorb too much information in the time available, or may not take into account the Receiver's prior knowledge of the subject.
- *Perception and attitude problems* include those related to false or unstated assumptions or misunderstood messages where the transmitter might use a word in one context or with one meaning while the receiver might use the same word in a different context or with a different meaning. Examples, albeit simple ones, of this would include words such as 'now', 'urgent' and 'quickly'. These problems can also occur when the Transmitter and Receiver have viewpoints that are so radically different that the shared understanding that might be generated by talking is not possible. History is full of examples, but recent ones have for a time at least, included Israelis and Arabs and nuclear armers and disarmers. The inability or unwillingness of the Receiver to understand or absorb the message is also part of this group, as is the behaviour of the Transmitter in withholding information from fear of the consequences, or for reasons of secrecy, deception or lack of trust.
- *Environmental problems* include:
  — Interference, e.g. distractions and noise.
  — Lack of channels, e.g. no formal meetings, no telephone.
  — Distance.

- Finally, there's the '*Chinese whispers*' or '*Telephone tag*' phenomenon: the longer the message chain, the more distorted the message.

CONCLUSION

The ability to communicate effectively is not something for experts or specialists – nor is it an add-on optional extra. It is, for effective managers (and should be for all managers), an essential integral part of their working life. Nevertheless, effective communication is a skill that can be learnt.

Communication can be seen as:

- A purposive social skill.
- Being both linguistic and non-linguistic in nature.
- A two-way process.

Non-linguistic communication involves the use of gesture, posture, space, touch, gaze and expression, including the paralingual aspects of speech, while linguistic communication is concerned with the use of written and spoken language. Models of the process of communication use the concepts of encoding and decoding with the use of media and channels. Noise interferes with this process and can be implicit in the process itself or originate from without the process. The objectives of communication are to affect other's thoughts or actions by:

- influencing and/or
- instructing and/or
- exchanging information.

The effective use of linguistic- and non-linguistic-based communication to achieve these objectives will require the manager to possess an understanding of:

- The desired purpose(s).
- The needs of the chosen medium and channel.
- The needs of the receiver(s).
- The causes of failure in communication.

The remainder of this book is concerned with providing the knowledge and information that will enable managers to enhance their communicative skills.

EXERCISES

1. What are the essential elements of the act of communication and how do they relate to each other?
2. List the relative disadvantages and advantages of writing to employees as opposed to talking to them.
3. You, as a manager, have to give two members of your work team:
   (a) some good news (a pay rise or a promotion).
   (b) some bad news (the sack or demotion).
   How would you give these messages and why?

4. Briefing groups are a common way of communicating with employees in large organizations. What are their strengths and weaknesses?
5. Many large organizations have house magazines or newspapers. What are the objectives of these and when would a small company use this communication channel?

REFERENCES

1. Ellis, R. and Whittington, D., *A Guide to Social Skill Training*, Croom Helm, Beckenham, 1981.
2. Kubr, M. (ed.), *Management Consulting*, International Labour Organization, Geneva, 1980.
3. McCall, M. W., Morrison, A. M. and Hanna, R. L., Studies of managerial work: results and methods, *Center for Creative Leadership, Tech. Report No. 9*, Greensboro NC, 1978.
4. Stewart, R., *Managers and Their Jobs*, Macmillan, London, 1967.
5. Peters, T., *Thriving on Chaos*, Pan, London, 1989.
6. Horn, J. H. and Lupton, T., The work activities of middle managers: an exploratory study, *J. Management Studies*, **2**(1), 1965, pp. 14–33.
7. Handy, C. B., *Understanding Organisations*, Penguin, London, 1985.
8. Smithson, S., *Business Communication Today*, ICSA Publishing, Cambridge, 1984.
9. Lowell, K., *An Introduction to Human Development*, Macmillan, London, 1971.
10. Morris, D., *The Naked Ape*, Corgi, London, 1967.
11. Business and Technology Education Council, *Common Skills* BTEC, London, 1991.
12. Engineering Council, *Management and Business Skills for Engineers*, Engineering Council, London, 1988.
13. Peters, T. J. and Waterman, R. H., *In Search of Excellence*, Harper & Row, New York, 1982.
14. Makridakis, S., Management in the 21st century, *Long Range Planning*, **22**(2), 1989.
15. Pedler, M., Burgoyne, J. and Boydell, T., *The Learning Company*, McGraw-Hill, Maidenhead, 1991.
16. Berger, S., Dertouzos, M. L., Lester, R. K., Solow, R. M. and Thurow, L. C., Toward a new industrial America, *Scientific American*, **260**(6), 1989, pp. 21–9.
17. Bartlett, C. A. and Ghoshal, S., Matrix management: not a structure, a frame of mind, *Harvard Business Review*, July–August 1990, pp. 138–45.
18. Little, P., *Communication in Business*, Longman, Harlow, 1981.
19. Kakabadse, A., Ludlow, R. and Vinnicombe, S., *Working in Organisations*, Penguin, London, 1988.
20. Hargie, O., Editorial introduction, in Hargie, O. (ed.), *A Handbook of Communication Skills*, Routledge, London, 1986.
21. Shannon, C. and Weaver, W., *The Mathematical Theory of Communication*, Illinois University Press, 1949.
22. Damasio, A. R. and Damasio, H., Brain and language, *Scientific American*, **267**(3), 1992.
23. Neisser, U., *Cognitive Psychology*, Appleton-Century-Crofts, New York, 1983.
24. Hargie, O. and Marshall, P., Interpersonal communication: a theoretical framework, in Hargie, O. (ed.), *A Handbook of Communication Skills*, Routledge, London, 1986.

ASPECTS OF COMMUNICATION

'In thinking about the many barriers to personal communication, particularly those that are due to differences of background, experience, and motivation, it seems to me extraordinary that two persons can ever understand each other.'
F. J. Roethlisberger

INTRODUCTION

Many writers view skill in communication as a social skill—logically so, since communication takes place within a social environment. As such, the communication contributes to, is a part of, and is influenced by, the complexity of the social interactions, relationships and groupings within that environment. This complexity has attracted substantial research effort, and has consequently generated a variety of views about what appear, at first glance, to be the most basic of processes within the complex network or web of social communication.

The purpose of this chapter is to examine briefly some of the strands from that complex composite of research work and knowledge about the social aspects of the communication process. But first, let us take a broad look at the richness and diversity of that research work and knowledge with the following examples.

Morris,[1] from the viewpoint of the animal behaviourist, identifies four basic types of verbal communication, with quite different objectives:

1. *Information talking*   Concerned with the exchange of ideas and information.
2. *Mood talking*   Concerned with conveying emotional states.
3. *Exploratory talking*   Described as 'talking for talking's sake, play talking'.
4. *Grooming talking*   Reinforces non-verbal signals and maintains 'social togetherness'.

From a different viewpoint, Senge,[2] in describing the role of team learning on the road towards the 'Learning Organisation' of the future, differentiates between two primary and very different types of communication process:

1. *Dialogue*, which he describes as having a purpose of going 'beyond any one individual's understanding', and in which 'individuals gain insights which simply could not be gained individually'.
2. *Discussion*, which he describes as a game in which the object is to 'win' and in which 'a subject of common interest may be analysed and dissected from many points of view'.

Tannen,[3] as a social linguist, states that conversations are made up of:

1. *Messages*   These are the information content of communication and are conveyed by the meaning of the words used.
2. *Metamessages*   These we are said to react to most strongly, and are about relationships, attitudes, feelings, etc., and often display themselves in how we speak those words.

From a management development and organizational behaviour point of view Kakabadse *et al.*[4] parallel Tannen's view by stating that the management of effective interpersonal communication must take into account:

- *Information passing*
- *Relationship building*

Nor is the work about communication limited to the traditional 'people-oriented' disciplines. Brand,[5] in describing work at MIT's Media Laboratory, cites Andrew Lippman's view of interactivity as being 'mutual and simultaneous activity on the part of both participants, usually working toward some goal, but not necessarily'. This definition, while generated in the context of computer–people interactions, could also be said to apply to people–people interactions, and, when effective, has five requirements:

1. *Interruptibility*   Mutual and simultaneous interruption, rather than 'your turn/my turn' alternation.
2. *'Fine grain' element structure*   Interruption at word level rather than sentence or 'paragraph' level.
3. *Graceful degradation*   The ability to handle interruptions without collapse of dialogue or the ability to degrade productively if the interaction cannot handle what it should.
4. *Limited look-ahead*   Limited thinking ahead of where you are talking.
5. *Impression of an infinite database*   No limitations or constraints on direction and route.

Dawkins[6] also transfers a concept from another scientific discipline when he draws the analogy between the genetic 'replicator' role of genes and the 'information replicator' role of concepts or ideas. Dawkins calls these concepts or ideas 'memes' and suggests that they can 'propagate from brain to brain' and change or mutate far more rapidly than their biological counterpart, genes. Examples of memes might include concepts such as 'democracy', 'heaven and hell' or even 'love'.

Having taken this broad look, what we shall now do is to focus in more detail upon a number of important strands in the research work and knowledge about the social aspects of the communication process. The strands or aspects that we shall look at are those that are significant in their influence upon the clarity and quality of the communication process in the workplace. They are:

- Perception.
- Transcultural communication.
- Gender.
- Sociolinguistics.
- Organizational culture.

PERCEPTION AND COMMUNICATION

A typical dictionary definition of perception is that of 'a process of becoming immediately aware of something' or 'insight, understanding'. However, our own experience and our observations of others tell us that:

- We may fail to see or hear things that are there.
- We only notice things when we pay specific attention to them.

- We only pay specific attention if we have a previous idea where to look.
- We see or hear what our experience prepares us to see.
- We sometimes think that we see or hear things which are not there.

Examples of these would include our inability to hear others when we are listening closely to another, a mother's ability to hear her child's voice above all other's, and our ability to drive through a red light when we are talking to our passenger. More subtle examples involve our presumptions about others. These include unproven and generalized assumptions about individuals because of their dress (torn jeans = scruffy), colour of hair (red hair = bad tempered), gender (woman driver = bad driver) and other aspects. De Bono[7] states that perception 'refers to the way that we see the world' and points out that we see 'mainly what we are prepared by experience to see'. Broadbent[8] reports the presence of two different kinds of mechanism associated with perception:

1. *Filtering*, which is described as a strategy for selecting and rejecting information.
2. *Pigeon-holing*, which is described as the occurrence of 'favoured' responses, even in the presence of limited evidence to justify their presence.

This and other evidence leads us to a definition of perception as a process by which:

individuals select and interpret information from their environment and their interaction with that environment and fit that selected information into previously identified patterns that their experience suggests are valid.

This process enables us to cope with the barrage of sensory information that we are subject to and to filter out what we believe to be surplus information or extraneous noise. It also adds certainty to our lives – if we want to see that something is so, then, by and large, we see it as so. However, this process also limits what we receive and decode to that which our experience leads us to expect, and in doing so it reinforces our biases and prejudices.

These biases and prejudices occur when we ignore or refuse to accept input about people that conflicts with that which our prior experience has led us to expect or when, on the basis of inadequate or incomplete information, we fit people into 'slots' or models or categories. Some examples of these were given earlier, but others would be statements like:

'Short men are always aggressive'
'Women cannot be logical'

In reality, there is substantial evidence to refute all of these examples. However, we have to allow that evidence to be received and decoded and also we have to be willing to modify what our prior experience might have lead us to believe is likely to be true.

The importance of this process to a manager is considerable, because, as Cook[9] states, 'the way people see each other determines the way they behave towards each other'. It will also be evident that, in some of the roles that a manager carries out, accurate and sometimes rapid perception is important. These roles could include, for example, those of selection interviewer, salesperson, conflict resolver, etc. Mintzberg's[10] analysis of the manager's job in terms of ten roles provides further evidence for the importance of effective perception with the interpersonal and decisional roles of disturbance handler, resource allocator, negotiator, liaison and leader all having high perceptive needs.

The ways in which each of us perceives what is happening around us reflects our individual experience and is one of the ways in which we use that experience. In so doing, we express our individuality. That perceptive process is influenced by a number of factors. An awareness of those factors and the biasing that can be introduced by them should enable us to perceive others and their actions more clearly, and so have a significant effect upon our ability to communicate and our ability to manage.

The factors that influence our perception about people operate at both a conscious and an unconscious level and begin to do so even before we actually start to communicate with those people. These factors can be grouped together as those that are relevant to:

- The other person.
- The situation.
- You.

For example, your expectation of a person that you have never met or spoken to before will influence the way that you perceive them on meeting. These expectations will be influenced by their job or position (Managing Director or Clerk?), their age (younger or older than you?) and what you have heard about them (friendly, trustworthy or the opposite?). When you meet them, you will, at both a conscious and an unconscious level, be looking for factors like physical appearance (tall/short, fat/thin?), how they are dressed (formal/informal, untidy/smart?), how do they speak (quickly/slowly, long/short words?) and how they shake your hand, look at you, etc. The circumstances and environment of your meeting (board room/bar/sports club) will also influence both your expectations and your perceptions. When several people are involved in the meeting, the process will become even more complex, since you also have your perceptions of the various interactions between these people to take into account.

Given the complexity of the process, it is not surprising that it has attracted considerable research interest. The results of that research have identified the following factors as being some of those that influence the process of perception.

- *The other person*
  The way in which you react to others is influenced by the way that you perceive and have expectations about their:
  — age
  — physical appearance
  — dress
  — gender
  — speech
  — motor behaviour, i.e. body movement, posture, etc

- *The situation*
  The influence of the situation includes:
  — roles
  — physical environment
  — rules for behaviour in that environment/situation

- *You*
  Factors such as
  — your beliefs, attitudes and prejudices

— your expectations
— your needs

will all influence the ways in which you perceive others.

We can influence and change others perceptions of us by, for example, the ways in which we dress, move and speak. We can also influence our perceptions of others by being aware of and, if necessary, by changing, our attitudes and expectations, our reactions to others and expressions of our individual needs.

The descriptions of the ways in which our biases and prejudices become manifest through our perceptions include the stereotyping process, which leads us to expect certain types of behaviour from certain categories of people, e.g. vicars, pop stars or lecturers. If we have limited information about a person we may well, quite incorrectly, classify that person in one of those categories in order to predict his or her behaviour. These ways also include the Horns and Halo effect, by which the perception of unfavourable (Horns) or favourable (Halo) behaviour by an individual in one area influences our predictions about their behaviour in other areas. The process of projection is also included in this group, and occurs when you attribute your feelings and perceptions to other people.

These individual biases and prejudices can limit both the quality and the scope of a manager's communications, and one of the ways in which managers can learn to improve and refine their perceptions is by use of the Johari window.[11] This framework was developed by two psychologists, Joseph Luft and Harry Ingram, and is named after the initial letters of both their forenames. The concepts of this framework can be illustrated, for the manager and others, by Fig. 2.1. This is divided into four areas, which represent clusters of aspects of the manager's behaviour or personality. These clusters are:

- *Both aware*   These are the aspects and characteristics of the manager's personality, behaviour and attitude of which are known to both the manager and others.
- *Manager aware, others unaware*   These represent the thoughts, attitudes and feelings that the manager keeps to him or herself.
- *Others aware, manager unaware*   These are those aspects of the manager's personality, behaviour and attitude which others see but which the manager is not aware of.
- *Both unaware*   Those personality, behaviour and attitude characteristics which neither the manager nor others are aware of.

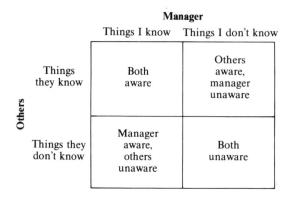

Figure 2.1   Manager—others interactions.

An awareness of these areas of perception helps managers to understand the nature and development of differences between:

- The way they perceive themselves.
- The way others perceive them.
- Others' reactions to their behaviour.

This awareness also helps managers appreciate other people's perception of and reactions to their behaviour. Increasing the openness of these relationships by, for example, self-disclosure and feedback, will enhance the quality of the communication in the relationship and hence enhance the manager's performance. For example, when we first meet others we tend to reveal little about ourselves and others gain little information about us. Consequently, the 'both aware' area of the framework is small. As we get to know others we usually begin to feel that we can be more open and disclose more about ourselves and our feelings. As this happens, the 'both aware' area expands and the 'manager aware, others unaware' area shrinks as others begin to know more about you. The size of the 'both aware' area can also be increased by feedback from others, which reduces the size of the 'others aware, manager unaware' area. When self-disclosure and feedback occur together, the size of the 'both unaware' area will decrease and our understanding of ourselves and others will increase, as shown in Fig. 2.2.

When the feedback we are given is not in agreement with our own view of ourselves we often react defensively and real skill is required from all involved in the process to maintain the relevant degree of 'openness'. Similarly, the process of self-disclosure requires confidence, and is not without its risks. However, it is important that managers have an awareness of these processes and that they are able to use them in relevant situations and at a relevant level. If used well they can and do enable others to be more open in their communications. If used inappropriately or excessively they can reduce the quality of those communications. For example, when you visit the dentist you do not expect the dentist to spend most of the session disclosing the detail of his or her own dental problems. That is, you have expectations of the role of the dentist which do not include hearing about the dentist's toothache. The same applies to the role of managers conducting annual appraisal interviews—they would not be expected by interviewees to spend time detailing their difficulties with their current job! However, some self-disclosure

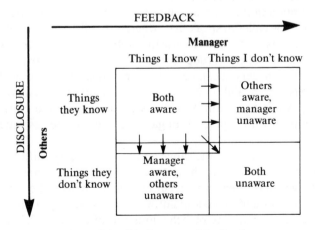

Figure 2.2 Disclosure and feedback.

can and will help the interviewee to feel that the manager is sympathetic and understanding and so likely to understand the interviewee's situation and feelings. In counselling situations particularly, self-disclosure can be very powerful, when used well, in getting people to talk freely and openly.

TRANSCULTURAL COMMUNICATION

As our organizations increasingly reach across national boundaries in both their structures and their search for customers it becomes increasingly important for managers to be aware of and responsive to the differences that culture will demand of their ability to communicate successfully. It is also evident that the nature of the society in which we live is also constantly changing, with increasing mobility, both within and across national boundaries, resulting in an increasingly cosmopolitan mix of races and creeds within our schools, universities, places of work and play—in fact, everywhere that people meet. The following represent a limited sample of the differences that result.

Gestures represent one type of communication whose meaning can change from one society to another. Morris[12] illustrates the change in meaning of one particular gesture called the 'chin flick'. This gesture, which is an insult in France and Northern Italy, is used as a gesture of negativity or disinterest in Southern Italy but returns to its insult status in some parts of North Africa. Another example is the V-sign with the back of the hand directed to the viewer. Argyle[13] reports that this represents '2' in Greece but is a 'rude sign' in Britain. This same sign is, however, converted to a 'Victory V' sign in Britain when the palm of the hand faces the viewer. The use of silence in conversations differs between societies. English speakers are said to find silences of more than four seconds uncomfortable while Trudgill[14] reports there are many societies which are more tolerant of longer conversational silences. Norms about the duration and volume of speech are different between North America and Northern Europe, sometimes resulting in North Americans appearing (to North Europeans) to be noisy and dominating. The process of bargaining or negotiating also differs, with some Arab societies strongly stressing the value of the given word rather than the written contract and societies on the Indian sub-continent never rushing into business discussions but prefacing these with extended periods of time in social discussion. These same cultures will often use the responses of 'Yes' to indicate that listening is continuing – rather than agreement. The use of impolite or aggressive language is viewed by Japanese negotiators as almost indecent behaviour, and loss of face by Chinese negotiators will result in a major disruption in the negotiating process. Many Japanese are said,[14] on answering the telephone, to expect the caller to speak first, whereas English speakers expect the answerer to speak first. Argyle[13] reports that while Americans prefer directness, Mexicans regard openness as a sign of weakness or treachery. Trudgill[14] states that in some Caribbean communities and among Black American teenagers, it can be, in some circumstances, normal for everyone to talk at the same time. Levels of gaze and body contact will also differ and Argyle[15] reports high gaze levels being shown by Arabs and Latin Americans, while Indians and Northern Europeans use low levels of gaze. Cultures with high levels of gaze are also reported as widely practising bodily contact.

These limited examples illustrate the range and variety of these differences. The extent and impact of these differences can be such as to create a state of anxiety and tension in the individual. This state, which is often termed 'culture shock', reflects the individual's reactions to the unfamiliar values, norms and behaviours of what can be seen as a hostile environment.

Many of these different patterns of behaviour are often described as being 'cultural' in origin, and the results of what Hofstede[15] called 'the collective mental programming of people in an environment'. Trudgill[14] suggests that these differences in cultures are manifestations of 'social distance', while Hofstede comments that culture is:

- A group characteristic, rather than a characteristic of an individual.
- An influence at many different levels (family, group, geographical area, professional environment, etc.).
- Difficult to change and often slow to do so.

Argyle[13] identifies that these differences can be manifest in a wide range of the aspects of our social environments, including:

- The language spoken.
- Rules about behaviour.
- The nature and patterns of social relationships.
- The desired goals and rewards.
- Beliefs, values and ideology.

Hofstede[15] reports on differences in national cultures identified by analysing questionnaires from a very large group of employees of a transnational company from forty countries. The results of this survey of work-related attitudes are expressed using four 'dimensions', which were said to represent the differences between national cultures. These dimensions were:

- *Power distance*   Indicates the extent to which unequal distribution of power is accepted, with a high value indicating high levels of acceptance.
- *Uncertainty avoidance*   Indicates the levels of perceived threat from uncertainty and ambiguity and the actions taken to avoid these. High levels indicate that uncertainty is seen as a threat which must be fought.
- *Individualism – collectivism*   A dimension that spans a range, with extremes of the spectrum being tight social frameworks (collectivism) and loosely knit social frameworks (individualism).
- *Masculinity*   High values are associated with the acquisition of money and objects, and low concern for others, quality of life or people.

The complex and detailed results of this analysis are expressed in a set of 'cultural maps' which display the data for each country with reference to two dimensions at a time. Examples of some of the results include:

- Low power distance/high individualist: Australia, USA and Great Britain.
- High power distance/high collectivist: Venezuela and Colombia.
- High power distance/low uncertainty avoidance: Singapore.
- Low power distance/low uncertainty avoidance: Denmark and Sweden.
- High uncertainty avoidance/high masculinity: Japan.
- Low masculinity/low uncertainty avoidance: Denmark and Sweden.

Hofstede comments that these differences are significant, and goes on to examine the implications of these cultural differences in terms of the application and relevance of management theories of motivation, leadership and organization. He also identifies the dilemma that transnational organizations face: whether to try to change the local culture or adapt to it.

One of the results of this, and other dilemmas that can result from cultural differences, is the need for managers to be able to communicate effectively across cultures that are represented by both their staff and customers.

A considerable amount of research has been conducted to establish the differences in the ways that different cultures communicate. This research has included factors such as language, facial expression, gesture, 'face', dress and rules. All of these and other factors can and do make a considerable difference to the way that people communicate in different cultures.

These cultural differences are real and significant – and will change as our societies change. Managers who can adapt to and use these differences in culture will undoubtedly be able to use their managerial process skills to greater effectiveness in a wider environment.

GENDER AND COMMUNICATION

Research has provided evidence that the differences between men and women lie not only in their physical characteristics but also in their cognitive patterns. This can be illustrated by the way that they perform in problem-solving tasks and examples are shown in Table 2.1. These differences lie in patterns of ability rather than levels of intelligence, and it has long been argued that their magnitudes are small and reflect experience rather than any more fundamental differences. However, Kimura[16] states that the bulk of research evidence now suggests that men's and women's brains are organized along different lines from very early in life, and that these differences result from sex hormone influences on the developing brain. These influences result in brains that are described as being 'differently wired' and in differences in, among other things, the ways in which speech and associated hand movements are organized within male and female brains. Given these differences, it is not surprising that differences in communication have been identified.

Tannen[3] reports that 'male–female conversation is always cross cultural conversation', but argues[17] that each style is equally valid – despite the considerable differences. Trudgill[14] points out that while many cultural linguistic differences originate from 'social distance', sex linguistic differences originate from 'social difference' and states that the ways in which men and women speak differ in many societies. These differences, he states, reflect the different social roles that men and women are given in these societies. When these differences in social roles are clearly defined, as they are, for example, in less technologically advanced societies than ours, then the language differences are larger – even to the point of being seen as separate varieties of the same language. These differences in the way men and women use language (and behave) seem to be acquired at an early age. Maltz and Borker[18] report that male and female children:

- Have different ways of talking to friends.
- Spend most of their play-time in same sex groups.

Table 2.1 Differences in performance of tasks by women and men

Tests in which women tend to do better than men	Tests in which men tend to do better than women
- Identifying matching items - Manual tasks involving precision - Verbal fluency - Mathematical calculation	- Guiding or catching projectiles - Mental object rotation or manipulation - Mathematical reasoning - Finding simple shapes hidden in complex figures

Male children are reported as playing outdoors in large hierarchical groups with leaders. Their games have winners and losers and 'who is best at what' is a subject of dispute and boasting. Female children are reported as playing in pairs or small egalitarian groups, with turn-taking cooperative games without winners or losers. Suggestions rather than orders and the absence of challenges were also noted.

Tannin[17] differentiates between the way men and women talk by using the concepts of report-talk and rapport-talk. For men, talk is said to be mainly about being in a hierarchical social order and preserving or protecting status. Men, it is said, learn as children to use talking as a way of getting and holding on to attention, and will do so by telling jokes or stories or demonstrating skill and expertise. They are said generally to feel more comfortable when talking in large groups with or to people that they do not know well. Tannen calls this style *report-talking* or *public speaking*.

Women's conversations are described as being about connections and relationships, with an emphasis on similarities and matched experience. Women who try to stand out from the group are subject to criticism, and their groups are small. Tannen calls this style *rapport-talking* or *private speaking*.

It is said, however, that these styles are not limited to conversations (as might be inferred for private speaking) or speeches (as might be inferred for public speaking), but are used in both conversational and speech-giving situations.

Given the significant and ongoing social changes occurring in all our social and working systems about the 'traditional' roles of both women and men it seems logical to conclude that linguistic changes will follow. Evidence of this already exists with the commonplace use of 'chairperson' to replace 'chairman'. Managers who fail to be aware of these changes and their social causes will limit their ability to manage.

LANGUAGE AND COMMUNICATION

Sociolinguistics is a branch of linguistics (the study of language) which is concerned with language in its social context. As such, it has many linkages to the traditional people sciences, e.g. psychology, anthropology, sociology, etc. The value of an understanding of sociolinguistics for the manager lies primarily in the way that it studies the use of language in conversations. This is not to dismiss the other aspects of this science, such as the study of language and social class or social context, but merely to identify that for the purposes of this book we shall look, albeit briefly, at some of the results of the sociolinguist's analysis of the way in which language is used in conversations.

In common with other disciplines, sociolinguistics identifies that conversations are not just about communicating information but also about relationships. In learning a language, at any age, not only do you need to learn what words to use and how to pronounce them, but also how to use those words in order to establish interactivity and a two-way conversation, i.e. to communicate.

This learning leads to an understanding of the rules for conducting and for interpreting conversations and how these differ from situation to situation and society to society. One example of this would be the use or non-use of formality in conversations. It would be grammatically correct, but formal, to say

   'Who is that man to whom is Fred talking?'

but in doing so you would risk sounding pompous, artificial and even pedantic. Most of us have learnt that to say

'Who is Fred talking to?'

is quite adequate for day-to-day informal conversations. Indeed, it may be that many of us would find it hard to imagine a day-to-day situation in which we would do other than use the second informal version.

Trudgill[14] defines conversations as 'structured, rule governed, non-random sequences of utterances'. He suggests that these rules or conventions include aspects such as:

- Turn-taking.
- Interrupting.
- Introducing new topics.

Other rules for conversations relate to their interpretation. for example, a conversation such as:

A: *'Are you going to change your car this year?'*
B: *'I haven't got enough money.'*

is far more understandable for most of us than a conversation such as:

C: *'Are you going to change your car this year?'*
D: *'My dog has died.'*

The reason for this is that, despite the lack of apparent connection between A's question and B's response, there does exist an acceptable linkage (*cars cost money*) which connects the two. It is more difficult, though not impossible, to identify the linkage between C's question and D's answer. An active imagination or a greater understanding of D and his or her background might enable us to identify a linkage related to D's grief at the dog's death or that, being blind, D needed a new guide dog to restore his or her walking mobility once someone else had driven him or her to a destination.

The existence of these conversational rules is not restricted to societies using the English language. Crystal[19] reports that the Japanese language uses different grammatical patterns depending upon the relative status of speaker and listener, and the French language uses *tu* and *vous* in different social situations. Bernstein[20] has put forward the concept of two types of language that are available to speakers. These are suggested to be:

- *Elaborated code* This is said to be used in formal situations and is described as imposing the speaker's individuality on the words spoken and as not being dependent, for effective communication, upon non-verbal language (facial expressions, etc.) or shared assumptions. Speech that uses this code involves a high proportion of the pronoun 'I', uncommon adverbs, passive verbs and adjectives.
- *Restricted code* This is used in informal situations and is described as stressing the speaker's group membership and as being based on shared assumptions. Speech using this code involves a high number of personal pronouns ('you', 'they', etc.) and uses questions to solicit agreement ('Wouldn't it?', 'Don't you think?').

The value, for managers, of an understanding of this area of sociolinguistics lies in its potential for the enhancement of their communicative skills and consequently their ability to manage.

ORGANIZATIONAL CULTURE AND COMMUNICATION

The richness, complexity and variety of organizational culture has led to a considerable amount of research into the how, why, when and where of the activities of different types of organization. While it is beyond the scope and intention of this book to conduct a comprehensive survey of this field, it is nevertheless worthwhile identifying that organizational culture has a significant influence on the communicative patterns of an organization and providing some examples of that influence. Ansoff[21] states that organizations can be viewed as 'purposive and goal seeking' and Lupton[22] states that an organization's internal life is composed of transactions, by individuals, across the boundaries of groups and subgroups within the organization.

For example, the bureaucratic organization, as described by Weber,[23] lays stress upon the use of written communication and records, even when oral communication is the norm. The differences between the mechanistic and organismic types of organization, as described by Burns,[24] are said to include the presence of a hierarchical structure of communication in the former whereas the latter has a network structure for communication. Leavitt[25] suggests that the appropriate organizational structure for effective communication is task-dependent, with repetitive programmed tasks needing centralized communication structures and new novel and/or ill-structured tasks needing 'wide-open' communication systems with large numbers of channels. Peters and Waterman[26] in reviewing, in 1982, the characteristics of then excellent companies, identify 'intensity of communications' as a critical factor. Informality is also cited as being significant, with use of first names, 'open door policies', 'Visible Management', 'MBWA – Management By Wandering Around' all given as examples. Morgan,[27] in describing the nature of organizational life, used a number of metaphors – some of which, such as 'Brain', 'Organism' and 'Political System', described organizations with implicit and obvious communication characteristics and needs. An organization's informal communication networks are said by Handy[28] to provide pre-warning of events, and to underline the formal communication channels. However, Pugh and Hickson[29] comment that one of the many contradictions of organizational life is that managers can claim to practice open communications but actually behave in ways which are defensive and win–lose oriented, and do not involve sharing feelings or thoughts. Thompson[30] discusses the different types of interdependence that exist within organizations and classifies the types of coordination and levels of communication effort required. These are said to include:

- *'Pooled' or generalized interdependence*, coordinated by standardization involving rules, routines and procedures and said to be least costly in terms of communication effort.
- *'Sequential' interdependence*, coordinated by plans and schedules and said to be intermediate in communication effort involved.
- *'Reciprocal' interdependence*, coordinated by mutual adjustment to changing situations with cross-hierarchical communication patterns and said to be most demanding in communication effort.

The 'ideology' of an organization is said by Harrison[31] to affect the behaviour patterns of its employees and its relationship with the outside world. Handy[28] uses 'culture' to describe these and other aspects of organizations. Both describe four organizational ideologies or cultures – all of which have structural and communication implications, as shown in Table 2.2.

Pedler *et al.*[32] writing about 'The Learning Company' identify the need for effective and open communication in the dimensions of such an organization. These include:

Table 2.2 Organizational ideologies

Ideology	Structure	Communication pattern
Power	Web	Through the chain of command.
Role	Temple	Limited cross-functional communication. Information flows up, directives flow down.
Task	Net	Information flows to and from centre of task activity.
Person	Cluster	Information flows from person to person.

- *Learning approach to strategy*, with feedback and experimentation.
- *Participative policy making*, with everyone discussing and contributing.
- *Informating*, using information technology to inform and empower.
- *Customer–supplier relationships* within the organization.

Bolwijn and Kumpe,[33] in providing a view of how multinationals evolve to meet the demands of the market place, describe the outcome of this evolution as the 'Innovative Firm'. This is said to have the characteristics of 'participation and democratization'. One of the evolutionary steps towards that outcome is termed the 'Quality Firm'. This is said to have the characteristics of communication and cooperation – both of which have very evident implications for communications.

A five-year study[34] of the differences between automobile manufacturers in Japan, North America and Europe has indicated that the growing Japanese share of this global market is due to substantial differences in organization, production method and communication. The Japanese 'lean production' method places a strong reliance upon communication between all the roles involved in designing, manufacturing, marketing and using the product – even when it is only a gleam in the designer's eye.

Whatever the purpose, goal, culture, structure or ideology of the organization, managers need to communicate with those around them. In order to make a worthwhile and valuable contribution to their organization, managers must ensure that their communication style and abilities are compatible with the needs and culture of the organization.

CONCLUSION

Communication has, as a subject, attracted considerable comment from workers in a wide range of disciplines. This chapter cites a limited number of examples from the fields of animal behaviourism, sociolinguistics, organizational development, genetics and information theory, before going on to examine the relationship between communication and a number of aspects of the social environment.

The ways in which we perceive others are seen to be strongly influenced by our experience and expectations, together with the situation and their appearance, movement, speech, age and gender. Our ability to perceive accurately can also be confused by those aspects of behaviour that are influenced by culture. Other cultures may have not only different languages but also different patterns and norms of behaviour. These differences can be significant and can influence many aspects of our social interactions. If not understood and accepted, they can easily lead to ineffective communication. Gender differences in communication can also be seen as 'cross-cultural' and as leading not only to different styles but also to different objectives for communication and to different use of language in social situations. The study of the use of language in social situations (sociolinguistics) reminds us of the relationship between the words we use and the situation of their use, as well as the relationship between speaker and listener. Conversations are seen to be structured verbal interchanges with rules about, among other things, turn-taking and interruption. The organizational environment within which communication takes place can influence the pattern, formality, channel and medium of these communications. Effective communication is seen as being able to make substantial contributions to the commercial success of an organization.

EXERCISES

1. Without any prior discussion, write down three words that represent your individual perceptions of someone known to all the group – then compare and discuss the differences and similiarities in these individual perceptions.
2. Identify how many different cultures are represented in your work group and what the communication differences are between these cultures.
3. You have to sack a long-standing but ineffective employee – identify the different ways in which you think it would be done if the employee was (a) female or (b) male.
4. 'Organizations exist to answer the needs of their shareholders rather than the needs of their employees'. Discuss in the context of communications.
5. Identify and discuss the patterns of communication that you believe will contribute significantly to commercial success in (a) a car manufacturer, (b) a hospital and (c) a leisure centre.

REFERENCES

1. Morris, D., *The Naked Ape*, Corgi, London, 1967.
2. Senge, P., *The Fifth Discipline*, Century Business, London, 1990.
3. Tannen, D., *That's Not What I Meant!*, Virago, London, 1992.
4. Kakabadse, A., Ludlow, R. and Vinnicombe, S., *Working in Organisations*, Penguin, London, 1988.
5. Brand, S., *The Media Lab: Inventing the Future at MIT*, Penguin, London, 1988.
6. Dawkins, R., *The Blind Watchmaker*, Penguin, London, 1988.
7. De Bono, E., *Word Power*, Penguin, London, 1977.
8. Broadbent, D., Relation between theory and application in psychology, in Warr, P. B. (ed.), *Psychology at Work*, Penguin, London, 1976.
9. Cook, M., *Perceiving Others*, Methuen, London, 1979.
10. Mintzberg, M., *The Nature of Managerial Work*, Harper & Row, New York, 1973.
11. Luft, J. and Ingham, H., The Johari window: a graphic model of interpersonal awareness, in Proceedings of Western Training Laboratory in Group Development, Los Angeles, UCLA Extension Office, 1955.
12. Morris, D., *Manwatching—A Field Guide to Human Behaviour*, Grafton, London, 1978.
13. Argyle, M., Inter-cultural communication, in Argyle, M. (ed.), *Social Skills and Work*, Methuen, London, 1981.
14. Trudgill, P., *Sociolinguistics: An Introduction to Language and Society*, Penguin, London, 1983.
15. Hofstede, G., Motivation, leadership and organisation: do American theories apply abroad?, *Organisational Dynamics*, Summer 1980, pp. 42–63.
16. Kimura, D., Sex differences in the brain, *Scientific American*, **267**(3), 1992, pp. 118–26.
17. Tannen, B., *You Just Don't Understand: Women and Men in Conversation*, Virago, London, 1992.

18. Maltz, D. N. and Borker, R. A., A cultural approach to male–female miscommunication, in Gumperz, J. J. (ed.), *Language and Social Identity*, Cambridge University Press, Cambridge, 1982.
19. Crystal, D., *Linguistics*, Penguin, London, 1990.
20. Bernstein, B., *Class, Codes and Control*, Vol. 1, Routledge, London, 1971.
21. Ansoff, H. I., Toward a strategic theory of the firm, in Ansoff, H. I. (ed.), *Business Strategy*, Penguin, London, 1965.
22. Lupton, T., *Management and the Social Sciences*, Penguin, London, 1971.
23. Weber, M., The theory of social and economic organisation, pp. 328–40, reprinted in Pugh, D. S. (ed.), *Organisation Theory*, Penguin, London, 1990.
24. Burns, T., Industry in a new age, *New Society*, 31/1/63, reprinted in Pugh, D. S. (ed.), *Organisation Theory*, Penguin, London, 1990.
25. Leavitt, H. J., Applied organisation change in industry: structural, technical and human approaches, in Cooper, W. W., Leavitt, H. J. and Shelly, M. W., (eds.), *New Perspectives in Organisational Research*, John Wiley, New York, 1964.
26. Peters, T. J. and Waterman, R. H., *In Search of Excellence*, Harper & Row, New York, 1982.
27. Morgan, G., *Images of Organisation*, Sage, London, 1986.
28. Handy, C. B., *Understanding Organisations*, Penguin, London, 1985.
29. Pugh, D. S. and Hickson, D. J., *Writers on Organisations*, Penguin, London, 1989.
30. Thompson, J. D., The structure of complex organisation, in Pugh, D. S. (ed.), *Organisation Theory*, Penguin, London, 1990.
31. Harrison, R., Understanding your organisation's character, *Harvard Business Review*, May–June 1972, pp. 119–28.
32. Pedler, M., Burgoyne, J. and Boydell, T., *The Learning Company: A Strategy for Sustainable Development*, McGraw-Hill, London, 1991.
33. Bolwijn, P.T. and Kumpe, T., Manufacturing in the 1990s – productivity, flexibility and innovation, *Long Range Planning*, **23**(4), 1990, pp. 44–57.
34. Womack, J. P., Jones, D. T. and Roos, D., *The Machine that Changed the World*, Rawson Associates, New York, 1990.

TWO

THE SPOKEN WORD

'The behaviour pattern of talking evolved originally out of the increased need for the co-operative exchange of information.'
Desmond Morris

'The tongue is more to be feared than the sword.'
Japanese proverb

LISTENING

'A long time ago in China there were two friends, one who played the harp skilfully and one who listened skilfully. When the player played about water, the listener would exclaim: 'Here is the running stream'. When the listener fell sick and died the player cut the strings of his harp and never played again.'
Traditional Zen story

INTRODUCTION

Skill in communication is often equated to the possession of skill or ability in the areas of reading, writing and speaking. The prominence given to these aspects of communication is illustrated by the way that we are taught as children both within our family groups and within our schools. In our schools this is reflected by the fact that reading and writing, as two of the 'three Rs' of reading, writing and arithmetic, are taught from an early age. In our families, the ability to speak is often seen as a significant milestone in our children's development, and as such is often the subject of considerable parental effort.

And yet there is another skill, often overlooked or taken for granted, which is at least as important as those skills – and that is the skill of listening.

The value and importance of this skill can be illustrated by the following examples. Peters[1] states that listening is a skill that is of considerable importance to modern managers. He identifies the need to shift from the 'talking and giving orders' mode to the listening mode, stating that an effective leader must become a 'compulsive listener'. Rogers and Farson[2] identify the need for managers to be able to listen 'intelligently and carefully' to the people with whom they work. Roddick,[3] in describing the growth of the Body Shop chain, relates how she 'wanted to hear from anyone' about better ways of doing things and about staff or customer complaints. Roodman[4] states that 45 per cent of total communication time is spent in listening, with speaking accounting for 30 per cent, reading 16 per cent and writing 9 per cent. So listening seems to be:

- Important.
- Something that managers do a lot of.
- Something that managers should be good at.

But are managers good at listening?

The answer to this question seems to be that people generally do not listen well, and as managers are people this appears to apply to them as well. Nichols and Stevens[5] state that 'people in general do not know how to listen' and report that one third to one half of what is heard is forgotten within eight hours. Smith[6] comments that:

- Few listen well.
- Skill in listening is not a natural ability.

Roethlisberger[7] comments, in the context of management, that 'the biggest block to personal communication is man's inability to listen intelligently, understandingly and skilfully to another person'.

And yet there are many situations in which the manager's ability to listen is a key factor in the management process. For example, in formal and explicit negotiating situations, the skill and ability to listen not only to what is said but also to the way in which it is said can provide cues which might enable an impasse to be overcome or an advantage exploited (see Chapter 5). Listening skills are also required in many social situations, including, for example, the less formal negotiations about who gets the coffee or 'where do we go for lunch?' In counselling situations, the ability to listen without judgement and in a manner which overtly displays a willingness to listen is often seen as contributing not only to the perceived warmth of the counselling manager but also to the freedom that the speaker has to talk. In job interviews (see Chapter 4), the willingness of the interviewer to question *and* listen skilfully is a key issue for both interviewer and interviewee. In routine day-to-day situations, the need to listen is just as important. Managers who listen in an effective manner will gain not only valuable facts, opinions and information but also the respect of their staff. All of these will influence the quality and ease of implementation of the decisions that managers take.

From these examples and from your own experience it will be evident that managers have to listen a lot and that the effectiveness or ineffectiveness of their listening can make a big difference to their job performance. So how can managers listen better?

In order to answer this question, it will be necessary to define listening, look at why managers listen, and then examine how managers can listen effectively.

WHAT IS LISTENING?

The process of listening to others starts, for most of us, with our hearing what they say. But is that action of hearing the same as listening? Hearing is defined, in the typical dictionary, as that 'faculty or sense by which sound is perceived'. As such it is a purely physical reaction to sound, which occurs when that sound is received at the ear. This description tells us that hearing is a necessary physical response without which we could not listen – but is it listening?

The typical dictionary describes listening as the process of 'attentively exercising the sense of hearing'. This definition tells us that hearing and listening are different and that the difference is something to do with the way in which we exercise the response of hearing. Most writers on this subject differentiate between hearing and listening by identifying the passive characteristics of the one and the active characteristics of the other. For example, Smith[6] states that hearing is a 'passive activity' while listening requires 'active participation' and goes on to describe listening as 'deliberate, active behaviour'. The fact that listening is not an indolent or passive activity is also stressed by Kakabadse *et al.*,[8] who describe listening as an active process that consumes both time and energy. It is also worth noting that observation of a conversation between individuals with hearing impairment will leave little doubt about the active and engaged nature of the listening taking place – albeit through the medium of sign and body language rather than spoken language.

So, having noted that hearing and listening are different, how do we define listening?

The range of definitions is considerable, but Smith[6] classifies them as focusing on or emphasizing one of:

- Language.
- Sounds.
- Verbal and non-verbal language.
- Concepts.

For example, a definition which focuses on verbal and non-verbal language would include not only the absorption, understanding and interpretation of the spoken word but also the absorption, understanding and interpretation of the gestures, facial expressions and body postures which add meaning and emphasis to those words (see Chapter 10). Definitions that emphasize the receipt of sounds or auditory stimuli appear to describe a process that would include the receipt and understanding of those 'uh huh' or 'mhm' sounds which Tannen[9] says that men use to indicate that they agree and women use to show that they are listening and understanding. Definitions that emphasize concepts or ideas might be concerned with interpretation of what is heard, while definitions that are based on language alone will concentrate on the receipt and decoding of what is said.

In order to try to simplify this rich complexity, it is worth revisiting the definition of communication that was introduced in Chapter 1. This definition states that communication occurs when ideas, information and feelings are conveyed. Based on that definition of the overall process, and remembering that hearing is the physical process of receiving sounds, then it would seem both logical and reasonable to suggest a definition of listening as:

The process of receiving, absorbing and understanding ideas, information and feelings by both aural and visual media.

This definition means that the listener not only hears what is said, but also:

- Absorbs or decodes what is heard and
- Understands the message.

That message will not just consist of the words spoken but will also include the paralinguistic 'message'. This paralinguistic message will consist of those other factors associated with the spoken word – other than the meanings of the words. It will include emphasis, with pitch, volume, stress and pauses all contributing. Pauses, for example, are reported by Argyle[10] to make up as much as 40 per cent of speech. They can be used to suggest thought or planning on the part of the speaker, but when used in excess, however, they can be interpreted by the listener to indicate anxiety, lack of self-confidence or uncertainty. The stressing of words is often used to give meaning to a sentence and to focus the listener's attention on the relevant part of the sentence. Pitch is often used to encode emotions in speech, with Frick[11] reporting examples that include anger (sudden increase), surprise (rising pitch), contempt (fall at end) and questioning (rise at end).

If the listening process takes place where the listener and speaker can see each other, then the message does not consist only of what is said and the way it is spoken. The gestures, facial expressions and body movements of the speaker will also give the listener information – that is if the listener is looking at the speaker! Gestures often emphasize the verbal content of the message, and as such are often described as 'baton' signals or gestures. Baton gestures are said by Morris[12] to account for the majority of the gestures that accompany speech, and are even used when the listener cannot be seen, e.g. during telephone conversations. Facial expressions can provide a wealth of information, usually about the emotional content of the message. Smiling, frowning, winking and a whole host of eyebrow movements are all examples of facial expressions which the listener is exposed to and which will also be used to provide feedback.

So listening is a process that involves the receipt of a considerable amount of 'data' – not only about the message but also about the speaker – and the subsequent absorption and decoding of those 'data'. Effective listening, in common with all communication processes, requires an active participative attitude on the part of the listener, and later in this chapter we shall examine the implications of that activity and participation. The next step is to take a look at why we listen.

WHY DO WE LISTEN?

Listening is one of those communication processes that we learn very early in life, since it ensures that we learn how to interact with those around us. Failure to listen means failure to relate to the people that we work, play and live with. However, in common with other communicative processes, listening is rarely undertaken for a single purpose. In Chapter 1 the purposes of communication were identified as:

- Instructing.
- Influencing.
- Exchanging information.

Listening, as a communication process, can help to achieve those purposes both singly and simultaneously. For example, listening can be undertaken in order to gain information and understanding. Managers who can listen will acquire, understand and evaluate information from, among others, colleagues, subordinates and customers. Failure to listen effectively and accurately will limit the quality of the decisions that managers take and will also limit their ability to manage their staff. Listening also enables feelings as well as facts to be received. Egan[13] states that speakers want a listener to be present 'psychologically, socially and emotionally'. This kind of listening, which is often called 'empathic' listening, is valuable for the manager not only in counselling or appraisal situations but also in all day-to-day working situations. Listening can also be or imply an act of social acknowledgement or recognition on the part of the listener. How many times have we heard about, or even said of, a bad or busy manager, 'he [or she] doesn't listen to me!'. A manager who listens is, in a very real and tangible way, acknowledging the value of the speaker and what the speaker has to say.

Smith[6] states that these multiple purposes of listening are 'frequently interwoven' and identifies several reasons for listening. In a management context the main reasons for listening are to:

- Acquire facts, figures, ideas.
- Understand thoughts, feelings and beliefs, i.e. to empathize.
- Consider and accept or reject what is heard.
- Affirm the value of the speaker.

However, whatever the reasons for a manager's listening, that listening will not achieve those objectives unless it is carried out in an effective manner.

THE LISTENING PROCESS

Earlier in this chapter it was suggested that listening could be defined as a process in which the listener receives, absorbs and understands ideas, information and feelings from the speaker. In common with all communication, this is a two-way process, as illustrated in Fig. 3.1. When speaker and listener can see each other, the spoken or verbal message will be supplemented by body and facial signals. Even when this line of sight contact is not possible, as in telephone

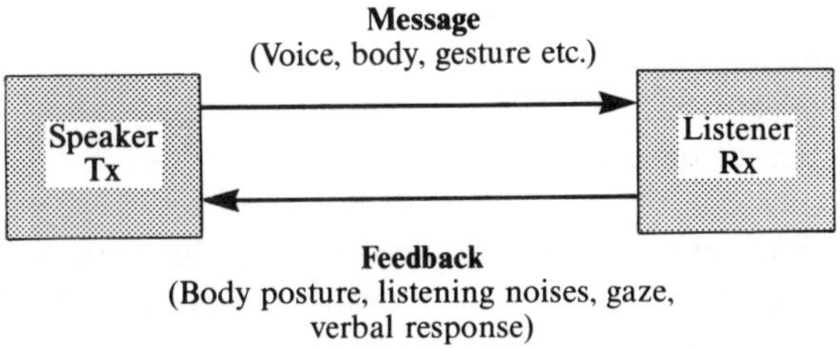

Figure 3.1 The listening process.

conversations, the words we speak are supplemented and given additional meaning by the way in which we speak them. However, the Speaker or Transmitter (Tx) will judge whether he or she is being listened to by the signals that the Listener or Receiver (Rx) gives. These signals will include eye contact, listening noises ('uh huh', 'mhm') and verbal responses. These are feedback, telling the speaker that he or she is being listened to. The quality and extent of this feedback from listener to speaker is what makes the difference between a good listener and a poor one.

So let's now take a look at some of the reasons why effective listening does not occur.

OBSTACLES TO LISTENING

Listening, as we noted earlier in this chapter, is often limited in its effectiveness. This ineffectiveness is not unique to managers, but is evident in many facets of all our lives. One of the problems facing a listener is that, while the average speaker talks at around 130 words per minute, the listener is capable of absorbing and understanding words at a rate which is at least five times faster.[5] This 'surplus' processing capacity is often employed in other activities, such as thinking about what to answer back or what needs to be done back in the office – and this limits the overall effectiveness of the listening process. Ineffective listening limits the freedom and effectiveness of communications within a working group and will ultimately limit the ability of the organization to respond to the environment in which it exists or market place and the needs of its employees. This ineffectiveness can be brought about by:

- *Environmental factors*, including interference, distractions, distance and noise. Examples include a noisy office or a conversation in the manager's office which is interrupted by the telephone constantly ringing.
- *Faulty message presentation*
  Examples:
  — Use of over-elaborate language, which confuses the listener.
  — Use of restricted or too simple language, which antagonizes the listener.
  — Use of jargon that the listener does not understand.
  — Too much information, which overloads and confuses the listener.
  — Spoken messages that say one thing and body language messages that say another.
  — Too low or high volume verbal message (too low volume = inaudible message, too high volume = distorted message).
- *Perception and attitude problems*
  Examples:
  — Unstated and inaccurate assumptions about the speaker (or listener).
  — Limited listener capacity, i.e. not able to absorb the message.

— Lack of trust.
— Listeners who pretend to listen.
— Listeners who select what they hear.
— Emotional content of message.

Earlier in this chapter we noted that people sometimes listen in order to consider and accept or reject what is said. However, this process of evaluation is also identified as one of the reasons why people do not listen effectively. Egan[13] and Rogers[14] identify evaluation as a significant barrier to effective listening. This viewpoint states that all listeners have a 'natural' tendency to evaluate or judge what is said to them. This tendency is said to be common to all communications involving language, but is increased when those communications involve feelings or emotions. The net result is, as Rogers describes it, 'nothing that could be called communication in any genuine sense'. Egan also identifies:

- *Filtered listening*, by which listeners allow their perceptions, biases and prejudices to limit or colour the content or interpretation of what is heard.
- *Fact-centred listening*, which focuses on facts but misses the person.
- *Rehearsing*, in which listeners start to think about how they are going to respond – and stop listening.

HOW TO LISTEN EFFECTIVELY

Effective listening is a skill which can be learnt, and is described, by Rogers and Farson[2] as 'active listening' or by Rogers[14] as 'listening with understanding'. However, it is also said to be a skill whose effective use is conditional upon the presence of a certain attitude on the part of the listener. Rogers and Farson[2] state that active listening is not effective unless it is 'firmly grounded' in the basic stance of the listener, and identify the need to respect the speaker's rights, potential worth and capacity for 'self direction' before effective listening can take place. Smith[6] identifies the need to be:

- receptive to the speaker and
- to pay attention to the speaker's words and actions.

Bolton[15] groups skills of listening under the headings of:

- Attending.
- Following.
- Reflecting.

Egan[13] differentiates between attending skills and listening skills, stating that attending refers to the physical and psychological presence of the listener while listening refers to the ability to receive and understand the verbal and non-verbal messages sent. Smith[6] reports that the American Speech Association has identified competences associated with the process of listening. These are said to be divided into two main groups:

- Those associated with the literal comprehension of the ideas and information transmitted, including the ability to recognize and recall individual concepts and their relationships to each other.

- Those associated with the critical comprehension of the ideas and information transmitted, including the ability to discriminate between fact and opinion and logic and emotion, and to detect bias and prejudice.

McKay et al.[16] outline the components of what they describe as 'total' listening:

- Gaze: good eye contact.
- Posture: leaning slightly forward.
- Reinforce what is said by paraphrasing and nodding.
- Asking clarifying questions.
- Moving away from distractions.
- By being and continuing to be committed, despite your own reactions to what is being said.

Egan[13] identifies the need to:

- Face the speaker with a posture that indicates involvement.
- Adopt an open posture, i.e. without crossed arms or legs.
- Lean towards the speaker.
- Make good eye contact.
- Relax.

Warmth and empathy are also significant factors in the listening process. Warmth is generally described as being the expression, by verbal and non-verbal language, of a genuine interest and concern in the speaker as a person. Authier[17] reports that warmth is demonstrated by:

- Willingness to listen.
- Respect for the speaker.
- Enabling the speaker's expression.

The expression of empathy involves being with and understanding the other. This can be demonstrated by both body and verbal language, with factors such as gaze, body posture, proximity and the focusing of questions and comments on emotional rather than factual content all being significant.

However, effective listening can also be about challenging the speaker. Egan[13] writes about 'tough-minded listening', which involves being aware of and challenging the flaws and gaps in the speaker's reality.

The word 'silent' is an anagram of the word 'listen', and the use of silence in the listening process is often almost ignored by writers on listening. Illich[18] identifies different types of silence, which include:

- The silence of the 'pure' listener, wherein the message becomes the 'he in us'.
- The silence of indifference and uninterest.

Slavson[19] states that creative listening is based upon 'the ability to remain receptively silent' while Douglas,[20] in writing about the environment of the group, indicates that silence can be perceived as threatening, but can also indicate any of the following:

- Uninterest.
- Support and confidence.
- Shared feelings.
- Reflection.
- Resistance.

However, there can be little doubt that silence can, with effective listeners, be an accepting and understanding space which will enable speakers to think through thoughts or experience their feelings before expressing them verbally.

There is also little doubt about the level of agreement on the value, power and importance of non-verbal messages. This non-verbal or non-language-based communication is explored in more detail in Chapter 10. However, it is worth noting that when used as feedback by the listener it avoids the complication and interruptiveness of verbal feedback, and when used by the speaker it adds considerably to the complexity and fluency of the message.

Paradoxically, two elements of effective listening are to do with verbal interchange. These are the processes of questioning and reflecting.

QUESTIONING

The skilful use of questioning can make a considerable contribution to the listening process. Later in this book (Chapters 4 and 5), we shall look at the use of questioning in both interviews and negotiations. In those situations, questions are primarily asked as requests for information or opinions, and can be initiated by either person involved in the communication process. However, in the effective listening process the question is primarily focused on the speaker and should be aimed at helping the speaker to say what he or she wants or needs to say. As such, 'listening' questions should:

- Be limited in number, as too many questions will at least disrupt the flow of the speaker and may even leave the speaker with the feeling of not being listened to.
- Be relevant to the content and context of what the speaker is saying and not be or appear to be random or irrelevant.

Examples of these 'listening' questions are described below.

Open-ended questions

Open-ended questions can be described as questions which require more than a simple 'yes' or 'no' as an answer. An example of a dialogue with an open-ended question would be:

A: *'I'm not happy about our sales figures this month.'*
B: *'Why is that?'*

A closed question would be:

A: *'I'm not happy about our sales figures this month.'*
B: *'Is Barnsley down again?'*

Both open and closed questions will be given an answer. However, in the context of effective listening, the important issue is whether the question enables the speaker to say more about the subject that he or she is talking about. Closed questions rarely do this.

Probing questions

Probing questions should focus the speaker and stop him or her talking in generalities or rambling. In so doing, however, they should not fall into the trap of the closed question, i.e. generating the specific limited answer. Again, the objective should be to enable the speaker to say more about the subject that he or she is talking about. Dillon[21] identifies these 'open' probing questions as 'narrative' questions and the 'closed' probing questions as 'directive' questions. Kahn and Cannel[22] identify that effective probes:

- Motivate the speaker to continue the conversation and provide more information in the area required.
- Maintain or enhance the speaker/listener social relationship.
- Achieve the above without introducing bias or changing the original topic.

Samples of probing questions and their purposes are given in Table 3.1.

Table 3.1 Samples of probing questions

Clarifying	'Can you explain that in more detail?'
Justifying	'Why do you feel that?'
Challenging	'Are you ready for that?'
Exemplifying	'Can you give me an example of when that happens?'
Extending	'Where did you go from there?'
Relevance	'How does this affect what we agreed yesterday?'
Accuracy	'Are you sure that the sales have fallen?'
Agreement	'Do you agree with that?'

REFLECTING

Reflections are those responses by which the listener feeds back, to the speaker, the listener's understanding of the speaker's statements. This can be undertaken by:

- Repeating what was said, word for word, or
- Paraphrasing or re-expressing what was said with a clearer meaning.

These reflections can be about:

- the facts, information and ideas, or
- the feelings that the speaker displays when transmitting the message to the listener.

The objective of reflections is generally to promote a more detailed or intense communication on the established subject or to ensure that communication continues on that subject. Reflecting can, however, be used as a summary and as a means of changing the subject or terminating the communication.

Table 3.2 Samples of reflections

'It seems to me that you feel strongly about John's unwillingness to recognize your contribution to the project.'

'As I understand it, you are claiming that this disciplinary action is unreasonable because your Head of Department hasn't followed the disciplinary procedure.'

'You are saying that we can't meet the project target date because the raw material supplier is letting us down.'

However, the process requires skill in its use and is not without risk. For example, repeating what was said, word for word, is generally viewed as being of limited effectiveness and can, if used without skill, be misinterpreted to indicate sarcasm or disbelief. Re-expressing what was said can be applied to feelings, though 'paraphrasing' is usually used to describe this action when the content is primarily concerned with facts, information and ideas. Reflecting is generally seen as a way of clarifying both feelings and facts. Its effectiveness depends upon relating directly to the speaker's current, rather than past, state. Samples of reflections are shown in Table 3.2.

THE LISTENING ENVIRONMENT

The environment in which the listening takes place can exert a considerable influence upon the quality and effectiveness of that listening. A conversation conducted in an open and noisy office will necessitate, if it is to be heard, higher levels of speech than would be required in a quieter environment. If that conversation is of a personal nature or about confidential information, then that environment is limiting both the quality, owing to a low signal-to-noise ratio, and the content, owing to the inappropriateness of the location. The layout of this environment can also effect the frequency of communication.

Allen[23] examined, in research and engineering laboratories, the effect of separation upon communication. His results indicate that if work positions are more than 10 m apart the probability of communicating once per week was between 8 and 9 per cent. When workstations were 5 m apart or less, this figure rose to 25 per cent. Managers who listen effectively will be aware of these factors and will ensure that their conversations take place in environments which contain limited noise and distraction and minimum potential for interruption.

In looking at the broader organizational environment, Peters[1] identifies several key social and physical factors for what he terms the 'listening environment'. These are:

- *A non-threatening forum*, in which listening and talking can take place. This must take place on a regular basis and have a no-holds-barred 'culture'. This can be formal (lunches with the Board) or informal (coffee meetings or Friday night beer groups).
- *A place to listen*, which can be a meeting room, but must be a room away from the intrusions and interruptions of the workplace.
- *Feedback and action*   These are needed so that people understand that managers are listening and are doing something about what they hear.
- *Training* to enable managers to listen effectively.
- *Frequent opportunities*   Not just annual meetings, but daily or weekly teams or work group meetings, held in working hours.
- *The right attitude*, from managers who believe that listening is important and productive and not an empty ritual.

There can also be, in the workplace, many opportunities for informal face-to-face conversations. These will only occur when people meet. 'Open door policies', 'visible management', 'management by wandering around' are all descriptions of proven ways in which managers meet and are able to listen to their staff.

Effective listening is an acquired skill, but it is worth the effort and practice that most managers need to undertake before being able to listen with understanding. To help that process, Appendix 3.1 contains a list of key issues for the listening manager and Appendix 3.2 contains a self-evaluation form for the listener.

CONCLUSION

It is evident that listening is different from hearing and that effective listening is neither simple nor straightforward. The listening process is a two-way process which can be limited by environmental or message-related factors as well as the perceptions or attitudes of the listener. Evaluation of the spoken message is seen as a barrier to effective listening. An attitude which displays, on the part of the listener, attentiveness and receptivity will contribute to effective listening, as will eye contact and posture. The use of reflecting, paraphrasing and open-ended questions are also seen as significant contributors to the effectiveness of this process. Managers need to listen to their staff if they are to develop them, delegate to them and encourage their contributions to workplace processes. Managers who do not listen will rarely be listened to, and by so doing will limit the effectiveness of both their own and others' roles.

EXERCISES

1. Choose a subject of common interest and in pairs discuss the subject. Each speaker will not, however, speak for him or herself until he or she has summarized correctly what the previous speaker has said.
2. Conduct a group discussion with six people within the group and six observers outside the group. Each observer will use Appendix 3.2 to evaluate one member of the discussion group. The discussion group members will fill in Appendix 3.2 after the discussion and compare with the observers' assessment of their listening.
3. Using silence, questions and reflecting, role play in groups of three (two role playing, one observing) an informal discussion between a manager and an unhappy (but reluctant to say why) employee. Alternate roles and give the manager role feedback on how his or her use of silence, questions and reflecting felt for the employee.
4. Discuss the following statement: 'The manager's job is not to hold employees' hands and listen to their troubles'.
5. In what sorts of organization would listening by a manager, to both clients and/or employees, be seen as irrelevant or ineffective?

REFERENCES

1. Peters, T., Thriving on Chaos, Pan Books, London, 1989.
2. Rogers, C. and Farson, R. E., Readings in communication, in Sigband, N. B. (ed.), *Communication for Management and Business*, Scott, Foresman and Company, Illinois, 1976.
3. Roddick, A., *Body and Soul*, Century, London, 1991.
4. Roodman, H. and Roodman, Z., *Management by Communication*, Methuen, Toronto, 1973.
5. Nicholls, R. G. and Stevens, L. A., *Are You Listening?*, McGraw-Hill, New York, 1957.

6. Smith, V., Listening, in Hargie, O. (ed.), *A Handbook of Communication Skills*, Routledge, London, 1986.
7. Roethlisberger, F. J., Barriers and gateways to communication – Part 2, *Harvard Business Review*, July–August 1952, reprinted as HBR Classic in *Harvard Business Review*, November–December 1991.
8. Kakabadse, A., Ludlow, R. and Vinnicombe, S., *Working in Organisations*, Penguin, London, 1988.
9. Tannen, D., *That's Not What I Meant!*, Virago, London, 1992.
10. Argyle, M., *Bodily Communication*, Routledge, London, 1988.
11. Frick, R. W., Communicating emotion: the role of prosodic features, *Psychological Bull.*, **97**, 1985, pp. 412–29.
12. Morris, D., *Manwatching: A Field Guide to Human Behaviour*, Grafton, London, 1978.
13. Egan, G., *The Skilled Helper*, Brooks/Cole, Belmont CA, 1990.
14. Rogers, C. R., Barriers and gateways to communication – Part 1, *Harvard Business Review*, July–August 1952, reprinted in 'The Articulate Executive', Harvard Business School Press, Boston, MA, 1991.
15. Bolton, R., *People Skills*, Prentice-Hall, Sydney, 1986.
16. McKay, M., Davis, M. and Fanning, P., *Messenger: The Communication Book*, New Horbinge Publications, Oakland, 1983.
17. Authier, J., Showing warmth and empathy, in Hargie, O. (ed.), *A Handbook of Communication Skills*, Routledge, London, 1986.
18. Illich, I., *Celebration of Awareness*, Penguin, London, 1978.
19. Slavson, S. R., Re-educating the Delinquent, Collier Macmillan, New York, 1961.
20. Douglas, T., *Group Work Practice*, Tavistock Publications, London, 1976.
21. Dillon, J. T., Questioning, in Hargie, O. (ed.), *A Handbook of Communication Skills*, Routledge, London, 1986.
22. Kahn, R. L. and Cannell, C. F., *The Dynamics of Interviewing*, Wiley, New York, 1957.
23. Allen, T. J., Communications in the research and development laboratory, *Technology Review*, October–November 1967.

APPENDIX 3.1: GUIDE TO GOOD LISTENING

1. *Indicate by your manner that what is being said is being absorbed*

   - Look, encourage by nodding, and reinforce – '*I see*'.

2. *Avoid self/others interrupting*

   - Don't interrupt, unless it is to ask for clarification.
   - Stop or avoid others interrupting.

3. *Resist distractions*

   - Listen for the theme of the message.
   - Focus on what the speaker is saying.
   - Avoid verbal, visual or physical distractions.

4. *Don't judge content or delivery*

   - Concentrate on hearing 'what' is said, not 'how' it is said.

5. *Avoid daydreaming*

   - Don't tune out.
   - Force yourself to listen.
   - Maintain eye contact, lean forward, occasionally summarize – '*So you are saying . . .*'.

6. *Let the speaker talk*

   - Don't rush to fill the speaker's pauses.
   - If the speaker stops, encourage them to continue – '*Go on*' or '*What happened then?*'.

7. *Keep your mind open*

   - Listen in an understanding way.
   - Don't prejudge what they will say before they've said it!

8. *Listen between the words*

   - Be alert for omissions; sometimes the essential message is contained in what is not said.
   - Listen for feeling as well as meaning.
   - Is the speaker:

     — Critical or neutral?
     — Open or evasive?
     — Optimistic or pessimistic?
     — Confident or defensive? (etc.).

9. *Check your interpretation of the speaker's message*
   - Clarify by: '*So the situation is . . .?*' or '*Do you mean. . .?*'.
   - Ask questions if you do not understand.
   - Ask yourself: '*Do I really know what they are saying?*'.

APPENDIX 3.2: LISTENING SKILLS SELF-EVALUATION QUESTIONNAIRE

Attending

1. *Gaze*
   We had good eye contact.   1 2 3 4 5 6 7   We had no eye contact.

2. *Posture*
   I adopted an open posture   1 2 3 4 5 6 7   I crossed my arms and legs.
   with no crossed arms and
   legs.

3. *Position*
   I faced the speaker and   1 2 3 4 5 6 7   I turned away and sat back.
   leant forward.

4. *Distractions*
   I did something about   1 2 3 4 5 6 7   I did nothing about the
   distractions.   distractions and allowed them
                                                  to continue.

Listening

1. *Silence*
   I allowed silences and did   1 2 3 4 5 6 7   I found silences difficult and
   not break them.   spoke to break them.

2. *Interrupting*
   I did not interrupt.   1 2 3 4 5 6 7   I interrupted persistently.

3. *Questions*
   I asked clarifying questions.   1 2 3 4 5 6 7   I asked irrelevant questions.
   I asked open questions.   1 2 3 4 5 6 7   I asked closed questions.

4. *Relaxation*
   I felt relaxed but attentive.   1 2 3 4 5 6 7   I felt tense and ill at ease.

Scoring

If your total score comes to 27 or less then you think that you are listening. Scores of 36 and above indicate that you may be having some problems listening to what is said to you.

FOUR

INTERVIEWS AND INTERVIEWING

'Our very eyes
Are sometimes, like our judgements, blind.'
William Shakespeare, *Cymbeline*, Act 4, Scene 2

INTRODUCTION

Being interviewed is a very common experience which takes place under a great variety of circumstances and for an equally large, if not larger, number of reasons. On many occasions this involvement with the interview process comes about when we interact with the systems of the social environment in which we live and work. For example, interviews happen when we want finance to buy a house or when we want to change our jobs. They also occur when we want medical treatment from a doctor, when we want to enter a course of study or when others need to know how we carry out our jobs – and in many, many other circumstances. So what is an interview and how does it come about?

A typical dictionary definition for interview includes such meanings as 'a formal meeting or conversation' or 'a meeting to test the suitability of a candidate for a post'. Other versions might include those situations in which a reporter questions someone about their views or personality in order to write about them or to inform a radio or television audience.

All of these and other definitions indicate that interviews are not chance or random social encounters, and that when they occur they always do so in a purposeful manner, i.e. they have a purpose or desired outcome. Further exploration indicates that all interviews, whatever their purpose or context might be, share a number of common features. These are that interviews:

- Are predetermined formal events.
- Involve two or more people.
- Usually, though not always, involve face-to-face contact.
- Take place because one or all of the participants believe that the interview will answer, or lead to an answer to, their individual need or needs.

The commonality of these factors to all interview situations has implications for the use and understanding, by participants, of a wide range of communication skills. Interviews are primarily conducted through the medium of language-based verbal communication, though they will also, when face-to-face, involve the use of non-linguistic communication, such as body movement, gesture, facial expression and the use of distance and territory. The skills involved in the interview process will include those of listening (Chapter 3), presenting (Chapter 7), use and awareness of 'body language' (Chapter 10) and even negotiating (Chapter 5). It has already been noted that interviews have objectives and purposes. In general terms these can be classified, in common with many communication processes, as the following:

- *Exchanging information*, as when applying to the bank for finance to buy a car. The bank manager will ask questions about the applicant's financial status, e.g. salary and outgoings, while the potential borrower will ask about interest rates and repayment periods.
- *Influencing* as when being interviewed for a job. Applicants will present their experience and background in as positive a way as is possible, in order to influence the interviewer(s) to offer them the job.
- *Instructing*, as when, on concluding an investigative interview as a part of a disciplinary procedure, the manager may instruct the interviewee not to repeat the offence.

Often these purposes will overlap, as, for example, in the selection interview, when the applicant will need to inform the interviewer in order to exert influence.

It is also evident that the patterns of communication that take place in these interviews are complex and involve two-way communication with all participants communicating via both language- and non-language-based media.

All of the above leads to a definition of the interview as:

a formal, purposeful and prearranged conversation between two or more individuals.

So how does the interview fit into the context and content of a manager's job? Certainly, exposure to the process of being interviewed is an experience that all managers have undergone at some time or another. For example, there can be very few managers who have not been interviewed as a part of the larger process of changing their job or moving to another company. For other managers, the process of interviewing others is a regular, even day-to-day, experience as a part of the duties of their managerial role. Examples of such management roles, in which interviewing is a mandatory core skill, will include those involved in market research, recruitment or management consultancy.

As identified earlier, these interviews take place for a very wide range of reasons and in a wide range of contexts. However, they can, in the general context of management, be classified as interviews that take place for one or several of the following reasons:

- For recruitment or selection.
- For information gathering or exchange.
- For feedback/discussion.

Each of these categories will be examined in more detail later in this chapter. The initial part of this chapter will, however, examine the basic process of the interview itself.

THE INTERVIEW PROCESS

The interview is an encounter between two or more individuals which, while it is primarily social in its nature, is also conducted for a purpose. The interactions contained within this encounter are complex, but reflect the roles of the individuals involved. For example, the interview is generally managed, controlled or conducted by one of the individuals involved. The individual carrying out this role is called the *interviewer* while the person being interviewed carries out the role of the *interviewee*. The person in this latter role, the interviewee, is generally expected to reveal more information than the interviewer, and under some circumstances, e.g. selection interviews or counselling interviews, this information may be of a personal nature. However, interviews are not social encounters between equals.

The interviewer can and often does exert considerable influence upon:

- What is talked about.
- When it is talked about.
- In what detail it is talked about.

This influence can be exerted directly and openly by an interviewer, who might, for example, ask direct questions on factual matters and expect the interviewee to respond in the same manner. However, overt and direct behaviour on the part of the interviewer is not the only method of displaying this influence. For example, interviewers might provide 'leads' which are, in their view, designed to enable interviewees to provide or reveal relevant information. The interviewer's influence can, in some circumstances, be much less direct, as, for example, in counselling interviews. In these, interviewers will often act in an indirect manner, limiting their actions and comments to those which they perceive to be relevant to the contributions of interviewees. However, even in this situation, interviewees are aware that the interviewer is watching and listening and will be aware of and will respond to the interviewer's body language or kinesic responses to their verbal, paralingual and kinesic messages.

In interviews where several people are involved in interviewing a single individual, e.g. selection boards or panels, the complexity of these interactions can be considerable. For this reason, the management or control of this interview panel will often be undertaken by one member. This role, which is often described as the 'chairperson of the interview panel', has many of the characteristics of the chairperson role as carried out in meetings devoted to discussion or problem-solving (see Chapter 6), but is primarily concerned with issues such as the timing, content, equality and standards of the panel's questioning of the interviewees.

An overall view of the nature of the interview process is shown in Fig 4.1, which displays the

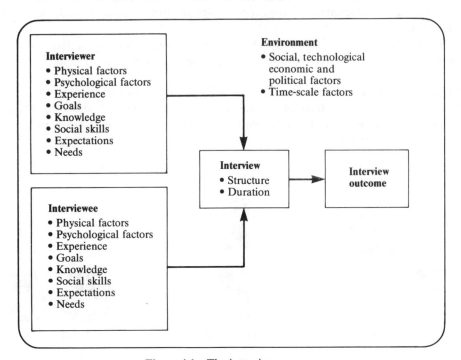

Figure 4.1   The interview process.

interaction of the interviewer, interviewee and the environment of the interview. The significant factors in this interaction are environment, perceptions and behaviour, as described below.

Environment

Environmental factors include not only the physical location in which the interview takes place but also the larger environment outside. This larger environment can intrude into and influence the interview, not only by external noise, e.g. telephone calls and traffic noise, but also by the knowledge and influences that the participants bring into the interview room with them. This knowledge and these influences relate to the social, technological, economic and political characteristics of that environment. Examples of influences would include:

- Unemployment levels, which could influence a selection interview favouring either the interviewee (high employment and growth levels) or the interviewer (high unemployment and low growth levels).
- Rapid changes in technology, which could cause a redundancy interview or influence a performance appraisal situation.
- The introduction of new safety legislation, which could lead to disciplinary interviews.

Let us move now from the larger and external environment to the environment of the interview itself. It has been observed that the layout of the interview 'space' can exert a considerable influence on the quality of the interview interactions. Korda[1] suggests that most offices can be divided up into two areas. These are:

- *The pressure area*, which exists around the desk and is the setting for formal conversations. These are usually characterized by the office occupant sitting behind the desk and leading the conversation.
- *The semisocial area*, which is away from the desk and might contain, in larger offices, easy chairs and low tables. Conversation in this zone is said to be on a more equal basis.

McCaskey[2] shows alternative office layouts and styles which illustrate these zones. Sommer[3] reports that conversations in which the participants sat at right angles to each other (Fig. 4.2(a)) contained six times the number of spontaneous conversations than face-to-face positioning (Fig. 4.2(b)) and twice as many as side-by-side positioning (Fig. 4.2(c)).

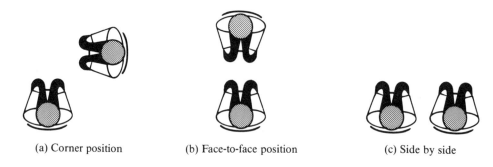

(a) Corner position   (b) Face-to-face position   (c) Side by side

Figure 4.2   Seating positions.

Finally, Hall[4] suggests that we use the space around us for different purposes and divides this space up into four main zones:

- *Intimate*   from contact to 18″ (0.5 m) of separation.
- *Personal*   from 18″ (0.5 m) to 4′ (1.2 m) of separation.
- *Social*   from 4–12′ (1.2–4 m) of separation.
- *Public*   from 12–25′ (4–8 m) of separation.

Hall suggests that the 'social' zone, with a distance of between four and five feet between interviewer and interviewee, represents the separation which was seen by most people to be not too friendly or informal, i.e. close, nor too formal or unfriendly, i.e. distant.

All of the above illustrate how the nature of both the outside environment and the actual interview environment and the ways in which the interview participants move in or use those environments can influence the interview quality and outcomes.

The quality and outcomes of the interview can also be influenced by the expectations, experience, goals and needs, social skills, physical appearance and attitudes of the participants. The next section will examine some of these factors.

Perceptions and behaviour

Goffman[5] uses the metaphor of drama or theatre to suggest that all interpersonal interactions consist of 'performances' that individuals and groups put on in order to influence and manipulate the perceptions and impressions of the 'audience'. Applying that metaphor to the interview situation it might well be argued that the larger environment influences the size and state of the 'stage' on which the 'set' of the interview location is used by the actors, i.e. the interviewer and interviewee, who may be playing not only to each other but also to their 'role set' (see Chapter 11), which exists outside the interview. This can be illustrated by a brief examination of some of those factors that influence appearance and over which there is some individual control and choice. These will include dress, hair, make-up, and spectacles. Hair is a factor of appearance about which there are often norms. Examples of these might include short hair being identified with soldiers, bank managers and monks and long hair being identified with hippies, musicians, artists and social rebels. Hairstyle is also often used to indicate membership of cultural groups, e.g. punk or Rastafarian hairstyles. Spectacles are reported[6] as indicating increased levels of perceived intelligence. Cash[7] reports that judgements about the suitability of women for management roles in a work environment are influenced by amount of make-up, jewellery and hairstyle. Dress is also a significant factor, with relationships reported[6] between choice of clothes and factors such as:

- Some aspects of personality.
- Emotional states.
- Social class.
- Perceived or expected behaviour.

Physical appearance is also said, by Argyle,[6] to be significant, with reports of taller men being more likely to be appointed and given higher starting salaries in American companies, while fat people are said to be less likely to be appointed to jobs involving high levels of people contact.

Social interactions in general have been modelled by several workers, including Argyle[8] and Hargie and Marshall.[9] These models have attempted to illustrate the relationships between such factors as perceived behaviour and goals and motivations. The relationships between some of

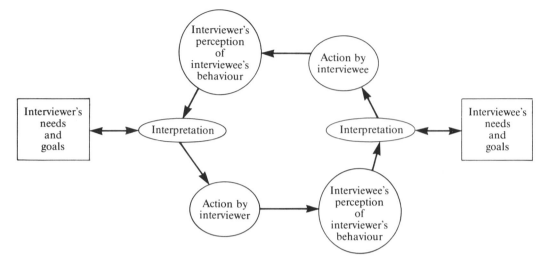

Figure 4.3   The interview as a social encounter.

these factors, within the interview, are illustrated in Fig. 4.3, which indicates that the behaviour of interviewers or interviewees is based upon their:

- Interpretation of the other's behaviour.
- View of how that behaviour is related to their own prior actions.
- View of how they might react to the other's future possible behaviour.
  Their individual goals and needs.

For example, an interviewer might, in the earlier stages of an information-gathering interview, perceive the monosyllabic responses of the interviewee to be symptomatic of nervousness or anxiety. Since the interviewer wants to have a successful interview, i.e. to acquire as much information as possible, the interviewer will modify his or her interview behaviour, process and timing in an attempt to reduce the interviewee's anxiety.

The behaviour that interviewers choose will reflect a number of factors:

- Their perceptions of and knowledge about the interviewee.
- Experience of the interview situation.
- The emotional and physical environment in which the interview is taking place.
- An estimate of the behaviour's likely success.

If, for example, the previous interviewer knew or had met the interviewee before the interview then the interviewer might feel more confident and relaxed about sharing his or her perceptions and asking what the cause of the apparent anxiety was. The response given by the interviewee will depend upon whether the interviewer's revealing/sharing behaviour is perceived to be appropriate or threatening. Alternatively, if the goal was to get the interview over as quickly as possible, the interviewee may view this interchange as a waste of time.

It will be obvious, even from this simple example, that the role of the interviewer requires skilled social behaviour. Argyle[8] identifies that the competent application of social skills has special characteristics. When these are considered in the context of the interview, they are found to include behaviour by the interviewer which:

- Establishes rapport with the interviewee.
- Displays accuracy in perception.
- Is flexible.
- Is proactive rather than reactive.
- Shows practised and smooth use of social techniques.

Interviewers will demonstrate the presence of these characteristics by the manner in which they:

- Prepare for the interview by identifying a desired content and structure.
- Communicate the above to interviewees at the beginning of the interview.
- Use questions which:
  — are open
  — contain relevant vocabulary
- Use techniques such as reflecting and probing.
- Close the interview effectively.

The effective interviewer will also need to display and use knowledge of and ability in both the language of gesture and posture and the paralingual elements of the interaction. The linguistic content of the interview is said to account for the minority of the 'messages' passing between interviewer and interviewee (see Chapter 10). The majority of the communication taking place is contained within the paralingual and the kinesic elements of the interaction. The paralingual messages that are contained within such features of the talk as voice pitch and stress on words and timing are concerned with emotions and covert thoughts. These can, for example, indicate to the trained interviewer whether the interviewee is:

- Anxious (raised pitch with long pauses).
- Extrovert (fast speech and raised pitch).
- Competitive and impatient (loud, fast speech with explosive emphasis).

Addington[10] identified a number of perceived links between speech and personality. These links indicate that listeners will attribute personality characteristics to speakers on the basis of the way in which they speak. For example, a person with speech that is thin in tone and lacking in resonance will be perceived as younger and possibly artistic, while speech with limited peaks and troughs, i.e. flat, is seen as cold and withdrawn. The characteristics of maturity, realism and balance or adjustment are said to be attributed to speakers with speech that is throaty, i.e. hoarse and guttural. Gestures are used by both interviewer and interviewee to illustrate and emphasize the spoken word. Butterworth and Beattie[11] found that gestures:

- Usually precede the related words or phrase.
- Occur most often during pauses.

The use of gaze, facial expressions and head movements all add to the messages exchanged during the interview process. Mehrabian[12] found that speakers who were attempting to persuade the listener:

- Looked more at the listener.
- Used more gestures and head nods.
- Spoke faster and with less hesitation.
- Smiled more.

Gaze is often used to send information and to emphasize words or phrases or to add to the eloquence of the spoken word. These and other areas of non-language-based communication are examined in more detail in Chapter 10.

Earlier in this chapter, management interviews were classified as taking place for:

- Recruitment or selection.
- Information gathering or exchange.
- Feedback and/or counselling.

Before moving on to examine these classes of interviews briefly, it is worth noting that an interviewer's self-evaluation questionnaire is provided in Appendix 4.1.

SELECTION INTERVIEWS

It is almost impossible to review the process of interviewing without examining those interviews that take place for the purpose of selecting people for a job or role. Most people who apply for a new job will expect that the selection process will include an interview. However, this interview is often not the only method used to select people, and psychological and aptitude tests are becoming an increasing feature of selection procedures. However, the content, value and use of these tests does not fall within the remit of this section and they will not be examined. This section will focus upon the use of the interview in the selection procedure and the strengths and weaknesses of that process.

The structure of the selection interview is portrayed by McHendry[13] as having four typical stages, which are said to be:

- *The rapport establishment phase*, during which the interviewer will, at the very least, tell the interviewee about the interview structure and duration. The objective of this phase is said to be that of getting the interviewee talking, and this can be achieved by questions about hobbies, etc.
- *The biographical questioning phase*, which will involve questions about the interviewee's past record. The techniques of open-ended questions, reflecting, probing and summarizing are used in this stage.
- *The answering queries phase*, which allows the interviewee to ask any questions and obtain any facts that he or she might need.
- *The parting phase*, during which both interviewer and interviewee agree on subsequent actions and procedures.

However, this view of the structure of the selection interview does contain some limitations, particularly when applied to the management selection interview in the rapidly changing environment of the 1990s. For example, had these stages been rigorously applied in the interview process for Russian managers in late 1990, that process would only have provided information of their abilities to operate under the pre-perestroika era of stability and certainty. As described it certainly would not have provided any information on the interviewee's ability to manage during the change process which subsequently converted the monolithic USSR into a fragmented group of independent states *and* to exploit that change process for the employer's benefit. The point of this (perhaps oversimplified) example is to underline the need for the selection process to take into account the larger environment or 'stage' on which the ritual of the selection process is being played out. It is also worth noting, in the light of the lack of social equality between the interviewer and interviewee noted earlier in this chapter, that the parting stage would be more likely to contain a 'telling' rather than a 'discussing' or 'agreeing' process. Nevertheless, this model can be adapted to provide an alternative, more detailed and perhaps more representative model, with the following stages:

- Objectives and expectations phase.
- Putting the interviewee at ease phase.
- Biographical information validation and enhancement phase.
- Exploratory phase.
- Consolidation phase.
- Completion phase.

Illustrative samples of the interviewer's comments and questions associated with each of the stages in this model are given in Table 4.1.

Whatever its structure, it is evident that the interview is a very commonly used component of the selection process. However, Argyle[8] notes that there are mixed views about whether this level of use is justified by the results obtained. The concepts of interview 'predictive validity' and 'reliability' are useful in this context. For example, when considering the manager's use of the selection interview, high levels of interview predictive ability would result in that interview providing sound and consistent information on the interviewee's subsequent job performance. There are, of course, a number of issues about how that future performance is to be measured. If, for example, that future performance was, for a manager, to be measured in the narrow but pragmatic terms of the profitability of the manager's unit or team, then the influence of the larger economic environment or the performance of associated support groups will be significant. These cannot, of course, be either measured or predicted by the selection interview process. Despite these difficulties, attempts have been made to measure predictive validity. Unfortunately the evidence does not indicate that interviews are able to predict job performance accurately. However, Arvey and Campion[14] comment that interviews which use a board or panel appear to display higher levels of both validity and reliability, and Trankell[15] suggests that teams of interviewers working independently but coming together for a consensus decision do display predictive validity levels as good as those of written tests. Nevertheless, the general picture that emerges is that the ability of the selection interview to predict subsequent performance is limited. However, Ulrich and Trumbo[16] and Anderson[17] do comment that the predictions made are generally, though not always, better than the predictions made from background information alone. Reliability as a feature of interviews is generally described as that feature whose presence should ensure that the same result or conclusion is reached at different interviews with the same interviewee or candidate. These can be with different interviewers (inter-rater reliability) or the same interviewer (intra-rater reliability). The research evidence appears to indicate that the use of structured marking schemes can raise the levels of both types of reliability. However, results obtained in the absence of such schemes are said[18] to be inconsistent and generally not providing evidence to support the presence of reliability in the interview process.

So why is this so? Why does such a selection process fail to produce results that are predictively valid and why is the process followed by the interviewer unreliable?

One of the factors that influence the interview process is bias. This can be described as a tendency, on the part of interviewers, to allow prejudice or inclination to influence their perception of or conclusions about interviewees. This is not unique to selection interviews, but also occurs in the other types of management interview discussed later in this chapter. Bias can occur very early in the interview. Webster[19] reports that during a series of 15 minute interviews,

Table 4.1   Samples of interviewer behaviour

● *Objectives and expectations phase*

   'What I would like to do during the hour that we have together is to take a brief look at what you have achieved in your career so far and then begin to explore how that experience might be used here at the Orange Computer Company.'

● *Putting the interviewee at ease phase*

   'Before we start can I offer you a cup of coffee?'

   or

   'I gather you've just been on holiday'

● *Biographical information validation and enhancement phase*

   'I see that you are currently in charge of the marketing at BZQ computers—that sounds a challenging job!'

   and

   'Looking back, what do you feel were your achievements during the time that you were Sales Manager?'

● *Exploratory phase*

   'Tell me why you think that your experience at BZQ is relevant to this job.'

   or

   'What do you consider your core skills are?'

   and

   'What do you need to know about this job and Orange Computers?'

● *Consolidation phase*

   'How would you summarize what you see that you would bring to Orange Computers?'

● *Completion phase*

   'We will have completed the interviews with all the candidates by tomorrow evening and I hope to be able to ring you, if that's convenient, with our decision on Wednesday afternoon.'

---

the average decision time was four minutes, with the remainder of the interview period being used to confirm or reinforce this early decision. Other sources of bias and error on the part of interviewers include:

● A like/dislike reaction to the interviewee.

- Overweighting of similarities in background/education, etc.
- Stereotyping.
- Physical appearance factors.

These and other pervasive factors lead to a situation in which bias on the part of interviewers is almost impossible to eliminate. However it can be reduced or limited, and this can be done by:

- The use of structured, systematic questioning.
- The use of several interviewers interviewing independently but deciding jointly.
- Interviewer training.

Another source of error in selection interviews relates to the nature and sequence of the questions asked. The relationship of these factors to the listening process was briefly examined in Chapter 3 and will be examined in relation to the process of negotiating in Chapter 5. Much of what was said about questioning in the listening process is equally applicable to interviews. In an interview, the questions are primarily aimed at the acquisition of information, opinions or judgements, and as such should:

- Be open rather than closed.
- Contain limited leads.
- Sequenced in a manner that indicates thoroughness and consistency.

The use of closed questions, such as:

> *'How did you put up with all that travelling?'*

results in less information in the immediate and subsequent linked response than open questions, such as:

> *'How did you find that amount of travelling?'*

Hargie[20] reports that leads can be:

- Simple: *'You have come by car, haven't you?'*.
- Complex: *'With the price of petrol rising, it's important that we all economize on costs. So don't you feel that you ought to travel to Glasgow by train?'*.
- Subtle: *'How large a rise in market share can we achieve?'* generates a different response from *'How small a rise in market share will we achieve?'*.

These and other sources of error can also occur in those interviews that are specifically targeted at gathering information.

INFORMATION-GATHERING INTERVIEWS

This type of interview can be associated with the acquisition of any or all of the following:

- Numerical data: *'How many times did that happen?'*.
- Objective facts: *'On which day did he say that?'*.

- Descriptions: '*Tell me what you do with this invoice*'.
- Subjective evaluations: '*Would you say morale is worse or better than last year?*'.
- Feelings: '*Do you like that way of doing it?*'

Examples of the use of information-gathering interviews by managers will include market research interviews, investigative interviews after a problem or accident, and interviews that aim to assess the basis of and case for change in an organization. The outcomes of information-gathering interviews often include or contribute to reports or study documents that might be used to identify areas of major organizational change, e.g. a new marketing policy. Pugh,[21] while reviewing the process of organizational change, identifies the necessity to establish the need for change as being the first step in effective change management. Information-gathering interviews are often a key stage in that initial step. Juran[22] and Crosby[23] both identify the need to identify the facts about failure rates, critical components, quality costs and operator attitudes, among others, as a key and critical first step on the road to improved quality in both service and manufacturing organizations. Again, information-gathering interviews are often a key stage in that initial step.

Despite the differences in outcomes and objectives, many of the features of the selection interview are evident in the information gathering interview. For example, a manager who is investigating a computer systems failure will display bias by responding to a factual description, by the operator, of his or her actions with the question, '*Why on earth did you do that?*' rather than '*Can you tell me why you decided to do that?*'. Closed questions, like '*That was unsatisfactory, wasn't it?*', generally produce limited answers. However, there are circumstances, e.g. market research surveys, where the manager is concerned with acquiring a large and statistically significant sample of answers for analysis. Under these circumstances closed questions will produce shorter and more easily recordable and analysable answers. Brenner[24] states, in the context of the research interview, that both the validity and reliability of the interview are strongly dependent upon:

- The questionnaire.
- The interviewee.
- The interviewer.

and cites the frequent use of structured questionnaires for this type of information-gathering interview.

The majority of information-gathering interviews have a number of stages. These are:

- *Background information acquisition* This initial stage involves establishing a basic factual framework that provides the answers to 'what', 'how' and 'who'. This may involve organization charts, production records and/or a host of other documents – all of which are needed as background information.
- *Preparation* During this stage decisions must be made about what information is needed from the interviews and how that information is to be acquired or accessed. These decisions will provide answers to:
    — Who is to be interviewed and in what order?
    — How long will the interviews last?
    — Where will they be held?
    — What questions will be asked?
    — How will the answers be recorded – notes or tape recorder?

- *Interview* The quality of the information acquired will depend not only upon the questions asked but also how those questions are asked. The skilled interviewer will use probing, open-ended questions and silence and will manage the timing and duration of the interview.
- *Analysis* After the interview it will be necessary to analyse both the information obtained and the effectiveness of the interview process.

As we saw earlier in this chapter, information gathering interviews are one of several types of management interview. The third and final type of interview concerns those interviews that are concerned with counselling and feedback.

FEEDBACK AND COUNSELLING INTERVIEWS

These interviews are generally concerned with those situations in which the manager and a member of staff will discuss issues associated with the member of staff's development. These types of interview can be classified as:

- Appraisal interviews.
- Counselling interviews.

As these are discussed in more detail it will become evident that there are major differences in both process and outcomes between these two types of interview.

Appraisal interviews

For the appraising manager the objectives of appraisal interviews are:

- To review the performance of the appraised individual over a specified period.
- To identify ways in which that individual's future performance might be improved.
- To set individual performance objectives or targets.
- To assess the training and development needs of the individual.

Warr[25] also identifies that these interviews can be used to provide data for staffing level planning and salary administration. As we shall see later, some of these aims might conflict with the objectives of the appraised individual. The type of appraisal interviews that we shall consider are those formal social situations which occur in those organizations that operate an 'open' appraisal system. In this type of appraisal system the appraised employee sees the written report and is allowed to comment on and perhaps sign that report. In closed appraisal systems the appraisal report is kept secret and not seen by the appraised employee. While closed systems might enable appraising managers to be more detached in their reporting, they can also lead to less rigorous or less thoughtful evaluations that are not challenged. It is also difficult to see how employees would react positively to 'secret' reports and also difficult to see how such reports would enable employees to improve their performance. However, even open appraisal systems have their problems. The individual being appraised will have a number of goals – some of which might conflict with the appraiser's goals identified earlier. The appraisee's goals might include:

- Increasing the chances of promotion or a salary increase.
- Influencing the boss's judgement.
- Finding out how the boss sees his or her performance.

- Finding out how to improve.
- Getting training, help or support.

The risks and the potential for conflict, for both employee and manager, cluster around their individual decisions about how open and honest their contributions to the appraisal process will be. Managers or appraisers who 'play it safe' and do not reveal their true assessment of staff members' performance, run the risk of the appraisal process becoming a bureaucratic form-filling exercise. Employees who are honest about their performance and faults run the risk of exposing themselves to undue criticism. These risks are lessened if a written record is made and if the interview and that record focuses on the task of objectively appraising behaviour, perform-ance and objectives rather than personality characteristics.

The level of objectivity achieved in this process will be influenced by those factors identified as generating bias earlier in this chapter. It will also be evident that, in order to review current performance and subsequently to identify ways in which that performance might be improved, it will be necessary to define:

- Job targets or content.
- What good performance is.

For many management roles, the outcomes or targets are difficult to identify in objective and/or quantified terms. As a consequence, the appraiser–appraisee dialogue runs the risk of being couched in subjective and judgemental terms. The limitations and conflict potential of such a dialogue are obvious, and steps should be taken to ensure that performance is evaluated against 'specific, jointly set and reasonable'[26] goals. Indeed, it is arguable that effective feedback on performance cannot take place without such goals. It can also be argued that the provision of feedback is such an important factor in the process of management that it should not be limited to a 'once a year' formal interview, but should be integrated into the day-to-day interactions between manager and managed. If and when that occurs the formal appraisal interview becomes a part of a less formal but continuing process.

The formal appraisal interview will, however, still have the potential to make a valuable contribution to the quality of those interactions. As such it should be planned, prepared and carried out with care. Many of the points made earlier in this chapter, in the context of selection or information-gathering interviews, are equally applicable to appraisal interviews.

The stages in effective appraisal interviewing are:

- *Preparation*   This will include the obvious steps of telling interviewees where and when the interview will take place, ensuring that the location is suitable and that adequate time is available for an unhurried interview. It will also require interviewers to read the background documentation, e.g. what was said and agreed last year, and most importantly, for inter-viewees to be told, *before the interview*, what their appraiser's aims are. This stage should also be long enough for interviewees to prepare their thoughts about their performance during the period under review.
- *Interview*   The first step will be for interviewers to remind interviewees of the stated objec-tives and to tell them about the interview structure and process. As the focus of the interview is the job rather than the person, interviewees should be encouraged, early in the interview, to talk about their views on task performance. Interviewers should use active listening skills (Chapter 3), probing, open questions and should ensure that both good and bad points are identified. The outcome of this part of the interview should be mutually agreed areas and

targets for improved performance. Notes should be taken, but not at a level or in such a way as to destroy or limit the rapport which has been built up. Indeed there may be some sensitive issues about which it is unwise to take any notes at all. The interview should be completed with a summary.

- *Post interview* The notes should be formally recorded and, if it is an open system, made available to interviewees for their signature. The agreed objectives/targets will also be recorded. These will often include or require action on the part of appraising managers. It is vital to the credibility of the appraisal interview that these actions are followed through and that any review dates are adhered to.

Handy[26] comments that appraisal interviews will only result in improved performance when they relate criticism to specific situations and occurrences and use the consequent dialogue as a goal-setting exercise.

Counselling interviews

Counselling is more than just helping or listening or providing a 'shoulder to cry on', and skills are required to ensure that the process is carried out effectively. The British Association for Counselling[27] defines this process as:

> *an interaction in which the counsellor offers another person the time, attention and respect necessary to explore, discover and clarify ways of living more resourcefully and to his or her greater well-being*

Egan[28] identifies the need for counselling to result in outcomes that are valued in the client's day-to-day life.

There are a number of views about the manner in which the counselling process should be carried out. These views are generally based on a particular theoretical approach and include the psychodynamic, cognitive, behavioural and person-centred approaches. The skills that are required to carry out the process of counselling will partly depend upon the approach taken. For example, the person-centred or non-directive approach pioneered by Carl Rogers describes[29] the need for counsellors to be:

- Genuine.
- Unconditional and positive in their regard for the interviewee.
- Totally acceptive of the interviewee.
- Empathic.

Other approaches, however, lay more stress on the ability of counsellors to interpret, analyse and evaluate what interviewees say or to probe beyond the problems that interviewees initially present.

While counselling skills are not the exclusive property of trained professional counsellors, it is important that the manager is aware that skilled counselling requires training. This training can involve several hundred hours of both theoretical and practical work, together with supervision by experienced counsellors. As a consequence, unless managers have had this training, their role in a counselling interview should be limited to:

- The initial stages of trying to resolve a problem that has an impact (direct or indirect) on job performance.
- Knowing when and where to refer an employee for professional counselling.

This basic level of counselling may be limited in its outcomes and may leave managers feeling that they have not done all that they could to help their staff, but it does ensure that staff get the professional help that they need. It also protects managers from overcommitment in an area for which they have little training. 'Amateur' counsellors operating out of their depth can be described as having the destructive potential, for the staff member and themselves, of a 'do-it-yourself' brain surgeon who uses an electric hobby drill. The skilled professional counsellor, who will have received extensive training, will operate with resources and support systems that are not available to the manager.

Given, then, that for the manager the counselling interview will have limited objectives, how is that interview best conducted? Before examining the answers to this question it is worth noting that, in this type of interview, the interviewee's perceptions, views and prejudices are of *overriding* importance. The feelings, reactions and views that the manager brings to or develops in the interview must not be allowed to intrude into or 'colour' what the interviewee needs to say or express. Failure to acknowledge and observe this basic rule of the counselling situation will not only limit the effectiveness of the interview but may also leave the interviewee more confused or distressed.

Despite the above, it is, however, evident that the stages of this type of interview are similar to those for the other types of interview covered in this chapter. They are:

- *Preparation*   It is important that a manager only agrees to a counselling interview if it is evident that a rapport exists between the manager and the interviewee. If the manager does not feel 'at ease' with the interviewee, then it is worthwhile reviewing whether the counselling should be provided by some other manager or the Personnel function. However, if the interviewee has specifically asked to speak to the manager, then the manager should go through with the interview, but should be aware of his or her feelings towards the interviewee and limit their influence. Preparation should also involve making sure that a quiet room is available in which the interview can take place without interruption and that the manager is available for an adequate length of time.
- *Interview*   This type of interview can be very time-consuming, and if the time that the manager has available is limited then this should be indicated at the onset with an option on another session if needed. Another primary issue which can present problems for managers is that of confidentiality. If the manager or the interviewee has any doubts or reservations about confidentiality then the interview should not proceed and a professional counsellor should be used. The aim of the interview should be for the manager to enable the interviewee to state what the problem is. The manager will need to listen and use effectively the skills associated with that process identified in Chapter 3. The manager's judgement and views are not needed – only the ability to listen and accept. If action is needed then the manager's role is limited to helping the interviewee to identify the options for that action. It is the interviewee's decision that is needed, since it is his or her problem – not the manager's. Many counselling interviews may not reach the decision stage, but those that do may also need a plan or projected time-scale. This, again, must be of the interviewee's choosing and can be the subject of a further interview.
- *Post interview*   It is important that after the interview managers 'self-assess' their counselling and whether it could have been better. Real indications of effective counselling in the workplace can include requests for repeat sessions, reduced friction or conflict, better time-keeping and better morale.

CONCLUSION

The interview is a social event which can be described as a formal, purposeful and prearranged conversation. This conversation is not, however, one which takes place between equals, and the interviewer often exerts a significant and controlling influence over the subjects, timing and level of detail of the conversation. This social interaction is also influenced not only by where it takes place, but also by the perceptions, expectations and motivations of those involved and the pressures and demands of the larger environment outside the interview itself. Managers who are competent interviewers are able to apply a range of social skills and to use these effectively in a number of circumstances. These include:

- Selection interviews.
- Information-gathering interviews.
- Feedback and counselling interviews.

While the objectives and focuses of these types of interview differ, they all require preparation and thought on the part of those involved.

EXERCISES

1. In the last interview that you were involved in, did you:
   - Prepare yourself?   Yes ☐ No ☐
   - Ask and answer questions clearly and succinctly?   Yes ☐ No ☐
   - Say all that you wanted to?   Yes ☐ No ☐
2. Write down the advantages and disadvantages, for the manager and for the appraisee, of the open appraisal interview.
3. Split your group up into pairs and interview each other, in turn, for 10 minutes. Then describe the other person to the whole group, taking no more than 5 minutes.
4. Examine the when, why and how of disciplinary and grievance interviews.
5. Review the strengths and weaknesses of:
   - Personality and aptitude tests.
   - Selection interviews.

REFERENCES

1. Korda, M., *Power in the Office*, Weidenfield & Nicolson, London, 1976.
2. McCaskey, M. B., The hidden messages that managers send, in *The Articulate Executive*, Harvard Business School Press, Boston, 1991.
3. Sommer, R., Studies in personal space, *Sociometry*, **22**, 1959, pp. 247–60.
4. Hall, E. T., *The Hidden Dimension*, Doubleday, New York, 1966.
5. Goffman, E., *The Presentation of Self in Everyday Life*, Edinburgh University Press, Edinburgh, 1956.
6. Argyle, M., *Bodily Communication*, Routledge, London, 1988.
7. Cash, T. F., The impact of grooming style on the evaluation of women in management, in Solomon, M. R. (ed.), *The Psychology of Fashion*, Heath, Lexington, 1985.
8. Argyle, M., *The Psychology of Interpersonal Behaviour*, Penguin, London, 1967.
9. Hargie, O. and Marshall, P., Interpersonal communication: a theoretical framework, in Hargie, O. (ed.), *A Handbook of Communication Skills*, Routledge, London, 1986.
10. Addington, D. W., The relationship of selected vocal characteristics to personality perception, *Speech Monographs*, **35**, 1968, pp. 492–503.

11. Butterworth, B. L. and Beattie, G. W., Gesture and silence as indicators of planning in speech, in Campbell, R. N. and Smith, P. T. (eds.), *Recent Advances in the Psychology of Language: Formal and Experimental Approaches*, Plenum, New York, 1978.

12. Mehrabian, A., *Non-Verbal Communication*, Aldine-Atherton, Chicago, 1972.

13. McHenry, R., The selection interview, in Argyle, M. (ed.), *Social Skills and Work*, Methuen, London, 1981.

14. Arvey, R. D. and Campion, J. E., The employment interview: a summary and review of recent literature, *Personnel Psychology*, **35**, 1982, pp. 251–69.

15. Trankell, A., The psychologist as an instrument of prediction, *J. Applied Psychology*, **43**, 1959, pp. 170–5.

16. Ulrich, L. and Trumbo, D., The selection interview since 1949, *Psychological Bulletin*, **63**, 1965, pp. 110–16.

17. Anderson, R.C., The guided interview as an evaluative instrument, *J. Educational Research*, **48**, 1954, pp. 203–9.

18. Robertson, I. T. and Cooper, C.L., *Human Behaviour in Organisations*, Pitman, London, 1987.

19. Webster, E. C., *Decision Making in the Employment Interview*, Eagle, Montreal, 1964.

20. Hargie, O., Saunders, S. and Dickson, D., *Social Skills in Interpersonal Communication*, Croom Helm, London, 1981.

21. Pugh, D., Understanding and managing organisational change, in Mayon-White, W. (ed.), *Planning and Managing Change*, Harper & Row, London, 1986.

22. Juran, J. M., *Managerial Breakthrough*, McGraw-Hill, New York, 1986.

23. Crosby, P. B., *Quality is Free*, McGraw-Hill, New York, 1979.

24. Brenner, M., Skills in the research interview, in Argyle, M. (ed.), *Social Skills and Work*, Methuen, London, 1981.

25. Warr, P. B., Judgements about people at work, in Warr, P. B. (ed.), *Psychology at Work*, Penguin, London, 1971.

26. Handy, C. B., *Understanding Organisations*, Penguin, London, 1985.

27. Palmer, I. and Chaytor, D., *Training for Counselling and Psychotherapy*, British Association for Counselling, Rugby, 1991.

28. Egan, G., *The Skilled Helper*, Brooks/Cole, Belmont CA, 1990.

29. Mearns, D. and Thorne, B., *Person-Centred Counselling in Action*, Sage, London, 1988.

APPENDIX 4.1: INTERVIEWER'S SELF-EVALUATION QUESTIONNAIRE

Preparation

1. *Background*
   I read all the background   1 2 3 4 5 6 7   I read them during the
   papers before the interview.   interview.

2. *Questions*
   I prepared a list of   1 2 3 4 5 6 7   I made the questions up during
   questions before the   the interview.
   interview.

3. *Recording*
   I decided how to record the   1 2 3 4 5 6 7   I have a good memory.
   answers.

Interview

4. *Layout*
   I put the chairs at right   1 2 3 4 5 6 7   I always sit behind my desk.
   angles and about 1.5 m
   apart.

5. *Beginning*
   I was welcoming and   1 2 3 4 5 6 7   I started straight into the 'real'
   opened with easy questions.   questions.

6. *Distractions*
   I did something about   1 2 3 4 5 6 7   I did nothing about the
   distractions.   distractions and allowed them
           to continue.

7. *Questions*
   I asked clarifying questions.   1 2 3 4 5 6 7   I asked irrelevant questions.
   I asked open questions.   1 2 3 4 5 6 7   I asked closed questions.

8. *Interrupting*
   I did not interrupt.   1 2 3 4 5 6 7   I interrupted persistently.

9. *Timing*
   I asked all my questions and   1 2 3 4 5 6 7   I felt rushed and missed
   did so in good time.   questions out.

Scoring

If your total score comes to 30 or less then you feel you are interviewing well. Scores of 40 and above indicate that you are having some problems—try to identify if they are to do with preparation or with the interview process.

FIVE

NEGOTIATIONS AND NEGOTIATING

'Let us never negotiate out of fear. But let us never fear to negotiate.'
John F. Kennedy

INTRODUCTION

Most managers, when asked about the level and nature of their involvement in negotiations, will reply that they have little or no involvement in wage or contract or purchasing negotiations, and that those activities are the responsibility of specialized functions such as the Personnel or Industrial Relations and Purchasing Departments.

And yet is this true? Do most managers have such a limited exposure to the negotiation process?

The answer is an unequivocal 'No', because we are all negotiators. We learn to negotiate from early childhood, and continue to use and expand these skills for the rest of our lives. These negotiations take place all the time and in all of our lives – at work and at play.

The importance of the negotiating aspect of all managers' jobs was recognized by Mintzberg[1] who, in his study of the roles carried out by managers, allocated the title 'Negotiator' to one of the 'Decisional' roles. The nature, formality and scope of the negotiations carried out by the manager will depend upon a number of factors, which will include the size and culture of the organization and the level of specialization evident in the managerial roles. For example, organizations which fit Harrison's Role culture (Chapter 2) will tend to have people in specialist roles who conduct those negotiations that take place at the interface of the organization and its environment. Examples of these roles would include purchasing or public relations experts. However, within that Role culture and within a People culture organization, the process of internal negotiation would be less specialized and more diffused throughout the organization. Nevertheless, there could be a degree of specialization, as not all managers would necessarily be seen to be either senior or experienced enough to undertake these duties.

However, not all the negotiations that managers are involved in are of a formal nature. There are, for example, those negotiations that occur on a day-to-day basis and are involved in the management and motivation of individuals and teams. These involve who will do what, when and sometimes why, and are often so implicit in the manager's role that they are not recognized as such. But they are negotiations – albeit informal negotiations of limited scope and consequence – but nevertheless negotiations.

The need for all these negotiations arises because human beings have strong drives to seek and achieve goals and to have their needs answered. These needs and goals exert considerable influence upon the way people behave. The ways in which they are displayed and the areas of their application are both diverse. As they can and do influence all the aspects of behaviour, these goals can be personal (e.g. to achieve a certain level of income), social (e.g. to do something about the homeless) or political (e.g. to change local government policies). They can also be complex (e.g. to write a book) or simple (e.g. to get enough food). Their frustration often leads to conflict.

This conflict occurs when the behaviour designed to satisfy one set of needs or to achieve one goal frustrates the satisfaction of another set of needs or the achievement of another goal. For example, a manager's need to finish a task may cause that manager to remain at work into the early evening and so begin to conflict with the need to have regular meals or a social life or to see his or her family. In this example, the resulting conflict could motivate the manager to finish the task quickly by working harder or to feel resentment about being late at work, with a consequent fall-off in work rate. It will also be evident that this conflict is of an internal nature, as no other person is involved. So conflict can be internal or external and can have results that are destructive or constructive. It can involve individuals at one extreme or groups of countries at the other, and can be controlled or uncontrolled. Conflict can also be covert or explicit and can manifest itself through the use of actions or through verbal and written language. For many of us, life is full of situations in which colleagues, friends, partners, relations and superiors differ with others and will not back down. The situational aspects of these conflicts will differ considerably, as will their subject and substance. The level of the desire or will for resolution or solution will also differ considerably. The presence or lack of effective communication can exert considerable influence upon the creation and resolution of these conflict situations. For example, those of you with children or with a partner who also works will be aware of the potential conflict between their apparently opposing needs. Considerable skill is often required in balancing the needs of all the members of the family group, and, in so doing, limiting the level or effects of conflict. Conflict within organizations can arise between departments, teams and individuals and over a wide range of issues, including aims, use of resources and power.

Handy[2] states that organizational conflict has two basic causes:

- Objectives and ideologies.
- Territory.

Lawrence and Lorsch[3] identify that the potential for interdepartmental conflict increases as a result of the increased functional differentiation between departments, which in its turn has arisen from the need for enhanced effectiveness. Morgan,[4] in viewing the organization as a political system, states that the Pluralist view of organizations regards conflict as 'inherent and ineradicable' while the Radical view perceives conflict to be 'inevitable', and a part of a 'wider class conflict'. Harrison[5] identifies the conflict that exists between the factors that best serve the welfare of people within an organization and those that advance the interests of the organization. Pascale[6] describes how conflict can be constructive and argues strongly that such conflict is necessary for an organization's growth and renewal.

So conflicts, in one form or another, together with the need for their effective resolution, are present in every manager's working life. These conflicts can, for example, arise over the use of scarce resources, e.g. money or skilled personnel, over territorial issues, e.g. whose department decides next year's production budget, or originate in individual likes, dislikes and prejudices. The need to resolve these conflicts in an effective manner can often make considerable demands of the manager. This conflict resolution role may also be an expressed rather than an implicit part of a manager's role if, for example, that role involves responsibility for industrial relations or purchasing. The conflicts experienced in those roles could be concerned with wage or salary levels, fringe benefits or the value of bought-in goods and services.

Given the complex nature of our societies, it is not surprising that a variety of ways have developed for coping with conflict. These have evolved in order to cope with a variety of conflict situations and to facilitate either their resolution or limitation. Thomas[7,8] identifies five basic styles of conflict management:

- *Avoidance*   (Ignore it and it will go away, put it into procedure). Generally used with trivial or low-priority issues, issues for which the cost of resolution outweighs the benefits, or those that cannot be won.
- *Competition*   (Use of power and rivalry, win–lose). Used in emergencies, with unpopular issues and as a tactic against others who exploit uncompetitiveness.
- *Accommodation*   (Submit and comply). Used when wrong, to minimize losses when losing or to 'keep the peace'.
- *Collaboration*   (Win–win solutions, unifying solutions). Used to learn, to gain commitment by consensus and to restore a relationship by working through interfering feelings.
- *Compromise*   (Negotiation, deals and trade-offs). Used with equal opponents to resolve incompatible goals, to generate appropriate solutions under time pressure and as an alternative to competing or collaborating when these are seen as too disruptive or demanding.

Negotiation should, therefore, be seen as one of a number of ways of resolving conflict. It is, however, a very commonly used process, both at the formal and informal level, and it is this process that will be examined in this chapter. During that examination we shall consider the characteristics of negotiation, how that process works and, finally, what 'good' negotiators do in order to ensure that the negotiation is conducted in a professional and effective manner.

WHAT IS NEGOTIATION?

The typical dictionary definition of the verb 'to negotiate' includes such concepts as the transaction of business, settling issues by discussion and bargaining, attempting to come to terms, and conferring and seeking agreement. The process of negotiating is also often seen to be synonymous with the process of bargaining, which the typical dictionary defines as involving haggling over terms. However, bargaining can also be seen as a particular form of negotiation in which the desired outcome is agreement.[9] This agreement may not be the only outcome of negotiations. Our own observations of major union–management negotiations and government–government negotiations will remind us that these are often conducted in an environment in which full use is made of press and TV attention to shift or influence public opinion by means of agreed statements. When negotiation is compared with persuasion (Table 5.1), it soon becomes evident that there are differences between these processes. Persuasion is usually seen as an informal one-to-one process in which the outcome is absolute, i.e. the persuasion either works or it does not, whereas negotiation is often seen to be a process of reaching a compromise solution, of 'an exchange of concessions',[10] which is not a process of mutual persuasion. Negotiation also differs from the processes of argument or debate, which are focused towards discussion rather than agreement.

These and other factors indicate that negotiation is a process which:

- Can involve two or several people acting as individuals or representatives.
- Can be formal or informal.
- Is usually, though not exclusively, face-to-face.
- Mainly involves verbal and body language.
- Has conflict both as a starting point and a continuing component.
- Involves joint decision taking.

Table 5.1 Persuasion and negotiation

	Persuasion	Negotiation
Objectives	Persuader wants to get the other to accept a point of view.	Negotiator wants to reach a compromise.
Flexibility	Little: persuader's point is or is not accepted, but can involve coercion, adaption, manipulation and exchanging information.	Considerable: the process of compromise involves change, and information exchange.
Formality	Often informal and face-to-face, e.g. salesman and customer.	Can be informal and face-to-face, but often, in the management context, involves groups or representatives of groups in formal settings.

As such, and as a communication process with a specific preferred outcome, negotiation can be described by Fig. 5.1, which also describes the process that is sometimes called full communication.

As a communication process, negotiation is used for the purposes of:

- Influencing.
- Exchanging information.

However, the balance of these purposes for negotiation is strongly shifted in favour of a primary purpose of influencing. Nevertheless, negotiations often include the exchange of information as a facilitating mechanism towards the achievement of that primary purpose.

But what about outcomes? Morley[11] describes these as a 'set of rules'. These 'rules' can describe, for example, how much people will be paid and for what or how people will behave under certain circumstances. Morley also points out that the outcomes could also include or be limited to an agreed 'story' about the 'what' and 'why' of the negotiations – an outcome that those of us who watch television news programmes will be familiar with.

From all of the above, it appears that the process of negotiation might be defined as:

A process by which people identify mutually acceptable decisions and agree outcomes that define the nature of future interactions.

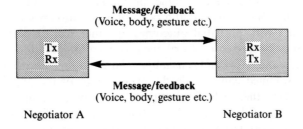

Figure 5.1 Communications in the negotiating process.

The subsequent parts of this chapter will look at how that process takes place and then attempt to identify some of the key factors of skilled negotiating behaviour.

HOW DOES NEGOTIATION TAKE PLACE?

The process of negotiation is a complex process with several stages, which comprises considerably more than a process of haggling over price or value. Even at the simplest level of negotiation, the negotiators need to prepare themselves before they enter the negotiating 'arena' and begin the bargaining process that might lead to a solution. That process of bargaining will involve choices about both strategic and tactical issues, some of which will need to be taken during the bargaining process and some of which will need to be decided well before the process itself begins. The final agreement will need to be approached through a trust-building process, resulting from the joint involvement of the negotiators. Each of these separate steps towards the identification of mutually acceptable decisions is itself complex, and can involve reference to other parties and groups who are not present in the negotiating arena. An example of this in the management negotiation field would be union–management negotiations that need to be ratified by reference either to union members or the company board.

However, the first of the steps in the negotiation process is always that of preparation.

Preparation

Whatever their level of skill and experience, negotiators who fail to prepare put at risk the outcome of the negotiations. At the simplest level, this process involves negotiators and their support teams:

- Recognizing the issues/problems and their causes.
- Generating potential solutions.
- Choosing strategies and tactics for the bargaining process.

This would, for example, involve answering questions such as 'exactly what are we negotiating about?' and 'what do we hope to achieve?'. The answers may not be either as easy to identify or as straightforward as might appear. For example, the negotiation of a long-term contract with a raw material supplier for supply of a key raw material, e.g. steel for the manufacture of motor cars, represents a key factor in that manufacturer's pricing policy. The stabilization or predictability of the price of this material will enable the car manufacturer to be increasingly competitive in a shrinking market. For the steel supplier, a knowledge of long-term demand patterns will enable capital investment decisions to be taken with greater confidence. These capital investment decisions might enable the steel supplier to enhance the conversion efficiency of its plant and so operate at lower unit costs and possibly higher profitability. The understanding of these factors will need to be quantified *before* the actual process of negotiation begins. With negotiations that are about major issues with potential outcomes of either real or perceived importance, e.g. nuclear disarmament or closure of a factory, the process of preparation can involve a significant expenditure of thought and effort and is usually, in larger organizations, undertaken by support teams. The factors examined can include the personalities of the opposing negotiators, their ability to withstand stress, their behaviour at previous negotiations and the location and timing of the negotiations. Some of these, e.g. the location and timing of the negotiations, may indeed be the subject of negotiations themselves, but not without preparation and research.

Most of this research will be focused on the mapping or identification of the bargaining

Table 5.2 Bargaining terrain checklist

1. *Background*
   What are the issues on which negotiation will take place?
   What are the historic facts and figures?
   Who is being negotiated with?
   What is known about their skills, experience, abilities, background and values?
   What is known about their needs and wants?
   Where will the negotiation take place?
   When will the negotiation take place?

2. *Objectives*
   What do we want to achieve?
   What is the best that can be realistically hoped for?
   What is the worst that will be settled for?
   What is known about the opponent's position on the above?

3. *Bargaining Strengths and Weaknesses*
   What are our strengths – technical, price, cost, cash flow, experience, time, etc?
   What are our weaknesses – technical, price, cost, cash flow, experience, time, etc?
   What information do we have about the opponent's strengths and weaknesses?
   What do we know about competitors and their strengths and weaknesses?

'terrain' or 'territory'. A detailed knowledge of the topography of this terrain is of considerable importance to the experienced negotiator, and Table 5.2 is a check list of factors associated with the preparation necessary to achieve a detailed and adequate mapping of that terrain. In addition to providing the answers to the questions outlined in this table, it is also necessary to take decisions about the strategy of the negotiations.

Strategic issues and decisions

Strategy and tactics are often confused. At the simplest level, strategy can be viewed as being concerned with:

- Large-scale issues.
- Final outcomes.

While tactics are concerned with:

- Small-scale issues.
- Short-term issues.

To put it another way, the strategic decisions about a journey will be about where the journey is to (London or New York?), what the mode of travel is (car, train, plane or boat?) and when the journey takes place (next Tuesday or next year?), while the tactical decisions will be about the detail of the route and the nature or style of the interactions with traffic or fellow travellers on the journey. In the general management context, strategic decisions are generally viewed as being about the future commitment of resources and strategy and as being a plan, pattern or position

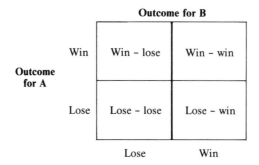

Figure 5.2   Negotiation outcomes.

or 'determination of long-term goals and objectives'.[12] In the specific context of negotiations, the strategic decisions are about the overall pattern and outcomes of the bargaining process, while tactics are about the detail of the bargaining interactions. Negotiations and bargaining are about change, and Kotter and Schlesinger[13] identify that, in the context of changing organizations, the choice of strategy depends upon a number of factors. These factors and some examples of their relevance in the context of negotiations are:

- Anticipated level and nature of resistance (e.g. negotiations with a city over a proposal to locate nuclear waste disposal facility within city limits will involve high levels of resistance).
- Relative power levels of those involved (e.g. negotiations with monopoly supplier of key component).
- Whether the other has information and energy which are key to the change (e.g. negotiations with potential agent for sale of Western pop records in Russia).
- Stakes involved (e.g. prototype of speculative housing modules for space environment: high cost/high risk).

One way of describing the desired outcomes of the negotiations can be illustrated by the use of a simple matrix, as shown in Fig. 5.2. This indicates that, for Negotiator A, the choice of outcomes lies between:

1. A wins and B loses.
2. A loses and B wins.
3. A wins and B wins.
4. A loses and B loses.

In common with all negotiators, A would not find losing to be an acceptable outcome, and so will be faced with a choice between outcome 1 and outcome 3.

These outcomes will result in different negotiating strategies:

Outcome	Strategy
Win–Lose	Distributive or competitive
Win–win	Integrative or collaborative

Table 5.3 Comparison of win–lose and win–win negotiating strategies

	Win–win	Win–lose
Interests	Complementary	In conflict
Information	Available to both sides	Facts are limited and presentation structured
Communications	Clear	Vague and ambiguous
Trust	Full trust needed	Only limited trust needed

The details of these strategies are described below.

Win–lose: distributive or competitive strategy Negotiators who, in the context of union–management negotiations, choose this type of strategy are described by Walton and McKersie[14] as having a primary objective of destroying their opponent's case rather than arguing their own. It is said to involve, when used with team negotiations, tactics of one on one 'marking' and exerting pressure on the less experienced members of the opponent's team. The interests of both parties are seen to be in overt conflict, which can be manifest in emotional outbursts, often premeditated, and it can also involve tactics such as the use of confused and vague communications and limited presentation of 'facts'. These tactics are said to be designed to confuse and disorient the opponent. As a negotiating process it involves limited levels of trust between the negotiators and views opponent's concessions as weaknesses. It carries the risk associated with its use that if A wins on this occasion, by the use of distributive strategy, then B will make sure that they win or both lose next time. This risk tends to ensure that the strategy is used in situations where the winners know that they will not meet the losers again or situations where the losers' feelings or short- and long-term responses are seen to be of no consequence.

Win–win: integrative or collaborative strategy Integrative strategy is based on the concept that both negotiators recognize and acknowledge the presence of shared interests. Pruitt[15] describes this strategy as a search for mutually beneficial agreements. As a strategy it seeks to satisfy both party's needs, and in so doing generate a better deal for all involved. It requires high levels of trust, an open exchange of information and the willingness to compromise, and as such is in many ways the complete opposite of the distributive or competitive strategy.

The characteristics of both of these strategies are summarized in Table 5.3. Whatever the strategy chosen, the core of the negotiation itself will often be associated with the process of bargaining.

THE BARGAINING PROCESS

Bargaining is often described as that process which involves haggling, dealing or bartering, and as such it is the process that lies at the heart of the negotiating terrain whose topography was outlined earlier. The presence of several stages in successful negotiations has been identified by a number of researchers, including Morley,[11] Douglas[16] and Morley and Stephenson.[9] These stages can be described as follows:

- An initial stage in which both negotiators undertake a formal ritual designed to depersonalize the process by emphasizing the representative nature of their roles, identify their positions and the incompatibility of their respective goals by long speeches and responses.

- A second stage in which negotiators engage in more informal and 'unofficial' behaviour designed to facilitate the process of searching for potential areas of agreement. Behaviour is individual rather than representative, and agreements made are not binding. This stage can be seen as one which prepares the ground for the next stage.
- A third and final stage in which behaviour returns to that of the formal representative role and is focused upon offers, decisions and agreements.

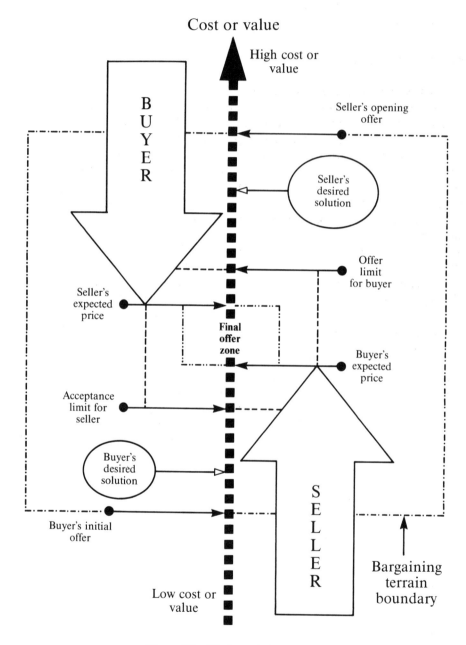

Figure 5.3 The bargaining process.

The process of preparation, which was identified as being so crucial earlier in this chapter, is a major contributor to all of these stages. The effective completion of these stages can demand much, in terms of stamina and skill, of the negotiator. A framework for some of the dimensions of this process can be illustrated by Fig. 5.3. This figure indicates, for the example of a commercial negotiation, the boundaries of both the bargaining terrain and the final offer zone in terms of the expectations and limits of both the buyer and the seller. These can be seen to include:

- *Buyer's offer and seller's acceptance limits*
  These represent the lowest figure that the seller is prepared to sell for and the highest figure which the buyer is prepared to buy at.
- *Buyer's and seller's expected prices*
  These represent the guesses that the buyer and seller have made about the expected outcome of the negotiation
- *Buyer's and seller's desired solutions*
  These represent the ideal outcomes for the buyer and seller respectively.
- *Buyer's initial and seller's opening offers*
  These represent the respective initial entry levels into the bargaining terrain.

It is worth noting that the differences between the above are as follows:

$$\begin{array}{rcl}
\text{Seller's opening offer} & > > > & \text{Buyer's initial offer} \\
\text{Desired solution for seller} & > > > & \text{Desired solution for buyer} \\
\text{Buyer's limit for offer} & > > & \text{Seller's limit for acceptance} \\
\text{Seller's expected price} & > & \text{Buyer's expected price}
\end{array}$$

where, '$>$' means 'greater than', '$> >$' means 'much greater than', and so on.

It is also worth noting that, for a successful negotiation, these values must ultimately converge and achieve parity within the final offer zone.

The process of bargaining is one that can demand much skill, stamina and experience from the manager. It is, however, a process that we are all exposed to in both our working and our social lives. The next section of this chapter will examine briefly how a successful negotiator behaves in the negotiating environment.

THE EFFECTIVE NEGOTIATOR

Much of the research conducted on how negotiators negotiate is based on laboratory simulations rather than real negotiation situations. This situation has arisen partly because the presence of an 'outsider', i.e. a researcher, during real and often delicate negotiations could put those negotiations at risk and, also and more pragmatically, because it would require the agreement of both parties. Nevertheless, there is enough evidence to provide clear indications as to how a skilled and effective negotiator behaves during the process of negotiation. Rackham and Carlisle[17] observed effective negotiators, who were defined as

- Being rated as effective by both sides of the negotiation.
- Having a record of successes.
- Having low levels of implementation failure.

Observation of the behaviour of these skilled negotiators indicated that they tended to *avoid* the

Table 5.4   Samples of unskilled negotiating behaviour

Irritators
Management negotiator: *'I believe that we are making an offer which, given the current state of the market, is not just fair but also downright generous.'*

Responsive counter-proposals
Negotiator A: *'I suggest that we have a coffee before we drive over to John's.'*
Negotiator B: *'How about having coffee when we get there?'*

Defence/attack patterns
Negotiator A: *'What you are asking is ridiculous. If you had any understanding of basic economics you would know what I'm talking about.'*
Negotiator B: *'If you had any understanding of people then you wouldn't be proposing such an arrangement.'*
Negotiator A: *'In all of my 20 years as a manager I've never met such an uncooperative attitude as yours.'*
Negotiator B: *'I don't care about your 20 years experience, etc.'*

Dilution by argument
Management negotiator: *'I believe that this proposal for revised working hours is the right proposal because it enables the company to be more responsive to its customers, make better use of part-time workers and solves our car parking problems.'*
Union negotiator: *'It's funny that you should mention the car parking – I've had it in mind to talk to you about that for some time.'*

Signalling disagreement
Negotiator: *'I disagree with your proposals because they don't go far enough to meet my needs and will cost me too much to implement.'*

---

following types of behaviour (examples of which may be seen in Table 5.4):

● *Irritators*
  These are described as words and phrases with negligible persuasive effect which cause irritation.
● *Immediate counter-proposals*
  These occur when a proposal by one negotiator is immediately followed by an alternative or counter proposal from the other negotiator.

  They are seen to:
  — Be perceived as blocking in nature.
  — Occur when the other negotiator is not receptive, as his or her attention is focused on their own proposal.
  — Diminish the focus or clarity of the negotiations.
● *Patterns of related defence and attack*
  These occur when negotiations become emotionally heated. Attack by one will lead to defence by the other, which, in its turn, is perceived as attack Rackham and Carlisle describe this pattern as 'Defence/attack spirals', thus indicating the increasing vigour of the sequential responses.
● *Dilution by argument*
  Rackham and Carlisle observe that unskilled negotiators used too many reasons to support their case. Too many reasons are said to:
  — Provide more material for dispute.
  — Introduce potential weaknesses.

Table 5.5   Samples of skilled negotiating behaviour

Signalling behaviour
Negotiator: *'I wonder if I might ask a question – how many times has this happened?'*

Not signalling disagreement
Negotiator: *'Because your proposals don't go far enough to meet my needs and will cost me too much to implement, I cannot agree to what you are suggesting.'*

Testing and summarizing
Negotiator: *'If I can summarize where I think we've got to – you have said that you will be able to accept our revised proposals about pay structures but have difficulty with the current working hours proposals. Have I understood you correctly?'*

Implementation concern
Negotiator: *'I would like to ask some more questions about the new duty rota and how it will work, since in the end my members will have to work this new rota.'*

Seeking information
Negotiator: *'At what size of order would I get a bigger discount?'*

Statements about feelings
Negotiator: *'We've been talking now for almost an hour and I'm beginning to feel some concern about the big differences that there still are between us.'*

However, observation of the behaviour of skilled negotiators indicates that they tended to *use* the following types of behaviour (examples in Table 5.5):

● *Behaviour signals or labels*
These are described as giving prior or advance notice of the following behaviour and are also said to:

— Slow the negotiation process down and thus provide time for thought.
— Keep the negotiation at a formal level.

● *Reason/disagreement patterns*
However, behaviour labels are rarely used to signal disagreement. Rackham and Carlisle report that skilled negotiators precede statements of disagreement with statements of reasons.
● *Testing and summarizing*
These are said to be used significantly more by skilled negotiators and were concerned with prevention of misunderstanding and the promotion of clarity. Associated processes are:

— Reflecting (see Chapter 3).
— Concern about implementation.

● *Seeking information*
The use of this behaviour is also said to facilitate control of negotiations and to provide time to think while the other party is occupied in generating the answer.

● *Statements about feelings*
Skilled negotiators were observed to give more information about feelings and motives.

Stephenson[18] also reports that the process of negotiating is influenced by the nature of the personal relationships established by the negotiators. Summarized evidence from several workers reports factors such as maturity, confidence in the other's cooperation and determination to avoid inter-personal hostility as influential upon the outcomes of negotiations.

CONCLUSION

The process of negotiation is often described as an 'art form' rather than a science. The aim of this chapter has, nevertheless, been to identify the main characteristics of that process and to identify how it has been undertaken with success. Negotiations are seen to be one way of resolving the conflicts that occur in many areas of the manager's working life. The effectiveness of this joint decision-making process is strongly influenced by the level and quality of preparation undertaken and the negotiation strategy selected. A collaborative or win–win strategy will require shared information, clear communications and high levels of mutual trust, while a distributive or win–lose strategy involves limited trust, communication and information. The bargaining process is seen to be at the heart of all negotiations and to involve three stages:

● Ritualized position identification.
● Informal search for agreement.
● Finalization and formalization of agreement.

The behaviour of effective negotiators is seen as including:

● Behaviour signals.
● Preceding disagreement by reasons.
● Testing and summarizing.
● Seeking information.
● Expressing feelings.

As with all communication processes, there is, in the end, no substitute for real experience, and Appendix 5.1 is designed to help you assess your own negotiating skill and ability.

EXERCISES

1. List the subjects and level of formality of negotiations which you take part in at work and at home.
2. In the last negotiation that you were involved in, did you:
   Have enough information?   Yes ☐   No ☐
   Plan how to use what you had?   Yes ☐   No ☐
   Decide what your objectives were?   Yes ☐   No ☐
   Decide what strategy to use?   Yes ☐   No ☐
3. Think back to the last negotiation that you were involved in, at work or at home, and list those of the behaviours that skilled negotiators do and do not use which you think you may have used.

4. 'Negotiations should only be undertaken by skilled practitioners': discuss and identify the implications for training and development of managers.

5. You are faced with conducting an annual price review negotiation with a supplier who is in a monopoly situation and who has a reputation for adopting a take it or leave it attitude in these negotiations. Identify in detail both the overall strategy you intend to take and your opening tactics.

REFERENCES

1. Mintzberg, M., *The Nature of Managerial Work*, Harper & Row, New York, 1973.
2. Handy, C. B., *Understanding Organisations*, Penguin, London, 1985.
3. Lawrence, P. R. and Lorsch, J. W., High-performing organisations in three environments, in Pugh, D. S. (ed.), *Organisation Theory*, Penguin, London, 1990.
4. Morgan, G., *Images of Organisation*, Sage, London, 1986.
5. Harrison, R., Understanding your organisation's character, *Harvard Business Review*, May–June 1972, pp. 119–28.
6. Pascale, R., *Managing on the Edge: How Successful Companies use Conflict to Stay Ahead*, Penguin, London, 1990.
7. Thomas, K. W., Conflict and conflict management, in Dunnette, M. D. (ed.), *Handbook of Industrial and Organizational Psychology*, Rand McNally, Chicago, 1976.
8. Thomas, K. W., Toward multi-dimensional values in teaching: the example of conflict behaviours, *Academy of Management Review*, **12**, 1977, pp. 484–90.
9. Morley, I. E. and Stephenson, G. M., *The Social Psychology of Bargaining*, Allen & Unwin, London, 1977.
10. Pruitt, D. G., Indirect communication and the search for agreement in negotiation, *J. Applied Social Psychology*, **1**, 1971, pp. 205–39.
11. Morley, I. E., Negotiating and bargaining, in Hargie, O. (ed.), *A Handbook of Communication Skills*, Routledge, London, 1986.
12. Moore, J. I., *Writers on Strategy and Strategic Management*, Penguin, London, 1992.
13. Kotter, J. P. and Schlesinger, L. A., Choosing strategies for change, *Harvard Business Review*, **57**(2), March/April 1979, pp. 106–13.
14. Walton, R. E. and McKersie, R. B., *A Behavioural Theory of Labor Negotiations*, McGraw-Hill, New York, 1965.
15. Pruit, D. G., *Negotiation Behaviour*, Academic Press, New York, 1981.
16. Douglas, A., *Industrial Peacemaking*, Columbia University Press, New York, 1962.
17. Rackham, N. and Carlisle, J., The Effective Negotiator, Part 1: The behaviour of negotiators, *J. European Training*, **2**(6), 1978, pp. 6–10.
18. Stephenson, G., Inter-group relations and negotiating behaviour, in Warr, P. B. (ed.), *Psychology at Work*, Penguin, London, 1976.

APPENDIX 5.1: NEGOTIATING SKILLS SELF-EVALUATION QUESTIONNAIRE

1. *Winning and losing*
   We should both win.   1 2 3 4 5 6 7   I must win, he or she should lose.

2. *The ideal negotiator*
   (a) Speaks circumspectly and precisely.   1 2 3 4 5 6 7   Speaks easily and skilfully.
   (b) Discreet and subtle.   1 2 3 4 5 6 7   Overbearing and sure of him- or herself.
   (c) Shows common sense clarity and open-mindedness.   1 2 3 4 5 6 7   Very analytical with a perfect memory.
   (d) Dresses in an unaffected way.   1 2 3 4 5 6 7   Dresses in a trendy way.

3. *Relationships*
   (a) Do you try to develop a human side to your interactions?   1 2 3 4 5 6 7   Do you keep it on a strictly business-like basis?
   (b) Do you ask for verification of false figures or statements later?   1 2 3 4 5 6 7   Do you interrupt to expose the error immediately?
   (c) Do you return what you think is rudeness with patience?   1 2 3 4 5 6 7   Do you return what you think is rudeness with the same?
   (d) Do you listen more than talk?   1 2 3 4 5 6 7   Do you talk more than listen?

4. *Bargaining*
   (a) Do you make concessions?   1 2 3 4 5 6 7   Do you refuse to budge?
   (b) Do you trade concession for concession?   1 2 3 4 5 6 7   Do you take concessions and give nothing back?
   (c) If you are buying, do you pitch your first offer well below what you hope to buy at?   1 2 3 4 5 6 7   If you are buying, do you pitch your first offer close to what you hope to buy at?

Scoring

If your total score comes to 36 or less then you appear to be negotiating well. Scores of 48 to 84 indicate that you are having some problems and may be looking for a quick fix or a win–lose negotiation.

SIX

GROUPS, TEAMS AND MEETINGS

'A committee is a group that keeps the minutes but loses hours.'
Milton Berle

INTRODUCTION

Robert Townsend expressed many manager's feelings about meetings when he wrote:[1]

'Generally speaking, the fewer the better. Both as to the number of meetings and the number of participants.'

Certainly, many meetings can waste a great deal of time and often appear to be held for reasons that have little to do with the business in hand. Hodgson[2] estimates that in the UK alone a total of four million hours are spent in meetings *each day* and Stewart[3] found that 32 per cent of the manager's time was spent in dyad meetings, i.e. with one other person, and 34 per cent in meetings with two or more persons. Mintzberg[4] also reports a commitment to scheduled meetings by chief executives of large organizations amounting to 59 per cent of their day.

But meetings do appear to satisfy a deep human need. They have occurred throughout human history and are a reflection of a need to interact socially that we continue to express despite our technology and tools. Katz[5] wrote that human beings, being social animals, are subject to one of the 'most potent' forms of motivation in the form of the stimulation, approval and support that are derived from our interactions with one another.

So holding a meeting appears to be something that groups of people do often, sometimes at considerable cost, and for a tremendous apparent variety of reasons.

The apparent reasons for or purposes of these meetings could be any one, or several together, of the examples shown in Table 6.1. However, Handy[6] suggests that these purposes can be classified as:

- Those required by the organization and concerned with management, control and coordination issues.
- Those which answer the needs of the individuals attending and concerned with individual social and psychological needs.

From a broader viewpoint, Jay[7] suggests that the purposes of meetings include the following:

- To define the group.
- To allow that definition to be revised and updated.
- To help individuals understand the collective aims of the group.
- To act as a status arena.

Table 6.1   Sample purposes of meetings

Taking decisions
Giving and receiving information
Negotiating
Resolving differences or conflicts
Planning
Generating new ideas or concepts
Reviewing progress or past activities
Coordinating activities
Controlling activities
Allocating responsibilities

The ways in which meetings can be described also show considerable variety, with assemblies, councils, boards, cabinets and committees all being samples of alternative titles. However, whatever their title, all of these meetings consist of groups of people who are communicating with each other. The purposes of objectives of that communication include, in common with many communication processes, those identified in Chapter 1 as being:

• Exchanging information.
• Influencing.
• Instructing.

The patterns of interaction associated with that communication are often complex and will be examined later in this chapter. They will, however, be those associated with two-way communication, which involves the use of both spoken and written language as well as those 'bodily communications' which supplement and complement our spoken words (see Chapter 10).

The purpose of this chapter is to examine the how and why of meetings. To do this we shall first examine some of the factors associated with those groups of people that are embodied in these meetings and how they function.

WHAT IS A GROUP?

The word 'group' is usually used in everyday life to describe a number of people, objects, animals, concepts or ideas which exist in a close physical, social or conceptual relationship to one another. The typical dictionary definition of a group involves comments about numbers of things or persons that are classed or belong together. This sort of definition indicates that, at least at a basic level, the concept of a group involves multiplicity, i.e. numbers of things or people, and proximity. However, further definitions begin to bring in other concepts, such as collectivism and cooperation, and characteristics such as shared views, social customs and beliefs. This is an important shift in definition, and can be illustrated by an examination of the differences between a baseball team and the crowd entering a London mainline railway station at rush hour. The rush hour crowd consists of a large number of people who are in close physical (often too close!) proximity. The same will apply to the baseball team in so far that it consists of players, manager, coach, etc. who are in close physical proximity when functioning as a team. But what about 'shared views, social customs and beliefs' and being a 'collective' unit?

Those of you with experience of London mainline railway stations at rush hour will be aware that the people in the crowd do share a common purpose – to get on the train, get a seat if possible, and to get home. But the individuals who make up that crowd are rarely aware of the detail of the objectives of the other people around them, and often only become aware of those objectives or purposes when they conflict with their own objectives, e.g. in conflicts over space or seating. It is rare for crowds of this nature to display a common purpose that involves cooperative action. A baseball team, however, needs that cooperative action in order to function. They will have learned to play together in order to achieve a common objective, i.e. to win the game or to be top of the league. They will have a team identity which for successful teams, will tolerate and accommodate individual ambitions but will ensure that these are achieved through the medium of the team.

Other more detailed and extensive definitions of groups have focused, either singly or together, on the factors of:

- Size.
- Purpose.
- Nature of internal interaction.

Cooley[8] identifies the *Primary* group, which is characterized by:

- Face-to-face interaction.
- Association and cooperation.
- Having a fundamental influence on 'social nature and ideas' of individuals.

An obvious example of the Primary group is the family, but it can also exist in the workplace as a small team consisting of a manager with a number of personnel under his or her direct control. The size of the group will be limited by the need for face-to-face interaction leading to cooperation and association. Communication within these groups is often based on the use of verbal language and non-verbal 'body' language.

Secondary groups are described[9] as being characterized by:

- Large numbers of people.
- Limited face-to-face interaction and cooperation.
- A declared common goal or objective which is often of lower priority than individual goals.

Examples of Secondary groups include the US Senate, the UK Parliament, political parties, large committees, etc. In the workplace, departments and divisions are generally secondary groups, with the large number of people involved limiting the opportunities for face-to-face interaction. Communications within these groups are often limited to the written medium, supported by verbal communication via the channel of the telephone. The size and culture of these larger groups can also often lead to the generation of rules and procedures about communication both within the group and with other groups or individuals outside the group (see Chapter 2). It is worth noting that Primary groups can and do exist within Secondary groups, as, for example, with the work team which exists within the department.

Both Primary and Secondary Groups can be created or designed, and as such are generally described as *Formal* groups. Many of the groups that exist in our workplaces are formal in nature and are:

- Created with a specific purpose or desired outcome.

- Hierarchical, with a formal leader and often with other designated roles for group members.
- Usually permanent, but can be temporary.
- Often subject to changes in individuals involved, but less often to change in the roles involved.

Examples of Formal groups would include departments, work groups and project teams, though the latter will often cease to exist on completion of the project. Roles within these formal groups can be the subject of written definitions, e.g. job specifications, and the nature of the communications patterns, media and channels will depend upon the size and culture of the group (see Primary and Secondary group definitions above). One example of a group which is both Formal and Secondary is the department. The department is generally permanent in nature and has its composition and role structure described in organizational documentation, such as an organization chart. The department will have a manager who acts as leader and coordinator and who will be responsible for the department's performance to his or her boss.

Informal groups exist to satisfy those social and emotional needs that are not satisfied by the formal groups. They can exist within formal groups or on their own and generally come into being because of chance or the choices and preferences of the individual members. They can often act as informal communication networks or 'grapevines'. Communication within these groups is often, as with Primary groups, based on verbal use of language and non-verbal 'body' language. Examples of these informal groups can be a coffee club, a car pool or a lunch group.

These classifications of groups provide a useful conceptual framework from which we can view the groups in which managers work or with which they have contact. Before we look at the way in which groups work it is worthwhile examining three other factors which significantly influence the group performance. These are the factors of:

- Group size.
- Group interaction.
- Group composition.

Group size

Group size and the effect which it has on the ways in which groups operate has been the subject of a considerable amount of research. McGrath and Altman[10] identify that small groups have a number of characteristics, including:

- Less perceived need for guidance and leadership.
- Members express less ideas and change less.

However, Krech *et al.*[11] comment that small groups tend to exhibit 'greater group cohesiveness' and members of these groups display higher levels of satisfaction. Increased group size is said to 'inhibit participation of some members' and generate issues about group leadership. Handy[6] observes that as group size increases, the range and diversity of skills and abilities within the group also increases, but the individual has, on average, less chance of contributing.

Handy also identifies that members who contribute or participate more are perceived to be more influential and vice versa. Hare[12] states that as the group size increases:

- More opportunities arise for subgroup formation.
- The gap between frequent contributors and others increases.
- Group leaders have to coordinate activity more.

- Less time is usually taken to complete a task.
- Communication patterns will change to more 'mechanical' and less interactive, owing to the larger numbers involved.
- The group may become less sensitive to minority issues.
- Fewer consensual and more autocratic decisions are taken.

It also seems evident that, with increasing group size, the quality and diversity of group discussion is changed, with, as Hoffman[13] observes, the introverted members becoming more inhibited and potential dissenters less willing to speak for fear of being thought 'deviant'.

The 'right' size of group is a compromise between the higher levels of representation, skill and knowledge diversity and creative conflict which larger groups engender and the higher levels of participation, cohesiveness and involvement that occur in smaller groups. Handy[6] states that if participation and involvement are key issues then five to seven appears to be an optimum size. Douglas[14] indicates that small groups can contain from five to fifteen members, but also states that maximum interaction within the group usually results from groups at the lower end of that size span. Argyle[15] identifies the changes in social interaction that follow increase in group size and comments that a group of five to six appears to meet most people's social and task needs.

Size is not, however, the sole factor in determining the effectiveness of a group, and the following section will examine aspects of the group interactions and composition.

How does a group work?

An effective group is the mechanism that converts the activities of individuals, working towards answering their own needs, into a cohesive, dynamic and interactive unit which works towards the achievement of compatible goals. So how does that happen?

Kakabadse et al.[9] identify that what goes on inside a group, i.e. its social interactions and dynamics, can be said to fall into three groups of behaviour patterns. These are:

- *Behaviours concerned with the task of the group*
  These are concerned with harnessing the collective skills and abilities of the group towards the chosen or given task. Behaviours such as decision taking and managing, giving and seeking of information and opinions, agreement and disagreement, testing understanding and summarizing all fall into this set of task-related behaviours.
- *Behaviours concerned with group morale and harmony*
  These are concerned with the quality and level of interaction taking place within the group, i.e. the group process rather than its outcome. Peace-keeping, harmonizing and providing feedback are all examples of these maintenance-related behaviours.
- *Behaviours concerned with individual member's goals and needs*
  These are related to the individual's need and wants and are concerned with issues such as power, status, prestige, belonging and friendship. Examples of these self-related behaviours include point scoring, withdrawing, seeking recognition, attacking and defending and trivializing.

Some samples of the behaviours associated with these groupings are given in Table 6.2.

Nor does the balance or ebb and flow of these behaviours remain static. Groups grow, mature, change and develop. Initially time is needed for the group members to get to know each other and assess their strengths, weaknesses, beliefs and value systems. Later, alliances and subgroups are formed, dissolve and reform. Studies of this development process indicate that it has a number of sequential stages. Tuckman[16] identifies these stages to be:

- *Forming* a time of inhibited, guarded, watchful, polite behaviour.
- *Storming* confidence grows and conflicts over personality, approaches, standards and beliefs emerge, giving rise to opting out behaviour and feelings of demotivation.
- *Norming* organization, systems, standards and procedures are established, as are understandings about individual skills and abilities – high task focus evident.
- *Performing* cohesiveness, mutual support, flexibility and productivity.

Table 6.2 Samples of group behaviours

1. **Task-related**
Initiating:

> *'I'd like to suggest that we take a look at the information available before we identify what our choices are.'*

Seeking information:

> *'Can we complete the indoor redecoration in time for the Sports Club annual dinner on 23 July?'*

Summarizing and decision management:

> *'I believe that we have now heard all the available information and been able to express our opinions of their relevance and accuracy. So may I suggest that we begin to think about what we are going to do?'*

2. **Maintenance-related**
Peace-keeping:

> *'I do see that you both feel strongly about this issue. Can we see if we can find some common ground?'*

Giving feedback:

> *'I do like the overall feel of your proposal, but I am a little unsure about some of the detail.'*

Encouraging:

> *'Well done.'*

3. **Self-related**
Defending:

> *'I really cannot understand why you are attacking this proposal since you yourself suggested something very similar last June.'*

Withdrawing:

> *'No comment.'*

Point scoring:

> *'I must express some surprise that the Accounts Department feels able to comment on some of the chemical formulation of our new perfume. Perhaps I should give up chemistry and take up accounting!'*

Whether a group will move, or needs to move, through all these stages to the mature performing stage will depend upon the nature of the task and the time available. For example, with a short time-scale, high-priority task, there may not be time to allow or encourage the full development process to occur. This does not necessarily mean that the group is ineffective – it may well achieve its task targets, but the interpersonal conflicts and barriers will not have been tackled and will, if the group were to remain together, emerge with a subsequent 'regression' of the group back from the 'norming' to the 'storming' stage. In some groups, a cyclic pattern of 'norming' → 'storming-' → 'norming' can occur. Even when time and organizational support is available for this development process, the transition out of the above 'storming/norming' cycle or just the 'storming' stage alone is said[9] to require high levels of skill from the group leader. That leader will need high levels of communicative ability allied with listening and counselling skills.

Group composition

The ability and willingness of a group to develop to the stage where it is capable of mature performance depends upon a number of factors. Some of these are external to the group, for example, the nature and time-scale of the task or the willingness of the organization to allow the group to develop. However, others are internal to the group. The key role of the leader in this development process has already been mentioned but there is also evidence that the ways in which team members work together are as crucial to the effective functioning of a team. Belbin[17] and Margerison and McCann[18] have both developed blueprints for the composition of the 'ideal' team. Belbin examined, via the use of psychometric tests, the characteristics of teams involved in playing management games. The objective of this research was to establish whether there were any common characteristics among those teams that were successful and those that were unsuccessful. Belbin established that successful teams are made up of people who can carry out eight different roles. The original outlines established for these roles were:

- *Chairman* described as being 'calm, self-confident and self-controlled', this role clarifies group objectives and sets agendas.
- *Company worker* a hard-working practical organizer who turns other team member's ideas into manageable tasks.
- *Shaper* 'outgoing and dynamic', this role is the task leader, uniting ideas and shaping the application of team effort.
- *Plant* 'individualistic and unorthodox', this role is the ideas generator for the team, but can be detached from practicality.
- *Resource investigator* often described as the fixer of the team; this role has high communicative skills and social acceptability.
- *Monitor–evaluator* the analyst of the team, who tends to be 'sober, unemotional and prudent'.
- *Team worker* 'mild and sensitive', this role listens and communicates well and often smoothes conflict.
- *Completer–Finisher* a perfectionist who has to check every detail.

According to Belbin, each individual has a preferred team role. That individual will also have a secondary role which he or she will act in if the preferred role is occupied by a more powerful individual or if no other is able to perform that secondary role. The original roles defined by Belbin were later modified to include a *Specialist* role and to change the role title for the *Chairman* role to *Coordinator* and the title for the *Company worker* role to *Implementer*. The

Specialist role is described as one which views the team task or objectives through the medium, and with the limitations, of their area of individual expertise. Unassertive behaviour by this role can lead to the team ignoring the functional skill and expertise it represents.

The presence of all these roles in a team is said to result in a balanced and effective team which:

- Makes the best use of its resources.
- Has the ability to bounce back from disappointments.
- Displays adaptability.
- Contains creative capability which is limited to a few members.
- Has limited dependence on key members.

Both the Belbin and the Margerison and McCann approaches to team composition management have developed self-assessment questionnaires to enable individual optimal roles to be identified.

MEETINGS

These groups of people come together and interact at the social gatherings that we often call meetings. As indicated earlier in this chapter, Jay[7] identifies the purposes of meetings as being:

- To define the group.
- To allow that definition to be revised and updated.
- To help individuals to understand the collective aims of the group.
- To act as a status arena.

Meetings can differ considerably in size, and this size factor has a significant influence upon the roles and actions of those involved in the meeting. For example, large meetings or gatherings involving several hundred people are usually formal and designed or structured in such a way as to enable the audience to be addressed by one or more speakers. There may be a coordinating or chairperson role, but very little opportunity is provided for formal audience participation. As a result, when contentious or emotive subjects are addressed, as for example at political election meetings or company shareholder meetings, then informal and interruptive audience participation occurs. This takes the form of heckling, catcalling or the Bronx cheer (a raspberry) and can be very disruptive. An example of a smaller but also formal meeting involving some fifty or so participants is that of a town council. These are formally chaired meetings attended by elected representatives and are structured in such a way that any member or representative may speak. These meetings usually have strict rules and procedures for the way in which the business of the meeting is conducted. However, informal subgroup meetings in which members will conduct conversations with other members often occur within these formal meetings. Members will also move about or leave the room while formal speeches are being made. In the UK, the televised proceedings of the House of Commons provides a graphic example of this type of meeting, with numbers of attendees ranging between dozens and several hundred depending upon the time of day and the issue under discussion.

A third and much more common type and size of meeting is that of the committee. These are very common in both the public and private sectors. Their title can be that of project meeting, sub-committee, working party, board, quality circle, control group or any other of dozens of titles. These meetings or committees can have up to around twelve members who function under the control and guidance of a chairperson. The members take part on at least a theoretically equal footing and contribute as and when they wish to do so within the limits of the Chairperson's perception of 'good order'. The proceedings of these meetings are generally organized and orderly and the meeting will have an objective or set of objectives which the parent organization has defined.

Examples of these objectives might be:

- To revise next year's budget.
- To agree a recruitment policy.
- To monitor progress on a project.

Membership of these committees can be on a representative basis, e.g. members representing their departments or work groups, or on an individual basis, e.g. because they have a skill or knowledge which the committee needs. The frequency of meetings of these committees can differ considerably, and is often related to the tasks or objectives of the committee. Examples of this would include a daily production scheduling meeting, a weekly sales review meeting, a monthly team meeing, a quarterly group performance review meeting and an annual board meeting.

It is these committee meetings which make up the majority of the meetings that a manager attends. Jay[7] estimates that some *11 million* of these meetings take place *every day* in the USA, and it is because these committee meetings are such a significant consumer of management time that this chapter will now examine the ways in which they can be made more effective. The first of the issues that will be examined is that of the *communication patterns* that exist within the meeting.

Georgiades and Orlans[19] state that these patterns of communication are about:

- Who speaks and for how long.
- To or with whom he or she speaks.
- Who speaks afterwards and how often.

For example, a meeting dominated by a limited number of members would display a communication pattern similar to that shown in Fig. 6.1(a), whereas a meeting with a strong and controlling chairperson who acts as the focus for all communication will display a pattern as in Fig. 6.1(b). It will be evident that these patterns reveal much about the meeting, including, for example, if and how the members are cooperating or forming subgroups. The interaction shown in Fig. 6.1(c) illustrates a meeting in which communication is not dominated by a few and is full in its nature, whereas the interactions in Figs. 6.1(a) and (b) are dominated or controlled by a few. The communication in these latter groups will still be two-way, but for some members may be restricted to 'bodily communication' (see Chapter 10). These patterns will define both the amount and the nature of the information to which each member of the meeting is exposed. Even when these patterns involve full and open interchange between all members, i.e. as in Fig. 6.1(c), the question remains as to whether they are relevant to or compatible with:

- The task.
- The skills and abilities of the group members.
- The information available.

For example, a task for which there exists very limited background information but which necessitates urgent decision taking may generate or even need communication patterns as in Figs. 6.1(a) or (b) if the meeting contains a limited number of members with experience of similar

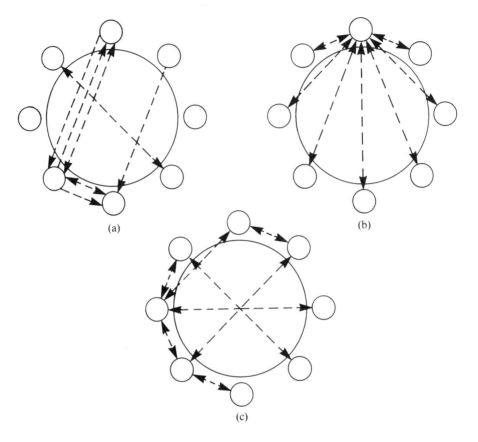

(a)

(b)

(c)

Figure 6.1 Examples of meeting communication patterns.

tasks. If, however, the meeting contains no prior experience but requires an innovative solution, then Fig. 6.1(c) will illustrate the type of patterns exhibited as the resources of the group are drawn into the generation of a consensus decision.

Von Bergen and Kirk[20] comment that strong pressures exist, within meetings, for members to increase the 'uniformity of their individual judgements'. They identify the phenomenon of '*groupthink*', which is described as occurring in groups which put a high value on the presence of cohesion, unity and *esprit de corps*. A meeting displaying the 'groupthink' phenomenon is said to display the symptoms of:

- Shared feeling of unassailability, moral and ethical rectitude and inordinate optimism.
- Strong internal safeguards to prevent internal challenge or threat to unanimity, including self-censoring by members and direct pressure on dissenters.
- Ability to collectively discount symptoms of potential problems or failure.
- Ability to collectively perceive information incompatible with or threatening to consensus as originating from the 'opposition', who are seen as being inept and incompetent.
- The illusion that unanimity has been achieved when vocal majority of members agree.

The implications of this pattern of behaviour are considerable. However, while most managers

Table 6.3 Chairperson behaviours

Task-related	Maintenance-related
Summarizing	Putting members at ease
Questioning	Listening actively
Encouraging	Harmonizing
Catalysing information exchange	Encouraging participation
	Creating atmosphere of trust
Coordinating	Setting standards
Diagnosing	Using humour
Evaluating	Defusing interpersonal conflict
Directing	Facilitating communication

will have experienced groupthink in one form or another, it is not intrinsic to the meeting process and can be avoided.

One of the most successful antidotes to groupthink lies in the way that the meeting is led. The role of leading a meeting is usually formalized in the role of the *chairperson*. A typical dictionary definition of this role encompasses the responsibility for 'presiding over a meeting' and the synonyms of presiding include the acts of moderation, arbitration and regulation. When the diverse nature of meetings is considered it will be evident that the range of behaviours expected from the chairperson role is wide. These range from that of controlling the highly formalized, almost ritualistic, proceedings of very formal meetings through to Belbin's coordinator, who is not formally appointed but acts, in less formal or informal meetings, in the chairing role.

One of the characteristics of skilled behaviour in the chairperson role is the ability to discriminate between the needs associated with group or meeting maintenance and those associated with the group or meeting task. Once these differing needs are identified, the skilled chairperson will also display the ability to focus on which of these will ensure the meeting's productivity. Earlier in this chapter, maintenance-related behaviour was described as being concerned with the morale and harmony of the group and the quality of the group interaction, while task-related behaviour was described as being concerned with harnessing the collective skills and abilities of the group towards a given task. The chairperson role would, in exercising these behaviours, undertake the functions identified in Table 6.3. It should be noted that several of the behaviours identified in this table have much in common with those identified in Chapter 3 as being concerned with the process of active listening.

However, Jay[7] reports that the chairperson has to concentrate upon tasks associated with social leadership, i.e. maintenance-related behaviour, rather than undertake task advocacy him- or herself. Jay also reports that skilled chairpersons will delegate that advocacy to others either before or during the meeting. Appendix 6.1 contains a chairperson self-assessment questionnaire.

The ideal chairperson's behaviours, which lead to effective meetings, are not limited to the actual meeting itself. Pre-meeting and post-meeting behaviour is also an important aspect of the chairperson role, and this is concerned with two features. These are:

- Papers, i.e. agendas and minutes.
- People, i.e. who should attend and who should speak on what.

AGENDAS AND MINUTES

These documents are usually only present at formal meetings and their purposes are described below.

Agendas

The word 'agenda' derives from the Latin and means 'things that must be done'; this root leads to the typical dictionary definition of 'items of business to be considered at a meeting'.

The generation of the agenda for a meeting is the responsibility of the chairperson, and this responsibility requires decisions to be taken, before the meeting, about the content and sequence of the business to be discussed. The agenda should be issued with any supporting papers required by agenda items and should identify:

- Date, time and place of meeting.
- Sequence of topics or subjects.

Supporting papers for the topics and subjects will influence the duration of the gap between the issue of the agenda and the actual meeting. For example, if these papers are voluminous and/or multiple then a gap of about a week seems adequate. With limited or no papers a gap of two or three days seems to be about right. Certainly, issuing the agenda too far in advance of the meeting does not necessarily ensure attendance, as less organized members will lose it or forget. The sequence of topics is also important, and an effective chairperson will, while generating the agenda, remember that:

- Some items will unite the meeting, while others will divide it, so the chairperson can influence whether the meeting starts or finishes with unity.
- The early part of any meeting is likely to be more creative and energetic than the later parts, so issues which need creativity and energy are best put early in the agenda.
- The overall meeting duration should not exceed two hours, so the chairperson's perceptions of the meeting time needed for individual items will influence both the content and structure of the agenda.
- Explicit and clear wording of agenda items gives members the opportunity to gather together their thoughts and information before the meeting and in so doing enhances the chances of an informed and effective discussion during the meeting.

Table 6.4 shows an example of a basic but typical agenda.

Some of you may notic that Table 6.4 does not contain that old agenda favourite and standby of 'Any other business'. Experience indicates that this item is often used as a cover-up for ineffective chairperson or member behaviour and often wastes time and causes frustration by its use. An effective chairperson will have prepared the meeting in such a way as to ensure that both he or she and the members know and understand what the objectives of the meeting are.

Minutes

In some formal meetings it is important to keep a detailed accurate record of what was said and by whom. Examples of this type of meeting would include a court of law or the proceedings of the UK House of Commons or the US Senate or House of Representatives. In all of these the

Table 6.4   A sample agenda

Orange Computer Company Inc.

Alpha Project Review Meeting
Date: Friday, November 4, 1994
Time: 2.30 p.m. start
Location: No. 2 Conference Room, B Block

Agenda
1. Apologies for absence.
2. Minutes of last meeting.
3. Matters arising from minutes of last meeting.
4. CPU progress report by Diane Johns.
5. Case design progress report by Dave Cass.
6. Software progress report by Joan Harris.
7. Date and time of next meeting.

Enclosures: Software progress report No. 7.
Case design progress report No. 2.
Note re software problems.

proceedings are recorded and published or stored for future reference in the event of dispute or appeal. Very few, if any, management meetings require that level of formal recording process and consequently the minutes, or records of the meeting, are often limited to a record of:

- What was agreed.
- Who is responsible for what consequent actions.
- By when.

Minutes should also contain information indicating:

- Who was present at the meeting.
- Who was invited but didn't come.
- When and where the meeting was held.
- Date, time and place of next meeting.

They should be written:

- With numbered paragraphs and subsections for future reference.
- Making limited use of names.
- With short sentences which record the core of what was said, by whom it was said and what was decided.

Table 6.5 shows samples from a basic but typical set of minutes.

Pre-meeting people issues

The chairperson will need to decide before the agenda is issued who should attend and who should speak on what. Since attendance at many management meetings is a function of

Table 6.5 Sample of minute structure

- *Title*

Orange Computer Company Inc.

Minutes of 6th Alpha Project Review Meeting

- *Date, place and time*
  1. Meeting held on Friday, November 4, 1994 in No. 2 Conference Room, B Block, starting at 2.30 p.m.

- *Attendance and apologies*
  Attended by Dave Cass, Diane Johns, Joan Harris, Irving Brown and Valerie Williams (Chairperson). Apologies for absence received from Jackie Stroller and Chris Pratt, with no response received from Ron Stanning.

- *Minutes of last meeting*
  2. These were agreed to be an accurate record of the last meeting

- *Matters arising from minutes of last meeting*
  3. Diane Johns reported that the marketing people were still all on holiday, so she had not been able to invite them to this meeting.

     Agreed action: Diane to invite on return from holiday.
     Completion by: Next meeting.

- *Progress report sample*
  4. Joan Harris reported that software development was on target and still had an anticipated beta version completion date of end of March. There were, however, still problems with Ron Stanning's lack of cooperation over graphics programmer availability.

     Action agreed: Valerie Williams to set up meeting with Ron Stanning and Joan Harris to resolve problems.
     Completion by: 21 Nov. 1994.

- *Date, time and location of next meeting*
  Next Meeting: Friday 25 November 1994, 2.30 p.m. in No. 2 Conference Room, B Block.

---

representation and/or functional responsibilities, the chairperson's influence is often restricted to limiting numbers to levels which enable the meeting to be effective. These limits have been discussed earlier in this chapter and effective chairperson behaviour will enforce these limits or run the risk of chairing an ineffective meeting. Options that are available to help the chairperson to do this are:

- Limiting attendance on an item by item basis.
- Having two separate meetings.
- Using subgroups to thrash out detail and have one or two representatives make recommendations to the main meeting.

The effective chairperson will also remember that discussions with meeting members outside the meeting and before the agenda is issued will often:

- Ensure that important points are raised.
- Ensure that the agenda includes perceived key topics.
- Prevent irrelevant and time-wasting issues being raised.

The ideal chairperson is one who rules by consent and with informal authority and of whom it is said: '*a good chairperson, but of course we did it all ourselves*'. Appendix 6.1 provides a checklist for chairperson behaviour.

MEETING PARTICIPATION

Even the ideal chairperson needs meeting members who are able to respond to his or her skills and contribute to the effectiveness of the meeting. In order to do this the meeting member will need to have:

- Relevant and adequate functional skills and knowledge.
- Adequate interpersonal skills.

For example, members who attend the meeting which sets next year's departmental budget will need to have adequate accounting skill and knowledge in order to be able to understand and contribute to the budgeting process, as well as adequate knowledge of the department's function and its future plans. In addition to these functional skills and knowledge, the members will also need to be able to plan and prepare their contributions. Members will also need to possess and be able to use adequate social skills to enable them to contribute effectively to the meeting.

These skills will include the ability to:

- Speak clearly and concisely.
- Listen actively.
- Compromise and negotiate.
- Withstand stress, yet avoid destructive conflict.
- Demonstrate independent judgement.
- Be creative and innovative.
- Carry out tasks and assignments resulting from the meeting with thoroughness and vigour.

and in stable groups:

- Be aware of their preferred and secondary Belbin roles and be prepared to carry these out.

These skills and their effective use are as important as the skills of a good chairperson, and Appendix 6.2 provides a self-assessment checklist.

CONCLUSION

Over four million hours a day are reported to be spent in meetings in the UK and some 11 million meetings are estimated to take place each day in the USA. All of these meetings involve groups of people. Groups and the interactions which take place within them have been the subject of considerable research. These can be primary or secondary groups and can also be informal or formal. Many management meetings consist of formal groups with specific tasks or objectives. The interactions which take place in these groups are not only concerned with tasks, but also with the morale and harmony of the group and the goals and needs of individual members. The size and the stage of development of the group are also important factors. Belbin has identified the behavioural characteristics, composition and individual contributions of effective groups of managers. The characteristics and behaviours of an effective chairperson can add to the effectiveness of a meeting, as will effective and clear meeting documentation, i.e. agendas and minutes. The characteristics and behaviour of an effective meeting participant have also been described.

EXERCISES

1. Simulate a committee by choosing and discussing a subject of common interest, with the lecturer or tutor acting as chairperson. Limit committee numbers to eight or nine, with the remainder of the class acting as observers, and limit discussion duration to 30 minutes. Review this 'committee meeting', starting with the observers providing feedback on roles, process and dynamics.
2. Imagine that you are the chairperson of a club, society or other recreational group with an activity that you are familiar with, e.g. golf, photography, etc. Draft the agenda and the minutes for the annual general meeting of that group.
3. Your boss is on extended sick leave and you have been asked to act as chairperson for the annual departmental salary review meeting. List the actions that you need to undertake before that meeting.
4. 'All meetings are a waste of time': examine and justify this statement with particular reference to the organizational culture or environment in which it might be true.

REFERENCES

1. Townsend, R., *Up The Organisation*, Michael Joseph, London, 1970.
2. Hodgson, P. and Hodgson, J., *Effective Meetings*, Century, London, 1992.
3. Stewart, R., *Managers and Their Jobs*, Macmillan, London, 1967.
4. Mintzberg, M., *The Nature of Managerial Work*, Harper & Row, New York, 1973.
5. Katz, D., The motivational basis of organizational behaviour, in Vroom, V. H. and Deci, E. L. (eds.), *Management and Motivation*, Penguin, London, 1989.
6. Handy, C. B., *Understanding Organisations*, Penguin, London, 1985.
7. Jay, A., How to run a meeting, in *The Articulate Executive*, Harvard Business School Press, Boston 1991.
8. Cooley, C. H., *Social Organizations*, Scribner, New York, 1929.
9. Kakabadse, A., Ludlow, R. and Vinnicombe, S., *Working in Organisations*, Penguin, London, 1988.
10. McGrath, J. E. and Altman, I., *Small Group Research: A Synthesis and Critique of the Field*, Holt, Rinehart & Winston, New York, 1966.
11. Krech, D., Crutchfield, R. S. and Ballachey, E. L., *The Individual in Society*, McGraw-Hill, Montreal, 1962.
12. Hare, A. P., *The Handbook of Small Group Research*, Free Press, New York, 1962.
13. Hoffman, R., Group Problem Solving, in *Advances in Experimental Psychology*, Vol. II, Academic Press, New York, 1965.
14. Douglas, T., *Groupwork Practice*, Tavistock Publications, London, 1976.
15. Argyle, M., *The Psychology of Interpersonal Behaviour*, Penguin, London, 1967.
16. Tuckman, B. W., Developmental sequences in small groups, *Psychological Bulletin*, **63**(6), 1965, pp. 384–99.
17. Belbin, M. R., *Management Teams: Why They Succeed or Fail*, Butterworth-Heinemann, Oxford, 1982.

18. Margerison, C. J. and McCann, D. J., *Team Management: Practical New Approaches*, Mercury, London, 1990.
19. Georgiades, N. J. and Orlans, V., The supervision of working groups, in Argyle, M. (ed.), *Social Skills and Work*, Methuen, London, 1981.
20. Von Bergen, C. W. and Kirk, R. W., Groupthink: when too many heads spoil the decision, in Fordyce, J. K. and Weil, R., *Managing WITH People*, Addison-Wesley, Reading, MA, 1979.

APPENDIX 6.1: CHAIRPERSON SELF-EVALUATION QUESTIONNAIRE

Preparation

1. *Purpose*
   I'm clear what I want the meeting to achieve.   1 2 3 4 5 6 7   I'm not sure why we are having a meeting.

2. *Agenda*
   I sent the agenda out at least two days before the meeting.   1 2 3 4 5 6 7   I gave the agenda out at the meeting.

3. *People*
   I chose or influenced the choice of people who will attend.   1 2 3 4 5 6 7   I left that up to departments being represented.

4. *Location and layout*
   I checked the room and the layout.   1 2 3 4 5 6 7   I didn't look at it until the meeting.

Chairing

1. *Summarizing*
   I summarized at relevant points in the discussions.   1 2 3 4 5 6 7   I let them work it out for themselves.

2. *Interrupting*
   I did not interrupt.   1 2 3 4 5 6 7   I interrupted persistently.

3. *Questions*
   I asked clarifying questions.   1 2 3 4 5 6 7   I asked irrelevant questions.
   I asked open questions.   1 2 3 4 5 6 7   I asked closed questions.

4. *Relaxation*
   I felt relaxed but attentive.   1 2 3 4 5 6 7   I felt tense and ill at ease.

Scoring

If your total score comes to 27 or less then you appear to be chairing well. Scores of 36 and above indicate that you are having some problems with the chairing role.

APPENDIX 6.2: MEETING PARTICIPANT SELF-EVALUATION QUESTIONNAIRE

Preparation

1. *Purpose*
   I'm clear what I want the meeting to achieve. 1 2 3 4 5 6 7 I'm not sure why we are having a meeting.

2. *Paperwork*
   I've read the agenda and other papers before the meeting. 1 2 3 4 5 6 7 I read the agenda and other papers at the meeting.

3. *People*
   I talked to other members to find out what they think about important agenda items. 1 2 3 4 5 6 7 I'll find out what they think at the meeting.

4. *Prior notice*
   I've told the chairperson I feel strongly about an agenda item. 1 2 3 4 5 6 7 I'll tell the chairperson in the meeting.

Process

1. *Speaking*
   I spoke clearly, concisely and relevantly. 1 2 3 4 5 6 7 I rambled and made irrelevant comments.

2. *Interrupting*
   I did not interrupt. 1 2 3 4 5 6 7 I interrupted persistently.

3. *Questions*
   I asked clarifying questions. 1 2 3 4 5 6 7 I asked irrelevant questions.
   I asked open questions. 1 2 3 4 5 6 7 I asked closed questions.

4. *Creation and innovation*
   I suggested new ways of solving problems. 1 2 3 4 5 6 7 I minded my own business.

5. *Relaxation*
   I felt relaxed but attentive. 1 2 3 4 5 6 7 I felt bored, tense and ill at ease.

Scoring

If your total score comes to 30 or less then you appear to be participating well. Scores of 40 and above indicate that you are having some problems with meetings and your role in them.

SEVEN

PRESENTATIONS AND PRESENTING

'Don't quote Latin, say what you have to say, and then sit down.'
Duke of Wellington

'A audience is two people or more with the power to vote you money'
Mark Twain

INTRODUCTION

It is difficult to imagine a managerial role that does not call upon that manager to undertake presentations in one form or another. The presentation is a very effective and flexible communication process. It can be formal or informal and enable the presenter to reach a wide range of both audience size and composition. The presentation process uses both the language-based and the non-language-based media (see Chapter 1) of communication. For almost all presenters, the primary medium is verbal and vocal in nature, though often supplemented by visual material involving the use of overhead projectors and transparencies, slides, flip charts, etc. However, effective presenters also make considerable use of gesture, gaze and facial expression to underline or reinforce what they are saying (see Chapter 10). Presentations can be an explicit and integral part of a management role as, for example, with selling and training roles. However, in today's business environment all managers can and do find themselves making some kind of a presentation. These can range from a presentation to a potential client or customer for a major contract or sale through to the after-dinner speech at a business function or a briefing meeting with a small work group. Increasingly, the presentation process is seen as an effective and economic means of communicating with groups of people. The size of these groups may vary from as few as two to as many as several hundred.

However, few managers are born with a natural aptitude for standing up and making a presentation. Most of them find the process stressful and have to work hard to produce a reasonable effort – and even then they are often aware of the faults and limitations of their efforts.

Nevertheless, a presentation does provide the manager with an opportunity, albeit a stressful one, to communicate. Some characteristics of this opportunity are unique to presentations. For example, audiences, at least initially, will assume that presenters know what they are talking about and that their role as presenter gives them the right to speak, without interruption, for a reasonable period of time. However, these are not unconditional assumptions, since if presenters speak for too long and/or show their audience that they do not know what they are talking about then the audience will lose interest and may, under extreme conditions, deliberately interrupt the presenter.

Presentations of a professional standard result in the ideas, concepts and information presented being understood and possibly accepted by the audience. Presentations of an unprofessional standard result in audiences not understanding or accepting the material presented, and they may even be antagonized by the way in which it was presented.

So undertaking a presentation or the act of presenting is a process that represents an

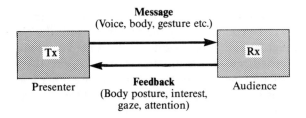

Figure 7.1 The presenting process.

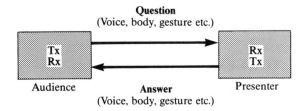

Figure 7.2 Questions after presenting.

important aspect not only of communication but also of the manager's role. Certainly, it is a process which is very often conducted in a very public manner, and the consequent success or failure can often result in the audience acquiring enhanced or diminished perceptions of the presenter's overall managerial abilities.

Presenting is often seen as a one-way process in which the presenter 'tells' the audience. However, the process of presentation is actually a two-way process, which can be illustrated by Fig. 7.1. Experienced speakers, presenters or transmitters (Tx) will be able to judge the effectiveness of their attempts to communicate with the audience (Rx) by the feedback signals given. These signals will include eye contact, body posture, questions and other manifestations of interest and attention. During the course of the presentation this body posture and eye gaze will provide feedback to speakers telling them that they are being listened to. However, presentations often include or encourage questions from the audience and this process can be illustrated as in Fig. 7.2.

Presenting in a professional manner is an example of skilled social behaviour, and as such it can be learned. Figure 7.3 illustrates how the inputs of skill, knowledge and method are

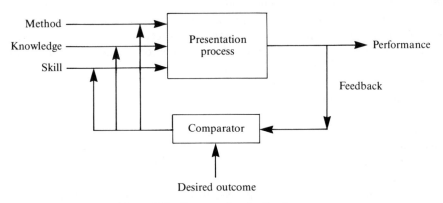

Figure 7.3 Presentation feedback.

combined to give a presentation performance. In this example of a feedback control system, the achieved performance will be compared, by the presenter, with the outcome desired, and any difference, e.g. not enough attention or laughter, will be used to modify the way in which the presentation is being carried out. These differences may require the presenter to draw upon different skills, to use different methods or to display and use other knowledge.

This chapter will focus on the provision of an outline of the knowledge and method aspects of the presentation process. In so doing it will consider the characteristics of a professional presentation and what the presenter needs to do in order to ensure that the presentation is conducted in a professional manner. However, given Bass and Vaughan's[1] definition of learning, i.e. 'a relatively permanent change in behaviour *that occurs as a result of practice or experience*', it should also be evident that practice and experience are also needed to produce a permanent professional standard of presentation.

PRESENTATIONS: THE KEY QUESTIONS

As an example of a communication process, the presentation is, in common with all other communication processes, used for the purposes of:

- Exchanging information.
- Instructing.
- Influencing.

Most managerial presentations are focused towards the purpose of influencing, as when selling to or persuading an audience. However, managerial presentations can contain elements of all three of the above purposes. One of these must, however, represent the dominant purpose. An example of this would be a presentation given by a data processing manager, on a new computer system, to a group of users. At first glance this presentation would appear to have the sole objective of giving information to the audience. This will be so if the DP manager perceives his or her role to be that of an 'expert' and presents in a didactic or 'telling' style. However, if the manager encourages the audience to respond and to discuss the material presented, i.e. to interact, then he or she will be receiving feedback information. This feedback may be about, for example, the audience's level of understanding or the potential problems which might arise with the new system or the effectiveness of his or her presentation style, method and material. The objectives of the didactic style and the interactive style are different. The didactic presenter has the objective of instructing the audience and does so by reviewing the subject or completing the 'syllabus' for the presentation. The interacting presenter has the objective of facilitating the audience's learning process and doing so by the use of feedback.

These different styles have implications for a number of aspects of the presentation process, including:

- The presentation material used.
- Scope of the subject.
- Time required.
- Size of audience.
- Layout of the presentation space.

For example, interactive presenters will need to allow time for the audience's responses and feedback, whereas didactic presenters will only be concerned with the time needed for what they need or want to say. Similarly, interactive presenters will lay out the presentation space in such a way that they can interact with their audience, while didactic presenters will be primarily concerned with a limited number of factors, such as the visibility and audibility of their presentation.

Another example illustrates the dominant purpose element discussed earlier. The manager who undertakes a presentation to the capital sanction committee, in order to get approval for a project, is attempting to influence that committee. But the presentation will also be designed to inform the committee about the technical and financial factors of the project, for example the payback period. The manager will inform the committee about the facts, but will also seek to present the information in such a way that the committee are persuaded or influenced to grant the capital – often in competition with other projects.

The key questions for all managerial presentations and presenters are:

- Who is the audience?
- What are the objectives?

The presenting manager needs to be clear about the answers to these questions before any presentation is undertaken. Failure to understand the needs and idiosyncrasies of the audience can result, in the extreme, in a presenter telling jokes about the Irish to an audience of Dubliners, jokes about the Scottish to an audience of Glaswegians or jokes about cricket to an audience of Americans – all high-risk strategies if the presenter's objective is to persuade or influence them on another issue! Uncertainty or lack of clarity about the objectives of the presentation will be equally disastrous and will result in a presentation which:

- Has several conflicting or overlapping objectives.
- Tries to cover too much ground.
- Leaves the audience confused and uncertain.

The importance of the presenter being clear about who the audience is and what the objectives of the presentation are cannot be overstated. Presenters ignore them at their peril and no amount of expertise in presentation method will make up for the absence of thoughtful and considered answers.

An examination of the factors associated with these questions indicates the following.

- *The audience*
  — Presenters need to bear the audience in mind *all the time* throughout their preparation and presentation.
  — Presenters need to list what they know about them in terms of how many of them there are, what their job titles and responsibilities are, and what their interests, biases, prejudices and concerns are.
  — Presenters can assume that, for most managerial presentations, the audience will be made up of experienced adults who will assume, *initially*, that the presenter is able to speak with authority on the subject.
  — The audience will have many other things on their minds and presenters will need to capture and keep their imagination and interest.
  — The audience's concentration will fade after around 10 to 15 minutes,[2] and the presenter will need to restimulate it.
  — The audience will remember what the presenter says if it has a clear structure and pattern and if it is repeated.

— The presenter's access to the audience's minds is through what they see and hear, with sight being the easiest.

- *Objectives*
  — The presenter should write down, *in a single sentence*, the objective of the presentation. Examples might be:
  '*To gain capital sanction approval for Project 34.*'
  '*To persuade the Board to agree to relocate the offices to Bristol.*'
  '*To get this client to buy one of our computers.*'
  '*To tell my team what the company results were like this year and why we need to do better.*'
  — The presenter will then need to decide if he or she is trying to:
    - Influence.
    - Inform.
    - Instruct the audience.
  — If the presenter is trying to do all three of these in the same presentation, then the objective needs to be reviewed and reshaped. Do not forget that while the audience will often need to be informed before they can be influenced, they can be influenced without first being informed.

PREPARATION AND PLANNING

Actors memorize their lines and rehearse, tennis players practice their strokes and get fit – so why shouldn't managers prepare for presentations? Hiller[3] reports a strong linkage, for teachers, between teachers' prior levels of knowledge and the clarity of their explanations to the pupils. Despite the old saying which states that 'to fail to prepare is to prepare to fail', many managers leave their preparation to the last minute and consequently find themselves with a presentation which:

- Is too long or too short.
- Contains too much material.
- Does not answer the audience's needs.
- Is delivered unprofessionally.

Thorough preparation is as important to the managerial presenter as it is to an Olympic athlete, and sometimes it appears to take just as long! To be effective this preparation needs to be focused on three aspects of the presentation:

1. The environment.
2. The method.
3. The material.

The relationship between these and the audience is shown in Fig. 7.4.

The environment

The physical environment within which the presentation takes place will have a considerable influence upon its effectiveness. Imagine, for example, trying to conduct a presentation in a hall with a considerable echo effect or on a hot summer's day and in a room adjacent to a busy main

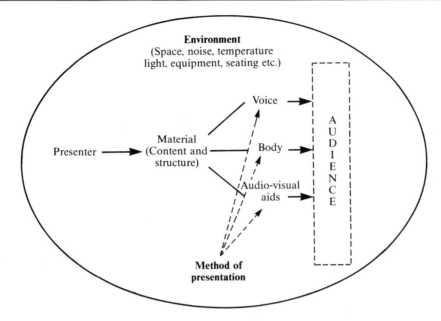

Figure 7.4   The presentation process.

road whose only method of ventilation is to open the windows. The effects of these particular environments upon both the presenter and the audience will be considerable, and will not help the quality or audibility of the presentation!

The physical or environmental factors concerned with presentations can be classified as follows:

- *Fixed factors*
  These are factors such as the size and shape of the room, the location and numbers of windows and pillars, the location, size and number of wall boards, screens, power points, etc. Often there is little that can be done about these short of rebuilding, but nevertheless the presenter should be aware of them and be prepared to ask for a different location if the one offered is very unsuitable.
- *Movable items*
  These include chairs, tables, audiovisual equipment and, by implication, the audience. The presenter should ensure that the environment is one in which he or she has continuous contact with the audience. Knapper[4] reports the importance of the presenter maintaining eye contact with the audience and identifies that this eye contact 'facilitates a certain degree of intimacy between speaker and listener'. Knapper also reports that glance exchange promotes inter-action and, when accompanied by nods and smiles, provides a source of reward for both audience and presenter.

The structure of the presenting environment can facilitate or limit eye contact. Figure 7.5 illustrates a number of seating arrangements which are designed to facilitate presenter–audience eye contact and, in the Horseshoe and Circle arrangements, also audience–audience eye contact. In configuring these movable items it is also necessary to consider the proximity factors. As we noted in Chapter 4, Hall[5] suggested that we use four main zones for different purposes:

- Intimate: from contact to 18″.
- Personal: from 18″ to 4′.
- Social: from 4′ to 12′.
- Public: from 12′ to 25′.

In most managerial presentations the interchanges take place within the social zone. This and other zones are influenced by other factors, such as whether those involved are sitting or standing and whether they like or dislike the others, as well as personality and culture. Nevertheless these zones do represent definite social norms, and deviation from these would be seen as 'breaking the rules'. As such the use of distance represents a factor worthy of serious consideration by the presenter.

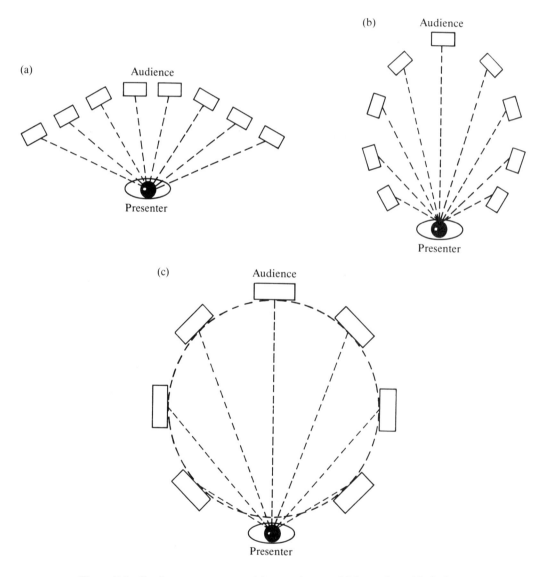

Figure 7.5 Seating arrangements: (a) curved rows; (b) horseshoe; (c) circle.

The presentation method

As we noted earlier in this chapter, many, if not most, managerial presentations are based on the use of the spoken word, though are often supported or embellished by overhead projector transparencies, slides, flip chart materials and even videos or films. All of these can be used to facilitate the audience's understanding and to gain and maintain their interest and attention. Chapter 12 examines the ways in which images can be used to supplement the spoken word.

However, a presentation will stand or fall by the presenter's abilities in the use of a number of 'core' skills. Several workers, including Brown[6] and Turney *et al.*[7] have identified these as including:

- Clarity.
- Emphasis.
- Using examples.
- Organization.
- Feedback.

In the following sections we examine these in more detail.

Clarity   Our own experience tells us that when we listen to presenters who speak clearly, do not use jargon or explain it when they do, make limited and/or reasonable assumptions about what we do and do not know or feel and tell us what they are, then we often feel that the process of listening to that speaker has been worthwhile. Not surprisingly, research supports this conclusion and identifies presenter behaviour which enhances understanding and retention as including:

- Defining new or technical terms and jargon.
- Increasing the clear-cut or explicit content and decreasing the inferred or implicit content of the presented material.
- Using crisp short sentences with minimum 'ums' and 'ers'.
- Avoiding all forms of vagueness, including ambiguity ('this sort of thing'), approximation ('about the size of') and indeterminacy ('a bunch of') among others.

Emphasis   Good presenters use emphasis to help the audience to 'see the wood from the trees'. It can be provided by gestures as well as by use of the voice.

Argyle[8] reports that while people speak they also make movements particularly with their hands and Morris[9] defines gestures as movements which send signals. These signals are used by presenters to emphasize the verbal content of their presentation and as such are often described as 'baton' signals or gestures. These baton gestures are part of a larger group of gestures termed 'illustrators', which include gestures which involve pointing, tracing shapes, etc. Morris[10] states that baton gestures account for the majority of the gestures which accompany speech and lists and illustrates as many as fifteen of the more important types of hand baton gestures, using self-descriptive titles such as 'hand jab', 'air punch' and 'hand scissors'. The use of the voice also provides emphasis with pitch, volume, stress and pauses all contributing. Pauses, for example, are frequently present in speech and make up as much as one third of speaking time. They often come before complex word sequences and can be used to suggest thought or planning on the part of the presenter. When used in excess, however, they can be interpreted by the audience to indicate anxiety or lack of familiarity with the subject. The stressing of the spoken word is often used to give meaning to a sentence. A sentence such as:

My cat sat on the mat

will take on quite different meanings when the stress is shifted. Try saying the sentence with the stress on the words that are not italic as follows:

My *cat sat on the mat*.
My cat sat on the mat.

This shift in stress is used to add emphasis and to focus the audience's attention on the relevant part of the sentence.

Pitch is often used to encode emotions in speech, with Frick[10] reporting examples which include anger (sudden increase), surprise (rising pitch), contempt (fall at end) and questioning (rise at end).

Examples The use of examples in a presentation is designed to reduce the level of the vagueness, ambiguity and indeterminacy of the material presented and hence to facilitate the understanding of this material by the audience. As such, examples need to:

- Offer support evidence.
- Enable the audience to relate new ideas and concepts to their own experience.
- Promote clarity and interest.
- Be related to and understood by the audience.

However, examples on their own are not sufficient and they need to be used in association with statements of principles or rules. Sequences which research has identified are:

- Rule → example → rule.
- Example → rule.
- Rule → example.

There is debate about the respective effectiveness of these sequences. However, Brown and Armstrong[11] suggest that the sequence used should reflect both the type of example used and the audience's level of knowledge of the topic presented. For example, the use of rule → example or example → rule would be appropriate when the audience has prior topic knowledge but needs to be reminded or to review their views of that topic. However the use of rule → example → rule would be more appropriate when the audience has limited or no prior knowledge of the topic presented.

Organization The evident presence of organization or structure in a presentation and the overt enunciation of this structure are said to be closely associated with clarity. Brown[12] identifies the use of four types of structuring statement as being valuable to both presenter and audience. These are:

- *Signposts*, which provide verbal points to the arrangements, order and objective of the material:

'I am first going to examine our performance over the last year and then identify how we should move forward.'

- *Frames*, which indicate the end of a point or issue and the beginning of another or the return to the main issue of the presentation:

  'So, having looked briefly at our competitors' performance in the market place, let's now return to the subject of how we might improve our performance.'

- *Foci*, in which the key points are highlighted:

  'The main issue here is that we do not lose sight of our long-term mission to dominate this market by the turn of the century.'

- *Links*, which bridge between an explanation and a rule, principle or a conclusion or between one part of an explanation and another:

  'So, as we can see, the reduction in selling price of this model led to a 10% increase in demand. This increase brings us to the next area of concern which needs to be addressed – the rising level of stock outs at the main warehouse.'

Feedback   The feedback which an audience provides to a presenter is a real and important measure of effectiveness. The managerial presenter of professional standards is always alert to this feedback, since it signals whether the audience is interested or bored and whether the presenter is achieving his or her targets in terms of understanding and interest. This feedback, which is usually but not always non-verbal, covers a range of signal types. Eye contact, facial expression and body posture all make contributions. Argyle[8] reports that people look more when they anticipate positive reactions and when they are cooperating. He also reports that speakers look intermittently at their listeners for feedback in the form of facial expressions, eye contact, head movements, etc. The amount of gaze varies with distance, liking, dominance and other factors, with figures between 40 and 70 per cent of the time being reported.[8] Another source of feedback is the presence, quality and number of questions and statements from the audience. These questions and statements are often best sited at the end of the presentation and may be initiated by the presenter or may occur spontaneously.

The material

The material presented and its 'internal' structure represents a key factor in the presentation communication process. The organization of the ideas or concepts contained in the presentation can make a considerable contribution to the clarity, understandability and audience retention levels of the material. There is a considerable body of research to support the view that, at least in teaching, student achievement is directly related to the teacher's ability to prepare, structure, organize and sequence information and concepts. Pemberton[13] proposes a structure for presentations which contains the following sequence:

- State proposition.
- Anticipate objections.
- Show evidence and proof.

Table 7.1   Presentation samples

Preface	*'Good morning ladies and gentleman, thank you for coming this morning and welcome to the launch of the Zenith – our exciting new saloon car. My name is John Davis and I and my colleagues Judy Smith and Eric Land will be showing you this morning how the Zenith will be an exciting and profitable addition to the range of vehicles which you sell. We will do that over the next hour, then break for refreshments, following which you have the opportunity to get your hands on and drive this exciting new vehicle. I'm sure that you will have many questions to ask about this exciting new venture, and Judy, Eric and I will be happy to answer these when we all take refreshment.'*
Situation	*'We currently hold 12 per cent of the saloon car market, having entered this market in 1990 with the Columbus and Idaho models, which, you will recall, we imported in assembled form. The shift to kit import and the opening of our new assembly plant in 1991 has provided us with an opportunity to give you and your customers a better and faster service.'*
Complication	*'The recent rises in gasoline prices, and the cost to your customers of vehicle insurance, have led to a downturn in saloon car sales. These now run at 10 per cent less than this time last year.'*
Recommendation	*'All of us at the Flagstaff Motor Company are committed to providing you, our sales people, and your customers, with the finest cars in the world. We believe that with the Zenith we are giving you a vehicle which you will be able to recommend unhesitatingly to your customers and which will continue to sell in the years to come.'*

- Provide practical evidence.
- Repeat proposition.

Jay[14] identifies a presentation structure as follows:

- Preface (welcome, self-identification, intention, route map and rules).
- Situation.
- Complication.
- Recommendation.

Samples of these are given in Table 7.1.

Jay also states that presentations which contain a review of alternatives can be better handled by a larger structure, which he summarizes in a six-part alliterative mnemonic:

Preface
Position
Problem
Possibilities
Proposal
Postscript

It will also be evident that, whatever the overal sequence used, there also exists a need to present material in an order that facilitates the audience's understanding. The alternatives are:

- Chronological order.
- Logical order.
- Descending or ascending order of importance.
- Descending or ascending order of complexity.
- Psychological order (from known to unknown).

The order used will depend upon the complexity of the material, the level of the audience's prior understanding and the outcomes desired. The impact of this material can be enhanced by the use of visual aids (see Chapter 12) and demonstrations. While the old saying states:

'They hear and they forget.
They see and they remember.
They do and they understand.'

there may be very real practical reasons (time, space, safety, cost etc.) which will limit the presenter's ability to allow the audience to 'do' and hence 'understand'. However, these limitations rarely apply to visual aids, and these can be used to considerable effect. The purposes of these include:

- Illustrating a point.
- Showing a complex diagram or graph.
- Explaining a complex process or sequence.
- Linking presentation sections.
- Posing a question.
- Summarizing points and proposals.
- Saving words.

However, it is important to ensure that these visual aids are legible at the limits of the audience and do not contain too many words. *'Never use more words than you would put on a T shirt'* is one version of the necessary limitation in word numbers. While visual aids have considerable impact it will also be evident that the use of multiple visual aid sources (overhead projector, slides, videos, flip charts) in one presentation will dilute the impact of this visual material and confuse the audience (if not the presenter). Chapter 12 contains further comment on the use of visual images to enhance communication.

BEGINNINGS AND ENDINGS FOR PRESENTATIONS

One of the several skills that are demonstrated by effective presenters is the way in which they start and close their presentations. The impact which is achieved by a well-chosen and pertinent beginning or ending can be considerable and these can exert a considerable influence on the audience. However, the beginning and ending used must be appropriate to the audience, the subject of the presentation and the environment in which that presentation takes place.

Beginnings

An effective beginning must:

- Set the agenda for the presentation.

Table 7.2   Sample beginnings

Sample 1: Question
   'I wonder if anyone here tonight knows how many children were born in America in the last 24 hours?'

   'I wonder how you would react if I were to tell you that many of you own computers that were obsolete when you bought them?'

Sample 2: Factual statement
   'The fathers of thirty children died in our city today – and these deaths could have been prevented.'

Sample 3: Reference
   'Every single one of you in this room today will recall the shock and pain that we all felt on hearing about the Lockerbie air disaster.'

Sample 4: Subject/agenda
   'My job tonight is to tell you about the exciting and new XR5 multiprocessor and to tell you how that computer can change the ways in which you run your businesses.'

Sample 5: Quotation
   'Marshall McLuhan said: "Everybody experiences far more than he understands". Yet it is experience, rather than understanding, that influences behaviour.'

Sample 6: Emotional appeal
   'It only takes 50p from each of your pockets to give this child a chance to live until next year's harvest.'

- Establish the presenter's credibility.
- Gain the audience's attention.

In order to achieve the above, the opening one or two sentences spoken by the presenter need to:

- Create impact and excitement.
- Generate interest, curiosity and involvement in the audience.

This can be done in a number of ways, of which specific instances of each are given in Table 7.2.

- *Ask a question*   This type of opening is often used with other ways of beginning, for example following a factual statement, and can be used directly or rhetorically.
- *Make a challenging or interesting factual statement*   As an opening this can create impact and credibility, but it does need to be a genuine and factually accurate statement which is simple enough to be grasped quickly by the audience. It also needs to be of interest to the audience and relevant to the material of the presentation.
- *Refer* to a person or event with which all the audience will be familiar.
- *Define the subject and agenda*   This is the commonest way of opening a presentation, and as such runs the risk, however, of not gaining the audience's immediate attention because of its common usage.
- *Use a quotation*   The use of an appropriate, relevant quotation can be an interesting way of gaining audience interest.

Table 7.3 Sample endings

Sample 1: Question
   'So, ladies and gentlemen, let me leave you with this thought – how would you feel if you were told that you were suffering from motor neurone disease?'

Sample 2: Reminder
   'Today I set out to try to convince you of the need for an increased and more professional marketing activity for our short course programme. I have attempted to do so by showing you that there is a huge untapped market waiting out there.'

Sample 3: Action
   'You have heard my proposals and you know that the time for delay is past. If we are to stave off imminent disaster we must act now. I urge you not to delay if you wish to ensure the future prosperity of this company.'

Sample 4: Choices
   'It seems to me that we have three options: to accept the union's ultimatum, ask for time to consider our position, or, lastly, to do nothing.'

Sample 5: Instil fear
   'So, ladies and gentleman, if we cannot improve sales by 10 per cent within the next month and sustain that level for at least two years, then we must close down the company now.'

- *Appeal to the audience's emotions*   This beginning differs from the preceding types more by the way it is used than its content. It is delivered emotionally and can be a question, a poem, or a statement.

Endings

The objectives for the ending used (see Table 7.3 for samples) can include:

- Reminding the audience about the content of the presentation.
- Asking them to do something.
- Providing inspiration or motivation.
- Giving the answer to a question.

Examples of how these objectives can be achieved include the following:

- *Ask a question*   This ending is aimed at getting the audience to think about a specific issue or question.
- *Remind them*   This ending involves either restating and re-emphasizing the objective of the presentation or summarizing a limited number of key points from the presentation.
- *Asking for specific action*   The emphasis with this ending is on urging or motivating the audience to actually do something.
- *Identify choices*   This involves leaving the audience with a choice, but one which is based on a limited number of clearly enunciated alternatives.

● *Instil fear* This ending is usually used to give a warning about the consequences of not following or following a specific course of action. It should never be used as an empty threat and must always be used with caution.

The skill of giving effective presentations is an important skill for the manager to acquire and to maintain. Appendix 7.1 provides a self-assessment questionnaire to help that process.

CONCLUSION

Most, if not all, managers undertake presentations on a regular basis and as an implicit part of their job. These are usually undertaken in order to influence or to inform others. Presenting is an effective and flexible communication process which can reach a wide range of audience types and sizes. The key questions which face the presenter are:

● Who are my audience and what are their jobs, interests, needs and prejudices?
● What are my objectives, and do these involve informing or persuading or influencing the audience?

The answers given must be borne in mind throughout the preparation and delivery of the presentation. The preparation of a presentation is a key stage and involves:

● The environment.
● The methodology.
● The material of the presentation.

Effective presentation beginnings and endings are seen to be the hallmark of an experienced presenter.

EXERCISES

1. You have been asked to give a 15 minute duration presentation to either someone from Britain on the subject of baseball or American football or to an American on the subject of cricket or soccer. Outline the structure and content of your presentation.
2. Working in a small group, undertake presentations of two minutes duration from a range of subjects selected at random. The group should concentrate on method rather than material and give constructive feedback to the presenter.
3. Prepare and deliver a five minute presention on a subject of your own choice. The audience will count the number of times that you say 'um' or 'er' and raise their hands when you do so.
4. When and under what circumstances would a presentation not be the appropriate communication process and why?

REFERENCES

1. Bass, B. M. and Vaughan, J. A., *Training in Industry – The Management of Learning*, Tavistock Publications, London, 1966.
2. Verner, C. and Dickinson, J., The lecture, an analysis and review of research, *Adult Education*, **17**, 1967, pp. 85–100.
3. Hiller, J., Verbal response indicators of conceptual vagueness, *American Educational Research Journal*, **6**, 1971, pp. 661–75.

4. Knapper, C. K., Presenting and public speaking, in Argyle, M. (ed.), *Social Skills and Work*, Methuen, London, 1981.
5. Hall, E. T., *The Hidden Dimension*, Doubleday, New York, 1966.
6   Brown, G., Explaining, in Hargie, O. (ed.), *A Handbook of Communication Skills*, Routledge, London, 1986.
7. Turney, C., Ellis, K. J. and Hatton, W., *Sydney Microskills Series*, Vol. 1, University of Sydney Press, Sydney.
8. Argyle, M., *Bodily Communication*, Routledge, London, 1988.
9. Morris, D., *Manwatching: A Field Guide to Human Behaviour*, Grafton, London, 1978.
10. Frick, R. W., Communicating emotion: the role of prosodic features, *Psychological Bulletin*, **97**, 1985, pp. 412–29.
11. Brown, G. A. and Armstrong, S., On explaining, in Wragg, E. C. (ed.), *Classroom Teaching Skills*, Croom Helm, London, 1984.
12. Brown, G. A., Two days on explaining and lecturing, *Studies in Higher Education*, **2**, 1982, pp. 93–104.
13. Pemberton, M., *A Guide to Effective Speaking*, The Industrial Society, London, 1982.
14. Jay, A., *Making Your Case*, Video Arts, London, 1982.

APPENDIX 7.1: PRESENTING SKILLS SELF-EVALUATION QUESTIONNAIRE

1. *Introduction*
   Concise, clear introduction which told audience what to expect.   1 2 3 4 5 6 7   No introduction given.

2. *Structure*
   Clear logical structure which was evident to audience.   1 2 3 4 5 6 7   No evidence of structure.

3. *Content*
   (a) Adequate but not excessive detail.   1 2 3 4 5 6 7   Too much detail.
   (b) All relevant information given.   1 2 3 4 5 6 7   Not enough information.

4. *Beginnings and endings*
   (a) Beginning got audience's attention.   1 2 3 4 5 6 7   They knew I'd started because I was talking.
   (b) Ending gave audience something to remember.   1 2 3 4 5 6 7   They knew I'd finished because I'd stopped talking.

5. *Presenting*
   (a) Words used were appropriate and free of jargon.   1 2 3 4 5 6 7   Words used were polysyllabic and technical.
   (b) Visual aids were well prepared, clear and interesting.   1 2 3 4 5 6 7   Visual aids were illegible, untidy and boring.
   (c) No irritating mannerisms.   1 2 3 4 5 6 7   Lots of 'ums' and 'ers'.
   (d) Clear audible voice with good pace of delivery.   1 2 3 4 5 6 7   Voice unclear, inaudible, too fast or too slow.

6. *Questions*
   Questions were encouraged and answered well.   1 2 3 4 5 6 7   No questions allowed or answered.

7. *Overall rating*
   Audience were interested and wanted to hear more.   1 2 3 4 5 6 7   Audience were bored and wanted presentation to finish.

Scoring

If your total score comes to 36 or less then you think that you are presenting well. Scores of 48 and above indicate that you seem to feel that there are problems getting in touch with your audience.

THREE

THE WRITTEN WORD

'I put the words down and push them a bit.'
Evelyn Waugh

WRITING: PROCESS, STYLE AND CLARITY

'Writing has laws of perspective, light and shade, just as painting does, or music.
If you are born knowing them, fine. If not, learn them.'
Truman Capote

INTRODUCTION

We all learn to speak before we learn to write and, perhaps because of this, most managers speak far more than they write. Nevertheless, the use of written language as a method of communication is still important. The earliest surviving forms of written material were created some five thousand years ago in an area in the Middle East between the Tigris and Euphrates rivers. In this area, then called Mesopotamia, what is thought to have been the earliest form of writing developed from its roots in pictographs or stylized pictorial representations of real objects and people (see Chapter 12). Recorded on clay tablets, this writing was created by a literate 'elite' of priests and merchants and was mainly used for commercial purposes, such as accounts and trading. Later these purposes changed and Oppheim[1] writes of the use of writing to:

- Record laws, events, etc.
- Write letters, decrees, decisions, etc.
- Record information associated with ritual or sacred texts.

The uses to which written material is put have continued to change and multiply since that time. For example, the Greek civilization extended the use of writing beyond commerce, government and religion into history, science, philosophy and literature. A further significant step in this change process was the ability to create written material, in volume, by the use of machines. This was brought about by Gutenberg's introduction of mechanized printing in the 15th century. Before that time, documents and books were generated and copied by hand using a variety of materials, such as papyrus, parchment, leather and cloth, and a number of writing implements such as styli, brushes or quill pens. The invention of the hand printing press and the increased availability of paper made it possible to print several hundred sheets of text per day compared to the output of hand copyists of about four sheets per day. This leap in the production of printed written material was further extended by the introduction of the cylinder press, with automatic inking. As a consequence, by the 19th century, printing rates had increased to some four thousand sheets per hour and by the mid-20th century to hourly production rates of forty to sixty thousand for a thirty to forty page newspaper. Toffler[2] provides a further example of this rate of change, stating that, between the 15th and 20th centuries, the output of books increased some four hundred-fold.

Nor has this change process stopped or slowed down. The explosion in the use of electronic computer based technology that has occurred in the second half of the 20th century has added to the rate and magnitude of that process. The use of personal computers, electronic mail (or 'email'), fax machines and laser printers has become commonplace and, in its turn, heralds even further change. The introduction of newspapers and books digitally recorded on 'compact discs' (CD-ROM format), the widespread availability of on-line computer information services and the growing presence of optical fibre-based cable TV and telephone systems are just three examples of the ways in which writing-based material is becoming an increasingly pervasive form of communication. These changes indicate that writing is becoming a process of communication which is increasingly electronic rather than paper-based in nature. This change process has had and will continue to have a major impact upon our society. As McLuhan[3] observes, 'Gutenberg made everybody a reader, Xerox made everybody a publisher'.

The increasing availability of the written word enabled large numbers of people to have access to information which had been, historically, available to a privileged few. In so doing it changed people's view of the world. So how does this potent and powerful written material differ from spoken material?

Both of these methods of communication are, by nature, discursive, and as such are:

- Expressions of knowledge, feelings or power.
- Controlled by conventions about their use and structure.

Ochs[4] describes a continuum of discourse which spans from unplanned, i.e. lacking in foresight and preparation, to planned, i.e. thought out and designed prior to expression. Most formal explanatory writing is said to lie at the planned end of this continuum, while spontaneous speech lies at the unplanned end. That is to say, in general terms, that most writing is prepared and composed, while most speech is not. But this is not exclusively so and the overlap area between these modes of communication will include the formal and prepared speech and the informal written note which is 'dashed off'. However, written language, when compared to speech, uses more words, more polysyllabic words and fewer personal words or references. It is also evident that written language differs from spoken language in both its organization and the rules and regulations it uses concerning the order and relationship of words (syntax) and the meanings that are allocated to words (semantics). For example, the written word will contain paragraphs, topic sentences and other structural elements which may provide the reader with signposts about the struture or logical sequence of the text. Speech, however, rarely does, and spontaneous natural speech will display false starts, changes of direction and will often ignore grammatical rules. The way in which the rules of semantics and syntax are applied to written language differ from those used in spoken language. For example, training in written English teaches the use of 'She will come to tea', whereas colloquial spoken English uses 'She'll come to tea'. Crystal[5] writes that 'many of the rules of traditional grammar apply only to the written language' and only possess meaning for spoken language after 'much qualification and addition'. Spoken language is also often strongly linked to the context in which it occurs, while written language is often free of that context. However, spoken language is also associated with or supported by non-verbal or bodily communication messages. As such, it can be seen as capable of multi-media message transmission, even when the supporting non-verbal communication medium is limited, as in a telephone call, to its paralingual content. This non-verbal or bodily communication medium is discussed in Chapter 10. Another of the differences between spoken and written language is identified by Trudgill,[6] who comments that English and other languages display more formality in the written form than in the spoken form.

It is also evident that differences exist in the ways in which we learn to speak and to write. Generally we learn to use the spoken language through social interaction with our parents, siblings and others. We learn to write and to read the written language, however, by exposure to others who are trained and paid to teach us and with the use of specialized materials, e.g. textbooks.

Despite these differences, written language can and does make a considerable contribution to the communication patterns of the manager. As identified in Chapter 1, the written word possesses, for the manager, a number of advantages, which include the following:

- Any feedback from the receiver is distant and delayed, thus enabling individuals to express ideas and feelings without having to cope with immediate responses.
- Words can be chosen with more care and thought and the written statement remoulded until satisfactory.
- The written word provides evidence that the content was sent to named people on a specific date and also provides a means of checking exactly what was sent.
- The written text can be simultaneously sent to a number of people, thus ensuring consistency of message.

Written language is distributed in a wide variety of forms. These include newspapers, magazines, books, letters, reports, posters, electronic mail, faxes, text on our television and computer screens, notices and signs. Written language is not frozen or limited by either time or location. It can be moved from place to place and can be kept as long as the material on which it is printed or stored survives. Faigley *et al.*[7] note that written material can 'transcend centuries and continents'.

This powerful communication medium can be used to fulfil all the purposes of communication, which were identified in Chapter 1, and are:

- Exchanging information.
- Instructing.
- Influencing.

Examples of the ability of written material to instruct include notices (Stop, Turn Here, etc.) and instructions (Part A is placed on top of Part D, etc.). Written advertisements are examples of its ability to influence and the reports and memos of the business environment provide examples of its ability to provide and exchange information. However, the ability of written language to fulfil the feedback needs of the communication process is limited by the separation, in terms of both time and space or location, between the transmitter and the receiver. Nevertheless, this feedback does occur, albeit in a delayed and indirect manner.

This chapter will examine the process by which writing occurs and some of the issues related to the style and clarity of that written material.

THE PROCESS OF WRITING

Studies of the ways in which written language is generated, composed or created initially identified a linear and sequential model of the writing process. Implicit in this model was the view that the act of writing was preceded by a period of preparation and planning and followed by a period of revision or rewriting. Faigley *et al.*[7] describe the evolution of models of the process of creating written material. Early versions are said to be linear and to typically consist of three stages:

Pre-writing → Writing → Rewriting

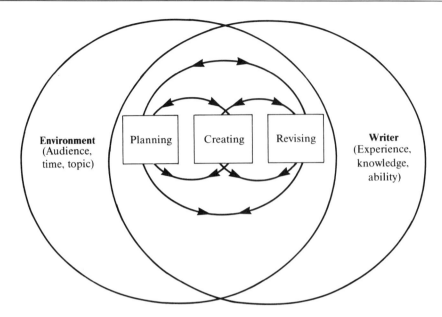

Figure 8.1   The overall writing process.

These early models took the view that there was little feedback or iteration between these stages. However, Faigley reports that further research indicated that feedback and iteration did occur. This work ultimately led to the view that these stages take place in a manner which is systematic but also simultaneous, parallel and interactive. This suggests that, for example, the writer's initial plans about what will be written and when, are revised and reordered throughout the actual process of writing. It also suggests that the process of rewriting or revising of the text will feed back influence into both these plans and the process of writing. It is worth noting that this later model concurs with recent neurobiological evidence[8] which suggests that the brain operates via a series of interacting and parallel systems. The planning stage might include such activities as identifying goals or targets and generating plans, while the rewriting stage will include the activities of assessing, reviewing and revising the written material. These three stages do not, of course, take place in a vacuum. The environment within which the overall process of generating text takes place will exert an influence, as will the skills, ability and experience of the writer.

Figure 8.1 displays the main characteristics of the relationship between these elements. Among the influences of the environment will be the nature, literacy, speciality and needs of the audience. This will mean that the writer who is generating a text for an audience of nuclear physicists will write that text in a certain style and with a certain vocabulary. A text on the same subject but for a less specialized audience would, however, be written with both a different style and a different vocabulary. Nevertheless, there will be features of these different texts which are common. These common features might include, for example, use of the English language and adherence to the same rules of syntax and semantics. However, the differences between these texts will be significant and might even be sufficient to limit the understanding of the text written for a 'specialist' audience by a 'non-specialist' audience. One way of explaining these differences is embodied in the concept of the 'discourse community'. This concept has its roots in studies of spoken language and is used to identify the norms of content and structure that are characteristic of a social group. An example might be the language used by a group of teenagers which has a particular and unique set of meanings for that group. Each linguistic group or 'discourse community' will have different norms and standards. Further examples of these can be found by an examination of papers published in specialist technical journals, magazines for special interest groups and even the tabloid newspapers. The ability of writers to write for these different discourse communities or audiences will reflect their ability to be aware of the different 'genres' required for those audiences and their ability to write in those genres. In this context the term 'genre' can be taken to include the form, structure, language and knowledge presumptions of the written material. The topic to be written about will also exert its own influence. For example, an article or book written about the practice of meditation will require the writer to use language to describe experiences and possibly even states of mind which can only be described in a subjective manner. This might involve using phrases and words such as 'relaxation', 'altered states of consciousness' and 'insight', together with specialist words such as 'samadhi', 'koan' and 'mettabhavana'. However, an article or book about gardening will describe actions and experiences which can be described in a more objective manner, and can be related directly to the experience of the reader. This might involve the use of phrases and words such as 'dig', 'water' or 'plant'. Even the specialist words, such as 'prune', 'compost' or 'deadheading', can be illustrated by either written descriptions or supporting diagrams.

The environmental influences upon the composing process will also include the time available for completion of that process and the topic to be written about. The process of creating text that is followed in generating, against the clock, the answer to an examination question may be such that it involves little review and revision – due to lack of time. However, the composing process followed in generating a company report may involve extensive review and revision. These reviews and revisions may be required by the complex nature of the material involved or because of the audience of senior managers, but more probably because the time was available.

The experience, ability and knowledge of the writer is also a significant influence upon the composing process. The knowledge of the writer can be said to consist of that:

- *Associated with the task*, e.g. knowledge of how to type, how to research, how to plan time usage, etc.
- *Associated with the topic*, e.g. knowledge of topic issues and data sources, knowledge and understanding of topic technology and specialist language, etc.
- *Associated with the audience*, e.g. knowledge and experience of audience, level of literacy or vocabulary, etc.

It will already be evident that the environment interacts with each of the elements of the overall process. The details and characteristics of these elements are described below.

Planning

Earlier in this chapter, most written documents, books, letters, reports, notes and memos were characterized as being planned discourses. It was also suggested that this planning activity is not only undertaken before, but also during, writing. This activity of planning is one of the major activities in the overall process, absorbing as much as half of the total time taken for composition.[9] Planning is concerned with creating goals, organizing material and activities and identifying potential content. These goals will reflect decisions the writer makes about, for example, what to write about or how to begin the text. They will develop and change as the text progresses and will interact with that text. The role of organization in the planning process is a key one and can make a significant difference to the quality and quantity of the written material.

Generating text

While the process of speaking is a familiar, everyday and almost automatic process, the process of writing is not. A simple view of the writing process might describe those physical actions associated with forming words on paper or on a computer screen. This view might even be extended to include the skills of spelling and punctuation. But the process of generating text is not that simple. Early research differentiated between the stages of forming an idea and that of converting that idea into words. These stages were not seen to be sequential but to be parallel and interactive. Our own experience will also tell us that the generation of text rarely results in instantly perfect and well-rounded phrases and sentences, and the writer must take decisions about when and how to revise that text, without inhibiting or losing the creative thread. This process of generating text is generally viewed as being complex and difficult to research or observe. As a result, the models and theories of this text production process are limited in number and are often as complex as the process itself. However, Scardamalia et al.[10] do suggest that written text is not a reproduction or transcript of a mental text, but that it is recreated or created when needed. They also comment that the writer's 'sophistication', needs and familiarity with the task will have a significant influence upon the writing process. Nor is this complexity diminished by the observations of practising writers. Bradbury,[11] in describing the act of writing from the writer's viewpoint, identifies the sequence of 'Work–Relaxation–Don't think' to describe the process that he has experienced as inducing creativity in writing. Complex as this activity of generating text might be, it is, nevertheless, a process which many managers embrace on a regular basis. It is also a process that can always be improved.

Revising

Revision can take place at any time during the overall process and can involve the re-examination of existing plans, goals, methods and text. However, most views of revision see it as a process which is applied to written text and as being concerned with identifying and implementing changes in that text. These changes can either be those that are concerned with the meaning of the text or those that are not concerned with meaning but with spelling or grammar, etc. These changes can consist of additions, substitutions, deletions, consolidations or extensions. Faigley et al.[7] summarize evidence which indicates that experienced writers often use revision to undertake changes in content and form, while less experienced writers use revision for minor changes. Experienced writers have also been observed to suppress concerns about the detail of the text until they had satisfactorily revised the core concepts of the text. The use of computer software with text editing facilities (word processors) has, without doubt, considerably helped the process of text revision. Nevertheless, revision is generally seen to be a process which takes up a limited and minor part of the overall time for composing process.

STYLE

The style of written material is an important factor with considerable influence upon the effectiveness of that material. Cooper[12] writes that style is very much to do with the writer's relationship with the reader, while Mulholland[13] comments that the written style can reveal much about the writer's 'personality and interests'. The style of writing used can result from a conscious choice, and as such it can reflect decisions taken by the writer about a number of factors. These include:

- The expectations and needs of the audience or discourse community.
- The relationship of the writer to that community.
- The nature of the document.

These factors mean that the CEO of a company would adopt a certain style of writing in writing a letter to his employees, but a different style in writing the annual report to the shareholders. Similarly, a manager will need to choose whether to write a letter in an informal or formal style when reminding team members of the need to observe good timekeeping. The style chosen will reflect the manager's relationship with the team, their expectations about the style of such a letter and, of course, the manager's view of their probable reactions to any given style. Written style is portrayed by the ways in which words are used and by the rhythms and structure of the written language. Whatever style is used, it should, to be effective, have a positive impact upon the reader. Table 8.1 lists the major choices available to the writer.

Table 8.1 Choices of style

Formal or informal
Specialized or lay
Indeterminate or precise
General or particular
Complex or simple
Rational or emotional
Reasoned or exhortative

As was noted earlier, style can be chosen, and some of the factors that will influence or result from that choice are as follows:

- *Sentence length*
  Brevity in sentences is generally seen to be a virtue. The number of words in a sentence should be such that the sentence is short, with, as Gowers *et al.*[14] comment, 'unity of thought'.
- *Sentence structure*
  Sentences should be designed or structured in such a way as to ensure that the reader clearly understands what is meant. Sentences can be simple, as in 'The cat sat on the mat', or compound, as in 'The cat sat on the mat and licked its paw', or complex, as in 'Because the cat sat on the mat when it licked its paw, we all laughed'.
- *Paragraphs*
  Gowers *et al.*[14] state that a paragraph is 'a unit of thought, not of length'. The general view seems to be that paragraphs should be short and start with a sentence which contains a proposition. For example: 'The sales figures for June show a fall in our share of the market' or 'The management training provided by the ANG Business School has not been up to the required standards'. All subsequent sentences in the paragraph should be related to that proposition. Long paragraphs are often tedious to read and the reader can lose the gist or thread of the argument. On the other hand paragraphs which are too short often appear incomplete and jerky, leaving the reader dissatisfied.
- *Punctuation*
  The rules of punctuation are fully reported elsewhere[14,15] and, important as they are, will not be repeated here. The purpose and use of punctuation is, however, worth comment. Cooper[12] comments that punctuation is used to 'denote separation of thought'. As such, the objective of

its use should be to ensure that the reader can quickly and effectively read, understand and absorb the thoughts that the written material is attempting to convey.

For example, the full stop should be used at a point in the narrative where the reader needs to pause before going on to the thought contained in the next sentence, i.e. as a signpost of a change in the direction of thought. However, not all the devices of punctuation are easy to use. Gowers *et al.*[14] comment that the correct use of the comma 'cannot be learned by rule'. The use of punctuation should be aimed not to obey the rules of punctuation, but towards making sure that the reader understands the meaning of the written material.

- *Jargon*

The word jargon is often used to describe gibberish or pompous language which is full of clichés. While the dictionary definition supports these uses of the word, there is another definition which will be examined here. That is that jargon is the word which is used to describe specialist language or language which is only understood by a limited or specialist group of readers. An example of this type of language is as follows: 'The solubility of tin in the alpha solid solution rises to 13.5 per cent at 798 °C. At this temperature a peritectic reaction occurs resulting in the formation of a beta intermediate solid solution'. This example contains specialist terms and words which will only make sense to a specialist, which in this case is a metallurgist. If the audience only consists of specialists, then the use of their jargon is acceptable. If, however, the writer is trying to reach others in the audience who are not specialists, then the use of jargon must be limited and explained.

- *Tone*

In the context of the style of written material, the tone of that material is seen as the attitude implied by the words used and ways in which those words are used. The tone of a letter can be direct or indirect or a report can be written with active or passive verbs. Both of these tonal features of style will tell the reader about the attitude of the writer. Other tonal dimensions include negative–positive and formal–informal. Examples of active and passive styles are:

Passive	Active
'When your order is received, the goods will be sent'.	'When we receive your order, we will send the goods'.
'The data was collated by Sid'.	'Sid collated the data'.

Most authorities argue that the active, direct, informal and positive aspects of tone are generally more effective in terms of the influence that they have on the reader. However, the formal, negative, passive and indirect tones do have their place, and should not be discarded. For example, the sentence 'It is hoped that payment will be made next week' may in some circumstances result in a better response than 'Payment must be made next week'. Which of these is used will, of course, depend upon the nature of the current or desired relationship between the writer and the reader. It will also depend upon the genre which is accepted by the discourse community.

For each writer, the evolution of an individual yet effective style is often only achieved by hard work and thought. There are no hard and fast rules for 'good' writing and writers' individual styles reflect how they feel about the topic as much as what they know or think about that topic. Individual style will also change and reflect the writer's exposure to alternative styles and techniques, such as the use of metaphor or analogy. The development and continued

Table 8.2   Readability indices

FOG Index
- Invented by Gunning in 1952.
- Gives the US school grade necessary for comprehension of text.
- Calculated by adding together the average number of words per sentence and percentage of words with more than three syllables, and then multiplying the sum by 0.4.

SMOG Index
- Stands for 'Simple Measure of Gobbledegook'.
- Calculated by multiplying the total number of words in text by 30, dividing the result by the number of sentences, taking the square root of the result and multiplying it by three.

Flesch Index
- Designed for adult texts.
- Calculated by:
  — Calculating the average number of words per sentence.
  — Multiplying by 1.015.
  — Subtracting the result from 206.8, giving Result 1.
  — Calculating the number of syllables per hundred words.
  — Multiplying by 0.846, giving Result 2.
  — Subtracting Result 2 from Result 1, giving the Flesch Index.

Power–Sumner–Kearl Index
- Designed for primary school tests.
- Calculated by finding the average number of words per sentence and multiplying by 0.0778, finding the number of syllables per hundred words and multiplying that by 2.029, and then adding the two results together.

Sticht Index
- Designed by US Army to test functional literacy.
- Calculated by finding the ratio of single syllable words to total words, multiplying that ratio by 15, and subtracting the result from 20.

evolution of an individual style of writing is often not a quick or an easy process. As the editor of *The Times* newspaper comments[18] 'Good style is hard work'. Nevertheless, for the manager who wishes to communicate effectively through the medium of the written word, such a process is mandatory.

CLARITY

The ease with which the reader is able to read, understand and absorb the written material is, to a considerable extent, dependent upon the clarity or readabiity of the text. That text may be grammatically perfect, with excellent use of punctuation and contain short jargon-free sentences and paragraphs – and yet may still not be easily read or understood. The clarity or readability of written text can be measured, and Table 8.2 defines a number of the most popular measures of readability. The most popular of these is the FOG index which was devised by Gunning[16] and is used to indicate the American school grade level of reading difficulty for the text. The scale of this index runs from six to sixteen, and Gunning views a value of twelve or more as indicating

Table 8.3 FOG, SMOG and Flesch indices

- *Before*

The fact that all organic and inorganic entities and artefacts go through, on this planet at least, cycles of change and decay is a well established and integral feature of life. The level of integration of this fact into human culture is total, encompassing and influencing religion, philosophy, psychiatry, economics and marketing and many other areas of our lives. One numerate view of the failure patterns associated with this cycle of change is shown by the bath tub curve. While not presuming to be all encompassing this view of failure patterns does coincide with significant areas of experience and evidence for both plant, equipment and human beings.

Totals: Words = 107
         Sentences = 4
         Syllables = 187
         Words with more than three syllables = 11

FOG Index   = 14.81
SMOG Index = 84.99
Flesch Index = 31.8

- *After*

The fact that all organic and inorganic entities and artefacts go through, on this planet at least, cycles of change and decay is a well known feature of life. This fact also influences many aspects of our lives including religion, philosophy, psychiatry, economics and marketing. One view of the pattern of change and failure is shown by the bath tub curve. Whilst this does not represent all types of failure, it does agree with much of the evidence for both plant, equipment and human beings.

Totals: Words = 85
         Sentences = 4
         Syllables = 131
         Words with more than three syllables = 5

FOG Index   = 10.85
SMOG Index = 75.75
Flesch Index = 54.85

---

that the text may be difficult to read. The Flesch Index[17] is an alternative which is designed for use on adult texts. The Flesch Reading Ease Index scale runs from zero to one hundred, with increasing ease of readability. 'Standard' writing is described as averaging around 17 words per sentence and 147 syllables per hundred words, with a resulting index of 64. It should be stressed that these and other indices are not measures of or guides to good writing. They represent mechanisms which can be used to support and refine the writer's personal judgement and knowledge of his or her audience. Table 8.3 shows samples of text with their FOG, SMOG and Flesch indices before and after editing to increase the text readability. However, the 'after' sample should not be taken as an example of 'good' writing, but merely as an example to illustrate how these indices operate.

Another aspect of readability or clarity in the written text reflects the use, or misuse, of words. Gowers *et al.*[14] state that writing should be 'terse, simple and direct' and should avoid the use of the 'unusual, longwinded, stilted and circumlocutory' phrases and words. Fowler[15] writes of the use of:

- The familiar instead of the far-fetched.
- The concrete instead of the abstract.
- The short instead of the long.

Examples of the *misuse* of words are:

- *Verbiage*
  There is no existing process that can do this instead of *No process can do this*
  At all times instead of *Always*
  For the reason that instead of *Because*
  It was noted that if instead of *Obviously*
- *Redundancy*
  Actual experience instead of *Experience*
  Equally as well instead of *As well as*
  True facts instead of *Facts*
- *Large vs. small*
  Optimum instead of *Best*
  Maximize instead of *Increase*
  Conceptualize instead of *Think of*
  Conjecture instead of *Guess*
- *Gender-biased*
  Man-hours instead of *Work-hours*
  Policeman instead of *Police officer*
  Salesman instead of *Salesperson*
  Chairman instead of *Chairperson*
- *Phrases instead of words*
  According as to whether or not instead of *If*
  A certain amount of instead of *Some*

The clarity of written language can also be reduced by misspelling. The 'Top Twenty' of misspelt words are reported[19] to be:

Word	Percentage spelling word wrongly
Practice/practise	54
Withhold	52
Occurred	52
Innovate	52
Benefited	48
Principal/principle	45
Incur	44
Grievance	40
Concede	40
Transferred	39
Competent	37
Calendar	35
Warranty	35
Acquire	34

Word	Percentage spelling word wrongly
Liaise	34
Truly	34
Expedite	33
Discrete/discreet	33
Affect/effect	32
Accommodation	32

Melkie[20] reports that a Gallup survey also reported that 10 per cent of the adult population were unable to spell any of six familiar words. So misspelling is a common problem. However, the misspelt word in a letter or report distracts and may even misinform the reader. While it is not necessary to know how to spell all of the half a million words contained in the *Oxford English Dictionary*, it is necessary to:

- Know how to spell words that are in common usage.
- Know where to find the correct spelling for the others.

Blake and Bly[21] suggest keeping a list of those words that you repeatedly misspell.

CONCLUSION

The process of generating written text has been in use for over five thousand years. During that time, the speed with which the text can be copied and disseminated has increased by several orders of magnitude, with the result that written text now makes a major contribution to modern patterns of communication. This text, which is generally formal and planned, involves the use of rules and regulations about the syntax, semantics and grammar involved in its structure. The process of creating written text is currently seen to involve the stages of planning, creating and revising in an ordered, interactive and parallel manner. Planning absorbs most of the time taken for this overall process and can make a significant contribution to its effectiveness. Few rules are evident about the creation of text from ideas and the process of revising is seen to involve the assessment and change of content, structure and meaning. All of these stages are influenced by aspects of the environment and the writer's experience, skill and knowledge.

Style is influenced by structural aspects, such as sentence length and structure, paragraph length and punctuation, as well as by jargon, tone and clarity. These are all important aspects of the written word – all of which can significantly influence the reader's ability to understand the writer's intent.

EXERCISES

1. Apply the FOG, SMOG and Flesch indices to a sample of your own writing and then see if it can be improved.
2. Comment on the use of: 'deplane', 'interface', 'subsume' and 'carcinogen'.
3. Identify those words that you repeatedly misspell or misuse – find out the correct spellings and meanings and keep them in your wallet or purse.
4. Identify which sorts of organization have rules about the style and content of their documents and the reasons for these rules.

REFERENCES

1. Oppheim, A. L., *Ancient Mesopotamia: Portrait of a Dead Civilization*, University of Chicago Press, Chicago, 1977.
2. Toffler, A., *Future Shock*, Pan, London, 1978.
3. McLuhan, M., *Understanding Media: The Extensions of Man*, McGraw-Hill, New York, 1965.
4. Ochs, E., Planned and unplanned discourse, in Givon, T. (ed.), *Syntax and Semantics, Vol. 12: Discourse and Syntax*, Academic Press, New York, 1979.
5. Crystal, D., *Linguistics*, Penguin, London, 1985.
6. Trudgill, P., *Sociolinguistics: An Introduction to Language and Society*, Penguin, London, 1983.
7. Faigley, L., Cherry, D., Joliffe, D. A. and Skinner, A. M., *Assessing Writer's Knowledge and Processes and Composing*, Ablex, Norwood NJ, 1985.
8. Damasio, A. R. and Damasio, H., Brain and language, *Scientific American*, **267**(3) Sept. 1992.
9. Gould, J. D., Experiments on composing letters: Some facts, some myths, some observations, in Gregg, L. W. and Steinberg, E.R. (eds.), *Cognitive Processes in Writing*, Erlbaum, Hillsdale NJ, 1980.
10. Scardamalia, M., Bereiter, C. and Goelman, H., The role of production factors in writing ability, in Nystrand, M. (ed.), *What Writers Know: The Language, Process and Structure of Written Discourse*, Academic Press, New York, 1982.
11. Bradbury, R., *Zen in the Art of Writing*, Bantam, New York, 1992.
12. Cooper, B. M., *Writing Technical Reports*, Penguin, London, 1964.
13. Mullholland, J., *The Language of Negotiation*, Routledge, London, 1991.
14. Gowers, Sir E., Greenbaum, S. and Whitcut, J., *The Complete Plain Words*, Penguin, London, 1986.
15. Fowler, H. W., *Modern English Usage*, Oxford University Press, Oxford, 1968.
16. Gunning, R., *The Technique of Clear Writing*, McGraw-Hill, New York, 1952.
17. Flesch, R., *The Art of Readable Writing*, Harper & Row, New York, 1949.
18. Jenkins, S. (ed.), *The Times Guide to English Style and Usage*, Times Books, London, 1992.
19. *Guardian*, Education Supplement, 20 October 1992, pp. 14–15.
20. Melkie, J., Five out of six adults trip up in spelling test', *Guardian*, 12 November 1992, p. 6.
21. Blake, G. and Bly, R. W., *The Elements of Business Writing*, Collier, New York, 1991.

NINE

BUSINESS DOCUMENTS

'What is written without effort is in general read without pleasure.'
Samuel Johnson

'You can stroke people with words.'
F. Scott Fitzgerald

INTRODUCTION

The typical dictionary definition for a document states that it is 'something written which gives information on facts' and defines the act of documenting as being the 'act of furnishing or supporting with written evidence'. The breadth of this definition means that the range of types of business document is enormous. The word document can be used, in the business environment, to describe letters, notes, bills, invoices, letters, reports, procedures, manuals, orders and many other pieces of paper with writing or figures on them. Each of these documents can also be described in a variety of ways. For example, reports can be described as project or formal or interim or final reports, invoices can be described as final or initial or monthly and letters can be described as confirmation, enquiry, appointment or dismissal letters. Several of the dimensions of this variety of descriptions are illustrated in Fig. 9.1.

Human beings have been creating documents for almost five thousand years,[1] and during that period of time the ways in which they have been produced has changed and evolved significantly. The first of these business documents consisted of inscriptions on clay tablets which listed the numbers of sacks of grain and head of cattle held by a temple. Over the passage of time, technological improvements enabled this primitive method of generating business documents to evolve to the marking of words or figures on paper with a pen, and then to the use of the typewriter keyboard and paper. More recently, this change process has led to the generation of documents which are written, viewed and stored solely on or by the use of electronic equipment.

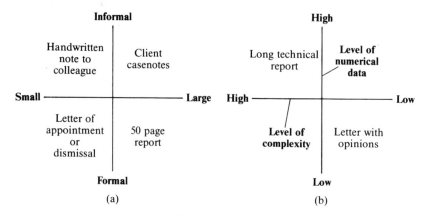

Figure 9.1 Dimensions of documents.

However they are generated, the common features of all these business documents are that:

- Their creation is deliberate and purposeful.
- Their contents are authentic in that they relate to or describe actual or proposed rather than imaginary events.
- Their contents can consist of numerical data, information, views, opinions and statements of fact.

The purposes of these documents can include:

- Recording information, events or views.
- Informing others or being informed by them about information, events or views.
- Persuading or influencing others.

For example, the purposes of a report could include the reporting of the evidence gathered and collated in response to a defined remit, while the purpose of an informal letter may have more to do with relationship building rather than information display.

It is also evident that both the nature and the visibility of the structure of these documents will vary with the purpose or the style of the document. For example, a formal report will be written with a detailed, well-defined and overt structure, while an informal letter will possess a beginning and an end but will display little overt evidence of structure between.

There appears to be little evidence to identify a quantitative relationship between the culture or other characteristics of an organization and the level or type of business documentation generated within that organization. It is, however, evident that some organizations are predisposed towards the use of documents. For example, the Bureaucratic organization[2] stresses the use of written communication and records even when oral communication is the norm, and the Mechanistic[3] type of organization has a hierarchical structure of communication with high levels of documentation in the form of procedures and manuals. Leavitt[4] suggests that, in an organization which handles repetitive programmed tasks, the type of structure which leads to effective communication is of a centralized nature. This type of structure will, in large organizations, establish and identify its norms, rules and procedures by the use of documents.

Whatever the purpose, size, formality, content or structure of the business document might be, it is intended as a way of communicating with others. Business documents need to be effective communication mechanisms and the key features of all effective business documents are:

- Clarity.
- Accuracy.
- Brevity.

Chapter 8 examined the process of creating the written document and commented on a number of factors which influence the clarity and brevity of that document. These included the excessive use of words (verbiage), the use of jargon, and sentence length and structure. The comments and observations made in that chapter are applicable to all business documents. It is, however, worth adding some comment on the subject of accuracy.

There are two aspects of accuracy in business documentation, and these are:

- Accuracy in the use of words.
- Accuracy in the use of figures.

The use of words in an accurate manner in business documents is important. For example, few customers will buy a product if its advertising brochure writes about the product's performance or capabilities in vague and non-specific terms. Nor will a manager persuade others to support a project if he or she is not accurate and precise about its objectives, time-scale and cost. One of the commonest ways in which word accuracy is lost is by the use of abstract words. Gowers et al.[5] comment that the vagueness of these abstract words is one of the reasons for their popularity, and that this 'safer obscurity of the abstract' is the 'greatest vice of present day writing'. An example of the use of vague and abstract words is as follows:

A high degree of demotivation, pre-project and post-project, on the part of some staff, was observed.

The meaning behind this sentence could have been expressed with more brevity, accuracy and clarity if this version had been used:

Some staff were seen to be unhappy both before and after the project.

Cooper[6] writes about the use of 'abstract tag words' which have lost precision through careless use in the past. Examples of these are said to include:

- Case
- Condition
- Implement
- Overall
- Facilities
- Situation
- Tendency
- Real
- Rather

Blake and Bly[7] write about words and phrases that 'hedge' and are used when the writer is unsure about the accuracy of what he or she is writing. Examples of these are said to include:

- In my opinion
- Virtually
- Probably

Table 9.1   Phrase generator

Column 1	Column 2	Column 3
Overall	Paradigmatic	Formulation
Systematic	Correlative	Projection
Conceptualized	Binary	Software
Optimized	Synchronous	Capacity
Operational	Logistic	Parameters
Integrated	Managerial	Programmes
Synergistic	Peripatetic	Mobility

Table 9.2 Spurious accuracy

Version A

Product	This month's sales	Year to date sales
X453	£134.50	£750.00
Multicore	£5,229.10	£21,474.10
D32 displays	£440.65	£1,002.65
H97 units	£800.00	£2,165.93
Total	£6,604.25	£25,392.68

Version B

Product	This month's sales	Year to date sales
X453	£135	£750
D32 displays	£441	£1,003
H97 units	£800	£2,166
Multicore	£5,229	£21,474
Total	£6,604	£25,393

- Is considered to be
- In some circumstances
- As I recall

All of these and other examples of 'abstract tag' and 'hedge' words and phrases are capable of correct use in the right context. However, their use in business documents can signal uncertainty on the writer's part and they do not add to the word accuracy of the document. Several illustrations of the use and meaning of abstract words in the context of business are given by de Bono[8] and include such words as cash-flow, syllogism, black box, etc. The use of an abstract phrase generator (Table 9.1) can enable the generation of even less meaningful phrases by the random combination of words from Columns 1, 2 and 3 in that order.

The use of numerical data or figures in a business document often faces the writer with a different problem – that of spurious accuracy. This is illustrated by versions A and B of the data given in Table 9.2. The differences between these versions are limited, but consist of:

- The omission of irrelevant detail.
- The rounding of the figures.
- The reordering of the rows so that the figures are in ascending order.

These changes are aimed at making the information:

- Easier to assimilate.
- More informative.

Any loss of accuracy is limited (in this case < 0.4 per cent) and can be countered by appending a comment to the table that all figures are rounded up or down to the nearest ten, or single digits, as relevant.

The following sections of this chapter will examine the preparation of business documents and then look at the key features of reports, letters and memos.

PREPARATION

Preparation is a key and major stage in the process of business document generation. The process model used in the previous chapter identified that this activity is not only undertaken before, but also during the actual creation of the document. Preparation was seen to be concerned with:

- Creating goals.
- Identifying potential content.
- Organizing material and activities.

All of these will reflect decisions made by the writer. Their nature will, however, develop and change as the actual generation of the text progresses. However, text does not appear upon the paper or computer screen spontaneously, and some prior thought and activity must take place. These will include a number of decisions which must be made before the generation of text can begin.

The first of these decisions should enable the writer to:

- Establish the purpose of the document.

The writer should identify, clearly and succinctly, for what purpose the document is intended. Is it, for example, intended to inform the reader or to act as a record of events or decisions? The document's purpose must be decided and understood before any further preparation is under-taken and must be capable of being expressed in a single short sentence. For example, the purpose of a letter might be expressed as:

To place on record my disagreement with Mr S's actions on 9 December 1991

or

To state my reasons for disagreeing with Mr S on 9 December 1991.

These different objectives will result in different letters, as one acts as a record while the other intends to inform and perhaps persuade. The generation of this purposive statement represents a key step in the composition of a business document. It will influence the style of writing and the structure and the formality of the document. It also leads to decisions about the subject and the scope of the document. The extent of this influence can be illustrated by the first of the above examples, i.e. the letter that was intended to act as a record. The style of this letter will be formal and it will be directly addressed to an individual, i.e. Mr S or Mr S's superior, though it could also consist of a formal statement attached to a letter to Mr S or his superior. It may or may not be concerned with relating the disagreement to other external events or actions, but may simply be a record which could be used at some time in the future. This letter will be structured in order to ensure that the reader understands its contents. However, as this letter is intended as a record, the circumstances of its future use may be unclear at the time of writing. Because of this uncertainty, the letter will also contain a level of detail which will be different from and probably in excess of that for a letter whose context of use is clear and defined. These characteristics can be contrasted with the style, content and structure of a brief handwritten note from a manager to a secretary. This will be informal, unstructured and intended to be discarded after receipt or, if it refers to an action, after completion of that action. The note can act as a way of transmitting a request and, after receipt, a reminder to the receiver that the request is awaiting action. These differences are significant in their influence upon the content and style of the document.

Nevertheless, even though the purpose of the document has been decided, the generation of that document cannot be started until a number of further decisions are taken. The next of these decisions is one which will enable the writer to:

- Establish who the readers are to be.

Writers, if they are to be effective in their written communication, must be clear about:

- Who the readers are.
- What they already know.
- What interests they have.
- What they want or need to know
- What language or terminology they will understand.

All of these will influence the style and content of the document. For example, a document written to describe the events which led up to the British Government's decision to leave the European Exchange Rate Mechanism in 1992 will be written in quite different ways when it is written for a House of Commons select committee and when it is written for the readers of a tabloid newspaper. These different groups of readers have different interests, vocabularies, levels of knowledge and needs. A conscious and considered decision about who these readers are and what their interests and characteristics are will enable the writer to ensure that the content and style of the document are both compatible with the document's audience. Once this decision is taken, then the writer can move on to the next decision. This should enable the writer to:

- Establish what the nature of the document will be.

Earlier decisions about the purpose of the document and its intended readership will have already had a significant effect upon the nature or genre of the document. If the intention of the document is to inform, then its nature and structure will be systematic. For example, a document whose purpose is to brief, i.e. inform, company board members about a hostile takeover bid should be:

- Systematic, so that the information is presented in a logical order.
- Succinct, so that it can be read quickly.
- Complete, so that no critical information is omitted.
- Accurate, in that its factual content is correct and verifiable.

Such a document will probably not exceed five sides of A4 paper and will possess a limited structure consisting of headings. However, a report which informs company board members about potential candidates for takeover bids will need to be:

- Comprehensive, so that all potential candidates and supporting data are given.
- Accurate, in that its factual content is correct and verifiable and that opinions and interpretations are identified.
- Clear, in that its conclusions and recommendations are identified and understandable.
- Structured in such a way that its contents are presented in an ordered and accessible manner.

Such a report will be large in size and will have several detailed appendices which contain detailed supporting information. Its structure will reflect the complexity and detail of the subject, but will, nevertheless, contain a short summary to enable busy or lazy readers to identify its main conclusions. The particular characteristics and demands of the report are discussed in further detail in later sections of this chapter. The writer's decision about the nature of the document will take into account such factors as size, formality, time and information available, existing conventions and previous relationship with the reader or reader group. Lack of time and a good previous relationship, for example, may lead a manager to write a brief and informal letter to a colleague, whereas a bad previous relationship will lead to a formal, detailed and thoughtful letter, whatever time is available.

Having established the purpose, readership and nature of the document, the writer must now:

- Establish what information is needed.

The previous decisions taken about the purpose, readership and nature of the document will exert considerable influence over the scope and amount of material needed. For example, a limited amount of information will be needed, by a manager, to write a brief and informal note to a colleague to remind that individual that he or she had promised to provide some figures. If, however, the same manager needs to write a formal report, for the Executive Committee, about sales trends over the past five years then a much larger amount of information will be needed. If the influence of these earlier decisions about the purpose, readership and nature of the document has not resulted in at least an outline of the document's information needs, then it is worth reviewing those decisions. With larger documents, a considerable amount of time and effort can be wasted collecting and collating irrelevant information. Even at this stage it is worthwhile, particularly for larger documents, classifying the material for ease of future reference. For shorter documents, such as letters, however, that classification may be limited to a few notes about topics or areas that the manager wants to cover in the letter. The larger the document then the greater the need is to classify, even at this early stage, and the more comprehensive will be the classification. A structured classification of material can also act as an aid to material collection. Whatever the size or nature of the document, the process of collecting the necessary information should ensure that:

- Only relevant, accurate information is collected.
- Facts are separated from both opinions and inferences.

The manager will not be ready to actually begin the process of creating the document until all of the above stages of preparation are complete. However, the overall process was seen in the previous chapter to be interactive and iterative. As a consequence, it may, for example, be necessary to revisit and review decisions about structure in the light of what has been written at that point in the overall process.

We shall now examine some of the characteristics and demands of the more common forms of business document.

Table 9.3 Example of report types

Special	Preliminary	Routine
Investigation	Interim	Operations
Planning	Valuation	Design
Feasibility	Test	Inspection
Construction	Work	Progress
Formal	Eye-witness	Informal

REPORTS

For most managers the task of writing a report is not one that is greeted with enthusiasm. But reports do get written on a very wide range of subjects and with a considerable variety of titles. Some of these reports are generated on a 'one-off' basis, while others may represent a routine task with a weekly or monthly frequency. The experience of writing a report appears to be one which all managers, whatever their age, experience or employment sector, have in common and has been described[6] as 'providing a challenge to the individual to be explicit and articulate'. But are these reports all the same?

Table 9.3 lists some of the commoner types of report. Even a cursory examination of this far from complete list will indicate that the word report is used to describe a very wide range of written documents. For example, the report of an engineering inspection on a vessel used in the manufacture of chemicals will be written out on a standard form (Fig. 9.2), which acts as both record and check-list. However, a sales report (Table 9.4) can consist of a table of figures which reflect the performance of a business unit and contain little or no written comment. An eye-witness report will usually consist of the written statement containing an individual's recollections of an event and will contain limited quantitative information. All of the examples given above are of reports which are brief, often consisting of no more than two or three pages of A4 paper, and which are focused towards providing information. Another report might be larger, consisting of fifty or more pages with diagrams and graphs, and focused towards persuading others, arguing the pros and cons, evaluating alternatives and making recommendations as well as providing information: in all, a report whose size, purposes, style and content are very different from the earlier examples. However, whatever their differences, all of these reports will be structured and formal documents, whose purposes will include those of all management documents, i.e. to record, inform or influence.

Table 9.4 Orange Computer Inc. sales report for January 1993

Week starting	Units sold (thousands)			
	X453	Multicore	D32 displays	H97 units
4/01/93	24.7	17.9	2.56	0.56
11/01/93	26.9	18.6	2.80	0.67
18/01/93	23.8	19.1	2.64	0.59
25/01/93	21.9	20.3	2.89	0.78

Vessel Inspection Report

PKG Resins Inc.

Vessel location: Identification No.:

Was vessel in service when examined?   Yes   No

If vessel was out of service when examined state date of last use:
Date of report: Date of examination:

Part 1: Description
Description:
Date of installation:

Part 2: Location

Part 3: Summary of inspected condition

	Internal condition	External condition
Shell		
Jacket		
Branches		
Instruments		
Paintwork		
Insulation		

Part 4: Further comments

Part 5: Recommended action

Signed:_____

Figure 9.2   Vessel inspection report.

The most basic structure for a report will be:

- Title.
- Contents (which can be divided into subsections).

The use of this basic structure is usually limited to the types of report shown in Table 9.4 and Fig. 9.2. The primary function of these reports is to record information, e.g. sales volumes or revenue, and to transmit that information to others. They contain little or no interpretation of or views about that information, and to be effective they will need to present that information in such a way that it is easily assimilated and understood. The value of diagrams in achieving these aims is explored in Chapter 12.

As the volume and complexity of the information contained in the report increases, so does the need for that information to be interpreted for the reader. As a result, the complexity of the structure increases to the following:

- Title.
- Summary.
- Table of contents.
- Main text.
- Conclusions and recommendations.

The introduction of a summary is intended to provide the reader with a preview or survey of the area covered by the report. It should be brief and factual, with a length less than 10 per cent of the report length. This summary is written after the report and should consist of statements which enable readers to understand the report's main issues and conclusions or to decide whether they wish to read the main report. The words 'abstract', 'synopsis' and 'summary' are often used to describe this part of the report. Their meanings are, to all real intents and purposes, identical.

Small reports do not require a table of contents, as the reader can, because of the report's limited number of pages, quickly identify the contents and their location in the report. With larger reports, i.e. those more than 5 pages in length, the inclusion of this table is mandatory. Its objective is to ensure that the reader can find any part of the report quickly and easily. Sections headed Conclusions and Recommendations are included to ensure that the reader is helped to interpret the information given and to understand what the writer sees as necessary future actions consequent upon that interpretation. In small and medium-sized reports, these conclusions and recommendations are often contained in the same section of the report.

As the complexity and size of the report increase further, this leads to further changes in structure. An example of the structure of an investigative consultancy report is as follows:

- Title.
- Summary.
- Table of contents.
- Introduction.
- Background.
- Findings.
- Conclusions.
- Recommendations.
- Appendices.

The introduction to this report will state:

- What the report is about.
- Its authority and terms of reference.
- Any required background, e.g. when, by whom, etc.
- How the report intends to develop the subject.

An example of the introduction to this type of report is shown in Table 9.5. It is worth noting that this introduction also contains the relevant acknowledgements, although if these are more comprehensive they can be located in a separate section.

The background section of the report will contain that material which the reader needs in order to understand the subsequent findings section. In the report whose introduction is shown in Table 9.5, the background section would contain that material which was necessary for an understanding of the subject of the review, i.e. the manufacturing function. This material would include, for example, a brief company history, roles carried out by named individuals, turnover levels, location of factories, organization mission statement, product range, number of personnel, typical contract values and some indication of known future changes and ambitions. In this report, this material would be reported briefly, as the readers, i.e. the Country Catering directors, already know these facts. In this example, however, the purpose of their presence is not to inform the reader but to indicate the writer's awareness and understanding of these relevant factors. The depth and detail of the material contained in the background section should, in common with all sections of the report, reflect the reader's prior knowledge and understanding of the subject.

Table 9.5   A sample introduction

---

1. Introduction
This review was undertaken at the request of Mr John Brown (Managing Director, Country Catering Equipment Ltd) following discussions with the staff of the Management Department of the ANG Business School.

The review, which was a part of a larger Business Development programme funded by the Southshire TEC, was undertaken during the summer of 1993 and had the following objectives:

- The outline identification and examination of the systems, procedures and practices followed in the manufacturing function of Country Catering Equipment Ltd.
- The identification of:
  — Current problem areas.
  — Areas which will cause future problems.
- The identification of potential solutions.

The discussions and investigative activities associated with the review were undertaken at the Dunesmead offices and factory of the company, on a part-time basis, during the months of May and June 1993.

Subsequent sections of this report are concerned with the following aspects of this review:

- Background.
- Methodology.
- Findings.
- Conclusions.
- Recommendations.
- The way forward.

Acknowledgement is made of the time given by all Country Catering personnel involved in this review.

The findings section of this report will contain the factual results of the investigation, which, for the example being considered, would be grouped under the headings of:

- Organization and roles.
- Systems.
- Personnel.
- Production facilities.
- Design facilities.

The presentation of material in this main body of the report should always be systematic and ordered. The choices of order used can include:

- Logical order.
- Chronological order.
- Geographical order.
- Order of importance.
- Order of magnitude.

The separation of the sections covering the conclusions and the recommendations reflects both the bulk of the separate sections and the need for the reader to understand the nature and inferences of the information reported. Conclusions should be written in clear, unambiguous and unqualified statements which do not contain any information or ideas that have not been written about previously in the report's findings section. At the end of the conclusions section, readers should be aware that they have reached a natural 'break point' in the report. All recommendations given in the report should be brief and sound. They should also be able to stand up to the test of the question: 'Can they be accomplished?'. The report's appendices should contain all of the detailed information which, if located in the main body of the report, would disrupt the flow of the narrative. Typical examples would include tables of detailed figures, graphs, test results, copies of other documents and photographs. The advantage of locating this information in an appendix is that while the reader is not obliged to read that section of the report, its contents are available for reference and support if required.

It is common practice to use numbers to identify and emphasize the different sections of a report. This practice can be extended to include subsections and even paragraphs. The nature and detail of the numbering system used must reflect the need that the reader might have to refer to and identify a particular paragraph or subsection. For example, while it is common practice in large reports to number down to subsection level, many Government reports number down to paragraph level. The objective of numbering is to aid readers to find their way through the report. For the main sections of the report, the numbering sequence used can involve either Roman numerals, I, II, III, IV, etc., or Arabic numerals, 1, 2, 3, 4, etc. Subsection numbering can involve Roman or Arabic numerals with small letters, I(a), II(b), or 1(a), 1(b), etc., or 'decimal' Arabic numerals, 1.2, 1.3 or 1.1.2, 1.3.2, etc.

A number of alternative structures for reports are shown in Table 9.6, and Appendix 9.1 contains a check-list for report writers which is intended to help the report writer to clarify issues about the subject, scope, audience and purpose of the report.

LETTERS AND MEMOS

By far the largest number of business documents consists of letters or memos. These can cover almost any subject and be written with any degree of formality. For many managers the task of

Table 9.6 Alternative report structures

Short (< 5 pages)	*Medium* (5 to 25 pages)
Title	Title
Background and introduction	Summary
Findings	Table of contents
Recommendations	Background and introduction
	Findings
	Conclusions
	Recommendations
	Appendices
Long (1)	*Long (2)*
Title	Title
Summary	Summary
Table of contents	Table of contents
Introduction	Introduction
Background	Background
Findings (a)	Findings (a)
Findings (b)	Conclusions (a)
Findings (c)	Recommendation (a)
Conclusions (a)	Findings (b)
Conclusions (b)	Conclusions (b)
Conclusions (c)	Recommendations (b)
Recommendations (a)	Findings (c)
Recommendations (b)	Conclusions (c)
Recommendations (c)	Recommendations (c)
Appendices	Summary of recommendations
	Appendices

writing letters or memos occurs on a routine, regular and frequent basis. However, it is often not realized that many of an organization's customers and clients make judgements about that organization based on the content, quality and style of its letters. Voss *et al.*[9] comment that the customer's perception of the level of quality present in a service organization's operations is often subjective and based on 'one or a small number' of the features of the service package. A study[10] of the application of quality circles within a major life assurance company provides data which indicates that over half of outgoing mail to customers was badly addressed. Nor is this effect restricted to 'external' customers. Oakland and Mortiboys,[11] in describing the concept of total quality management, stress the concept of the 'internal' customer and the need for effective communications within the quality organization. It is also true that many managers develop views of their colleagues based on the style and content of their memos.

For many managers, letter or memo writing is a routine and uninspiring task that is often delegated to others, but these letters are important to both the reader and the sender.

Letters can tell others that the writer is efficient, effective and willing to treat them with sympathy and understanding. Alternatively, the letter can tell them that the writer is uninterested, difficult to understand, vague and verbose. Little of the impression that the reader gains will come from the factual content or grammatical accuracy of the letter. Most of their impressions will arise from the way in which the letter is written, i.e. its style.

That is not, however, to say that correctness of grammar and accuracy of content are not important. Both of these or their absence will contribute to the impression that the reader gains about the writer and the writer's organization. For example, few readers react positively, promptly or constructively to those official letters which start by addressing them as the 'occupier'. Another example is that of the job-seeking manager who lovingly and carefully crafts a job application letter and CV, only to receive a rejection with grammatical errors and his or her name misspelt! Neither of these examples provides the recipient of the letter with the impression that they are dealing with an organization which is interested in or concerned about them as an individual.

But even when the letter has correct grammar and accurate content, it still is possible to create the wrong impression. For example, the writer of a letter that starts with:

Further to your letter of the 4th inst., we are pleased to enclose herewith . . .

is probably under the impression that Charles Dickens is still alive and, more importantly, stands little chance of developing a profitable business relationship with the reader, because of a written style which is too formal and stiff.

Style is important, and the main issues are:

- The use of clear, simple and exact language.
- Avoidance of clichés, jargon, abstract language or superfluous words.
- The use of short sentences.
- The use of a friendly, natural and sympathetic style.

Gowers *et al.*[5] write that the effective letter-writing style should be 'simple but also friendly' and Blake and Bly[7] comment that customers like 'to deal with people who are warm, friendly and pleasant'. Fielden[12] writes about and illustrates that the written style has the potential to produce an 'emotional reaction' and stresses the importance of tone (see Chapter 8).

	Writer's address and telephone number
Reader's name, title, and address	
Date Reference	
Dear	
	Subject of letter
	Text of letter
Yours sincerely Signature of writer Name and job title of writer	

Figure 9.3 Typical letter layout.

Appendix 9.2 contains a check-list for letter writers which is intended to help the writer clarify issues about the subject, audience, content and style of the letter.

The layout of a letter is often governed by 'house rules' which represent the conventions for letters in that organization. These conventions may also include the use of headed paper, define the size of margins and fonts used, and specify the use of titles and reference formats. Figure 9.3 shows a typical sample layout. Letters are generally used for written communications with others outside the organization, while memos are used for written communication within the organization. However, the style, grammar and accuracy issues identified earlier for letters are also applicable to memos. One of the pitfalls for the memo-writing manager is the dangerous presumption that the knowledge level and memory capacity of the reader(s) matches, in all respects, that of the writer. This is often aided and abetted by the fact that the memo generally has a lower level of formality than the letter. These factors can result in memos which are marvels of brevity but which communicate little. An example of the resultant memo might be:

To: *John*
From: *Fred*
Subject: *XYZ Project*
I totally agree with the proposals that we discussed over lunch last week and look forward to receiving my new portable computer.

The obvious danger is that Fred remembers different proposals to the proposals which John remembers. This could have been avoided by a simple recapitulation of the proposal content, as shown below:

To: *John*
From: *Fred*
Subject: *XYZ Project*
I was very interested to hear your latest proposals for improving our inter-office communications, over lunch last week. I shall be happy to support these proposals at the Review Meeting next week. In the meantime I look forward to being involved in the test run of the portable computer fitted with a modem.

From:
To: Date:
Copies to:

Subject

Text of Memo

Signature of writer
Name of writer

Figure 9.4 Typical memo layout.

The layout of memos is also usually governed by house rules. Figure 9.4 shows a typical sample layout.

AGENDAS AND MINUTES

The subject of meetings and their associated agendas and minutes is discussed in Chapter 6.

CONCLUSION

Business documents come in all shapes and sizes and are created for a wide variety of purposes. Some aspects of this variety are formality, size, complexity and level of numerical data. However, all of these documents are deliberately created with a purpose in mind and have contents which are concerned with describing actual, rather than, fictional, events and consist of numerical data, information views and opinions. In order to be effective as a means of communication these documents need to display:

- Clarity.
- Accuracy.
- Brevity.

in the use of both words and numerical information. The presence and use of abstract words tends to increase the vagueness of the written document. The key steps in preparing a business document are seen to be those of establishing its:

- Purpose.
- Readership.
- Nature.
- Information needs.

Reports, letters and memos are found to have different purposes and structures. The importance of using an appropriate style in writing letters is also identified.

EXERCISES

1. Examine several examples of recent business letters that you have written and, using Appendix 9.2, see if you can improve them.
2. Write a memo to your boss explaining why you cannot work overtime on the evening that you are about to celebrate, with your family, your wedding anniversary or birthday.
3. List the uses that your organization has for reports.

REFERENCES

1. Jean, G., *Writing: The Story of Alphabets and Scripts*, Thames & Hudson, London, 1992.
2. Weber, M., *The Theory of Social and Economic Organisation*, pp. 328–40, reprinted in Pugh, D. S. (ed.), *Organisation Theory*, Penguin, London, 1990.
3. Burns, T., Industry in a new age, *New Society*, 31/1/63, reprinted in Pugh, D. S. (ed.), *Organisation Theory*, Penguin, London, 1990.
4. Leavitt, H. J., Applied organisation change in industry: structural, technical and human approaches, in

Cooper, W. W., Leavitt, H. J. and Shelly, M. W. (eds.), *New Perspectives in Organizational Research*, Wiley, New York, 1964.

5. Gowers, Sir E., Greenbaum, S. and Whitcut, J., *The Complete Plain Words*, Penguin, London, 1986.

6. Cooper, B. M., *Writing Technical Reports*, Penguin, London, 1964.

7. Blake, G. and Bly, R. W., *The Elements of Business Writing*, Collier, New York, 1991.

8. de Bono, E., *Word Power*, Penguin, London, 1979.

9. Voss, C., Armistead, C., Johnston, B. and Morris, B., *Operations Management in Service Industries and the Public Sector*, Wiley, London, 1991.

10. Department of Trade and Industry, *Quality Circles: An Executive Guide*, Department of Trade and Industry, London, 1992.

11. Oakland, J. and Mortiboys, R., *Total Quality Management and Effective Leadership: A Strategic Overview*, Department of Trade and Industry, London, 1991.

12. Fielden, J. S., What do you mean you don't like my style?, in *The Articulate Executive*, Harvard Business School Press, Boston, 1991.

APPENDIX 9.1: REPORT WRITER'S CHECK-LIST

1. What is the subject and title of this report?

2. Who will be the readers for this report?
   Main reader(s):

   Other readers:

3. What are the reasons for writing this report?

   - To get the reader's support.   Yes ☐ No ☐
   - To report the results of an investigation.   Yes ☐ No ☐
   - To influence or persuade the reader.   Yes ☐ No ☐
   - To provide answers to questions asked by the reader.   Yes ☐ No ☐
   - To explain issues.   Yes ☐ No ☐
   - To provide answers to questions asked by others than the reader.   Yes ☐ No ☐
   - To record facts, information or opinions.   Yes ☐ No ☐
   - To report on progress.   Yes ☐ No ☐
   - To sell.   Yes ☐ No ☐
   - To establish authority or reputation on a subject.   Yes ☐ No ☐
   - To inform a large group.   Yes ☐ No ☐
   - To provide evidence of work undertaken.   Yes ☐ No ☐
   - To publicize efforts and results inside and/or outside the organization.   Yes ☐ No ☐
   - To initiate or contribute to debate on topic.   Yes ☐ No ☐
   - To instruct.   Yes ☐ No ☐

APPENDIX 9.2: LETTER WRITER'S CHECK-LIST

A. *Before writing*
   1. What is the subject of this letter?

   2. Why are you writing this letter?

   3. Who will be the readers for this letter?
      Main reader(s):

      Other readers:

   4. What does the reader already know and need to know about the subject.
      Current knowledge:

      Needs to know:

B. *After writing*
   Is the letter you have written:

   - Clear.   Yes ☐   No ☐
   - Arranged in logical order.   Yes ☐   No ☐
   - Grammatically correct.   Yes ☐   No ☐
   - Free from jargon and slang.   Yes ☐   No ☐
   - In simple and direct language.   Yes ☐   No ☐
   - Sympathetic, polite and helpful.   Yes ☐   No ☐
   - Accurate.   Yes ☐   No ☐
   - Complete.   Yes ☐   No ☐
   - Prompt.   Yes ☐   No ☐

If any Nos are given to the above questions, your letter needs revision or redrafting.

PART
FOUR

THE OTHER WAYS

'Things are seldom what they seem
Skim milk masquerades as cream'
W. S. Gilbert

TEN

GESTURE, GAZE, SPACE AND MOVEMENT

'If we want to understand human social behaviour we shall have to disentangle this non-verbal system.'
Michael Argyle

INTRODUCTION

The ways in which people communicate with each other are not restricted or limited to those ways that involve the use of spoken or written language. There are other ways of communication, which involve, for example, the use of gesture, movement, space and gaze. These and other non-linguistic ways of communicating are often, in popular literature, grouped together under the general heading of 'body language'. However, academic literature uses the designations of 'bodily communication' or 'non-verbal communication' for this type of communication. Lewis[1] writes that the term non-verbal communication is applicable to all messages that are 'not coded in words'. Whatever title is used, the range and power of this type of communication, which does not exploit spoken or written language, is considerable. Indeed Mehrabian[2] goes as far as to state that the semantic content of our communications only accounts for around 10 per cent of the total message, and comments that non-verbal messages are more effective when used to communicate like/dislike, power or status and responsiveness.

Porter[3] identifies four broad areas of non-verbal communication:

- *Physical* sense of touch and smell, facial expressions, body motions and proximity, gaze, etc.
- *Aesthetic* music, dance, mime, painting, sculpture, etc.
- *Signs* flags, alarms, horns, sirens, peal of bells, etc.
- *Symbolic* religious, status or ego-building symbols, e.g. crosses, cars, etc.

The typical dictionary also recognizes the existence and use of these non-verbal media or channels in a definition which states that language is 'any system of signs, gestures and symbols, etc. used as a means of communication'.

Some indication of the capability of these alternative communication media and channels is manifest in the power and the plurality of sign languages. These languages, which are used by people with severe hearing impairment, are said by Sacks[4] to have arisen spontaneously all over the world and to involve a 'linguistic use of space'. Stokoe[5] describes the American Sign Language and states that it consists of signs which are 'complex abstract symbols'. The dictionary of the British Sign Language[6] contains a variety of hand shapes, hand locations and types of movement which are portrayed in 1800 photographic sign entries. This theme of the expressive use of space and movement is, of course, one which is also amply demonstrated in the fields of dance and mime. A typical dictionary definition for mime describes it as 'the art of theatrical communication solely by use of gestures and facial expression'. The use of dance to enable the expression of feelings by the medium of body movement is well established and needs little comment here. However, it is worth noting that the physical movements associated with dance, which can be either spontaneous or predetermined, can be documented using an 'alphabet' of signs which can be combined to produce 'words and sentences' of movement. This 'language of dance' can be documented, and Parker and MacMillan[7] write about the development and use of the Benesh dance notation system as a way of doing so. The use of space, movement and gesture is not, of course, limited to those who mime or dance or those whose hearing ability is impaired. The use of complex and special gestures is also evident under circumstances where speech would be, for example, difficult or undesirable. An example of this use of gesture and space is the use, by bookmakers on racecourses, of a 'tic-tac code' to communicate shifts in betting volume or other information. The use of gestures in situations where silence or secrecy is required is also familiar, as is their use in very noisy environments. Even under normal circumstances, the use of gesture, space, gaze and movement is seen to be significant. Margerison,[8] writing about conversational skills for managers, reports that over half of the messages that are transmitted are 'coded' in facial and body expressions.

Given the widespread nature and obvious power and value of these uses of body movement and space, are they an alternative to verbal or written language based communication – and how did they come about?

The answer to both these questions lies in the fact that body movement, gesture and space have been exploited by mankind as a method of communication for a long time and that they are used to complement, supplement and add emphasis to our verbal communications. It is also evident that this use of body movement, gesture and space has at least some of its beginnings in the early history of our species. Leakey and Lewin[9] suggest that, some two to five million years ago, 'gesture language' may have been part of human-kind's first attempt to break through the communication barrier. They also suggest a possible link between the manipulative skills needed to produce and use more complex tools and those needed for complex signing. Argyle[10] writes of the similarities in non-verbal communication between human beings and monkeys. These are said to include:

- Indicating feelings by facial cast or expression.
- Indicating attitude by manner and direction of gaze.
- Greeting and grooming by touching.
- Signalling by pointing or beckoning.
- Indicating dominance/submission by posture, gesture and movement.

However, Argyle does stress that the ways in which monkey and human bodily communication are 'fundamentally different' include our ability to choose if and how we express emotions, the influence of social mores and patterns and our extensive use of speech. However, some of the ways in which we communicate with our bodies are, as they also are for animals, inborn or innate. Examples of the innate nature of use of movement, gesture and space for communication include reports of how mentally handicapped children and their carers communicate. Kingman[11] reports that the parents and carers of profoundly mentally handicapped children use innate non-verbal communication to overcome the child's inability to speak or even to use sign language. This non-verbal communication takes the form of looks, nods, nudges and other forms of physical contact. These physical contacts, which include patting, stroking, shaking and tapping movements, are reported to take place at different frequencies which relate to the carer's intention. For example, slow patting or stroking is said to indicate reassurance, while faster movements happen during playful interaction. It is also reported that many of these movements are also used by mothers of non-handicapped children and with the same range and level of frequency of movement as the parents or carers of the handicapped children.

The face is also said to provide a large part of our bodily communications, with Darwin[12] writing that facial expressions are concerned with the expression of emotion, and Mehrabian[2] reporting that facial expressions can provide as much as half the 'meaning' content of any message.

Whatever the origins or causes of this use of movement, gaze, gesture and space, it is evident that it has attracted considerable research interest and that this research has traversed many aspects of human behaviour. Knapp[13] and Argyle[10] both suggest that the modes of this non-language-based or non-verbal communication can be identified as including:

- *Kinesics* hand, arm, leg, head and eye movements, posture changes, gaze and facial expressions.
- *Proxemics* distance and spacing, territorial factors.
- *Tacesics* body contact and touching.
- *Bodily appearance* body shape, skin colour, smell.
- *Use of ornamentation* clothes, jewellery, wigs, etc.
- *Environmental factors* physical setting or location.
- *Paralinguistic factors* content free or non-verbal vocalizations and patterns.

Patterson[14] suggests that non-verbal behaviour has five basic functions:

- Supply of information.
- Control, alignment and development of interaction.
- Expression of intimacy.
- Persuasion and influence.
- Facilitating interaction goals.

However, Knapp[13] identifies several uses for bodily communication during a verbal interaction. These are:

- *Repeating*, in which the speaker's gesture repeats what is said. Example: pointing while saying, *'This way, please'*.
- *Contradicting* in which the actions or gestures contradict what is said. Example: saying, *'I'm happy'* without a smile.
- *Substituting*, in which the gestures or facial expression substitute for actual words. Example: responding to question, *'Can I come over and have a chat with you?'* with a shake of the head.
- *Complementing*, in which verbal and non-verbal messages are the same, but the non-verbal supplements the verbal. Example: saying *'I like that'*, while leaning forward and smiling.
- *Relating and regulating*, in which, for example, single nods, eye movement and posture shifts indicate that the speaker is being listened to and should continue talking while double or triple nods and other posture positions indicate that the listener wants to speak.

Rozelle *et al.*[15] stress that all non-verbal behaviour must be viewed within the context in which it occurs and that failure to do so may lead to incomplete or limited interpretations.

Whatever the context or the nature of this bodily communication, its prime purposes, in common with all communicative behaviour, are those which were identified in Chapter 1 as:

- Exchanging information.
- Influencing.
- Instructing.

There can be little doubt that care and thought in the observation and use of bodily communication can make a valuable and powerful contribution to the communications of the manager. This chapter will briefly examine some of the key issues relating to a number of the ways in which this non-verbal or body-based communication takes place.

GESTURES

Gestures are one of a number of bodily actions which send visual signals to the viewer. Gestures can be deliberate, as when the gesturer waves, incidental, as when the gesturer sneezes, or unconscious, as when an anxious and preoccupied person scratches his or her head. Many of these gestures involve the use of hands, but the head or other parts of the body can also be involved.

Ekman and Friesen[16] identify three main categories of gestures:

- *Emblems*
  These are deliberate gestures which have a direct verbal equivalent. They usually involve the use of hand movements and are often used in situations where verbal communication is difficult or for communications between members of a specific group. These gestures can be used to ensure speed of message transmission or privacy or visibility over a distance. They are also used when high noise levels limit the use of audible signals or when there is a need for impact. Morris[17] writes about and illustrates technical emblem gestures. These are said to be used by a wide range of occupations, including fire-fighters, crane drivers and TV studio floor managers and to be usually common to a particular activity or occupation. Argyle[10] writes that emblem gestures can be very widespread in their use, crossing cultural and language boundaries.
- *Illustrators*
  Illustrators are generally also deliberate gestures which are directly linked to speech and are intended to illustrate, repeat, complement or underline the verbal content of the message. Examples include pointing to objects or people, drawing a shape in space and beating a rhythm. Illustrators can be of several types:

  — *Baton* signs, which Morris[17] describes as *'beating time to the rhythm of the spoken thought'* and as such provide emphasis to the words spoken.
  — *Guide* signs, which indicate direction and include pointing and beckoning.
  — *Spatial* signs, which are about movements such as 'up' or 'around'.
  — *Form or shape* signs, which describe a shape in space.
  — *Concept or idea* signs about patterns of thought.
  — *Bodily action* signs, which mimic or replicate body actions.

- *Regulators*
  These are described as maintaining and regulating an interaction. They include waving, nodding and some eyebrow movements and can be often deliberate in their use.

Unconscious or leakage gestures are bodily movements which display our inner or 'true' feelings and thoughts. They occur despite our conscious efforts and the pressure to conform to social norms and control our gestures. They can involve us in touching our own bodies in ways which provide comfort, for example, at times of stress. These unconscious actions replicate or mimic the actions of others touching us. An example is the action of stroking the face or hair. Morris[17] reports that the most frequent of these unconscious gestures include those involving support of the jaw, chin, cheek or temple, together with touching the hair or mouth. Other unconscious self-comforting gestures involve self-hugging with arms, leg hugging and thigh clasping, leg crossing and hand interlocking or clasping gestures. Other gestures of this type take place when we experience tension, frustration or inner conflict and consist of small and irrelevant movements. Morris describes these as 'displacement activities', which we use, unconsciously, to fill the gap between the often conflicting desires we experience at these times. Airport departure lounges are said to often reveal high levels of these activities. We also use unconscious gestures when we attempt to deceive or mislead others. Hand to face contacts, and particularly the mouth cover gesture, increase at these times. These gestures will often display the conflict that we are experiencing and can indicate to the informed observer that we are trying to deceive them. All of our gestures transmit signals to others. For managers, the use of clear and well-defined gestures and a knowledge and understanding of others' gestures can contribute to the effectiveness of their communications.

FACIAL EXPRESSIONS

The expressions that we exhibit on our faces provide many signals about our thoughts, feelings and intentions. As with gestures, these expressions can be deliberate, as with the polite smile, incidental, as when we screw our eyes up in bright sunlight, or unconscious, as when we are genuinely surprised or shocked.

During social interactions, these facial expressions are often observed closely and can provide considerable information about emotions and attitudes. Some of these expressions, such as the smile, the laugh and the frown, are said by Morris[17] to be capable of being faked 'with ease'. However, others, such as small movements of lip and jaw muscles and the muscles around the eyes, are more difficult to fake and are more likely to provide genuine signals about feelings and response. Facial expression is generally associated with the communication of emotions, and even very young children are able to display expressions of fear, hunger, anger, surprise and happiness. These early facial expressions are later modified and extended by an acquired ability to control the expression of emotions and the influence of social norms. Facial expressions involve facial movements of considerable complexity, with the coordinated movement of muscles in and around the eyes, forehead, eyebrows, brow, cheeks, nose, jaw and lips. The control of these movements result in the ability to express a wide range of emotions, including the basic and easily recognized emotions of anger, fear, surprise, sadness, happiness, disgust and contempt. These can be expressed either separately or together as, for example, with disgust and anger. Considerable research has been undertaken on the structure and classification of these facial expressions. The results have included the identification of over thirty basic elements of facial expression[18] as well as 45 positions for the lower face, 17 for the eye, and eight brow and forehead positions.[19] However, it is possible to recognize emotions from a limited number of facial 'cues', as illustrated in Fig. 10.1.

Our ability to 'decode' or recognize these and other, often asymmetrical, facial expressions can be influenced by the context of their expression, our experience of the expressor or the expression and the number of emotions portrayed. However, it is a very unwise manager who does not read and take note of the messages 'writ bold' on the faces of his or her staff and peers.

GAZE

To gaze involves the act of looking. When gaze takes place in interpersonal interactions, it can involve extended or brief periods of looking, can be done by both persons or one and can be

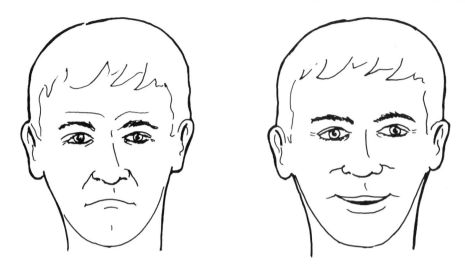

Figure 10.1   Facial expressions.

undertaken while talking or listening. It can also be expressive, direct or indirect and can result in a wide range of responses on the part of the observed person. Animals gaze a lot, and do so not only to collect visual data but also to signal to other animals. For example, monkeys use gaze either to threaten, as in 'staring someone down', or to signal alliance and affiliation. Human children use gaze to recognize and communicate with their mothers, and adults in intimate love relationships will often gaze into 'each other's eyes' for extended periods of time. People will also use gaze to express status, with gaze in groups being directed at the highest status person. Dominance and aggression are both indicated by extended direct gaze and the need to influence another will also result in increased levels of gazing. The act of being gazed at can influence behaviour. Knapp[13] reports that high-gaze speakers are seen to be more persuasive and credible by their listeners. However, in many other circumstances extended gaze will induce negative reactions in the observed.

Research indicates that gazing is usually a discontinuous process involving glances of limited duration and one which is influenced by context and activity. For example, a manager and a subordinate will look at each other less while examining together an engineering drawing or document and more when engaged in discussing, in the abstract, how to solve a production line problem. Gaze can be used to signal the desire or willingness to communicate or start a conversation. It can also be used to indicate the desire to finish that communication. We look at those we wish to communicate with and generally do so before we start to speak. Speakers will glance at listeners to confirm their attention and to underline or accent what is being said. The end of a conversation is generally signalled by shorter glances between speaker and listener and increased gazing at other people or objects.

However, Morris[17] writes that, in social interactions, most gaze behaviour is 'mild and muted', and damped or even hidden due to social norms about polite or acceptable behaviour. Nevertheless, even small changes in direct gazing do signal, albeit in general terms, an intent on the gazer's part. These changes must, however, be interpreted in association with the other non-verbal behaviour evident at the same time. Gazing is a pattern of behaviour that is common and well used despite the fact that the 'rules' of gaze are complex. As such, the manager can use the medium of gaze to add to the communications pattern of the workplace.

TOUCH

Body contact is a way of communicating which we first experience as small children, when much of the warmth and affection we receive from our parents is signalled by strokes, caresses, pats, hugs, kisses and embraces. As we grow older this level of contact declines and changes. As adults, our body contact with our parents becomes limited to kisses, embraces and handshakes and most of our close and extensive body contact with others takes place with our sexual partners. However, body contact does take place, albeit to a lesser extent, with other people who are not part of our families or sexual partners. These body contacts can consist of either non-social or social touching. Non-social touch occurs in our contacts with people whose functional roles require them to touch us, e.g. doctors, hairdressers, dentists, etc. This type of touch can involve body zones in which we would normally only allow touch under conditions of trust and intimacy, e.g. hair, genitals, etc. Social touching takes place with a larger group of people with whom we work, play and socialize. It is generally restricted in both its nature and body location. This section will briefly examine the role of social touch in the workplace and the contributions which it can make to the communication process.

Social touching is usually undertaken or intended as an expression of either warmth or dominance. However, it can also be concerned with attracting attention, guiding others and adding emphasis to the spoken word. In the workplace the extent of social touching is usually limited, but can include:

- Greeting and parting by shaking hands.
- Influencing by touching, while speaking, the other's arm, hand or shoulder.
- Gaining attention by a brief touch to the arm or shoulder.
- Directing or guiding movement by a light clasp on the arm or a slight touch to the back.

But even these limited touches can have variants which reflect the nature and intimacy of the relationship, at least on the toucher's part. Handshake variants are illustrated by Morris[17] as including the handshake with hand clasping, the handshake with arm clasping, the handshake with shoulder clasping and finally, at the highest level of warmth and intimacy, the handshake with shoulder embrace. An example of signal duality in touching is contained within the apparently warm and welcoming guiding arm or back touch which can also be intended to indicate the guider's dominance. There are, of course, some occasions even in the workplace when emotion causes the conventions of limited touch to be broken. These can involve people in hugging and embracing when, for example, a large contract, which involved a lot of teamwork and effort, has been won. A more familiar example is often seen when a soccer team scores a goal. The expression of dominance by touch is common in hierarchical organizations, with high status individuals generally initiating touch with lower status personnel. For example, many managers will put an apparently friendly hand on the shoulder of their secretary, but would react badly to a reciprocal touch. This use of touch to express dominance is also exhibited in behaviour which is often associated with sexual harassment. Nevertheless, we do, as a species, communicate with each other through the process of touch. However, the level of and type of touch are said to vary considerably between different cultures and even subcultures. Argyle[10] reports that these can be classified as contact or non-contact cultures. Arab, South American and Southern European countries are identified as contact cultures, with Japan, Britain and United States showing low levels of touch.

For the average manager, touch in the workplace can be a sensitive issue and one that must be treated with care. To be effective, the use of touch, as with all methods of communication, must take into account the needs, capabilities and attitudes of the receiver.

POSTURE

The postures that we adopt will often reveal our attitudes towards others. For example, a stiff and rigid posture can indicate tension, dislike of another or unease, while a relaxed posture may indicate high status relative to another or liking of another. We adopt postures when we sit, stand and lie, and do so by the way we lean, place or cross our arms and legs, and raise, lower or tilt our heads. Argyle[10] reports some 100 recorded postures, though the commonality of use of some is culturally dependent. Context as well as culture influences the postures that we adopt. For example, sitting on the floor is not a common posture in many European or North American organizations, though it is common for many European and North American parents when playing with their young children. These influences mean that there are postures which are seen as 'appropriate' to many of the social situations that we find ourselves in. These social norms for posture influence the ways that we and others expect people to sit or stand when negotiating, presenting, listening, working and being interviewed. Those who fail to adopt these 'appropriate' postures, without good and evident reason, can be perceived as displaying a range of less desirable characteristics which might include being tense, withdrawn, uninterested, bored, shy or even violent. However, as with other aspects of non-verbal behaviour discussed in this chapter, posture on its own will rarely provide all the information that we need, and other simultaneous signals, such as facial expression and gesture, will also contribute and can be just as significant. The way that we perceive another's posture can lead us to draw conclusions about his or her attitude, degree of tension or relaxation, level of like or dislike and even their personality. Posture is also used differently by men and women. Argyle[10] reports work by several observers that indicate that men generally sit with knees and ankles apart while women sit with knees and ankles together or slightly apart. Posture can be used to express or reflect the nature of our relationships. Morris[17] describes the process of 'postural echoing' by which close friends will unconsciously adopt similar body postures and the 'superior signal' of the tilted back head combined with half-closed eyes which gives rise to the expression 'looking down one's nose'. These and other bodily positions are part of the rich postural vocabulary that we all use both in and outside the workplace.

SPACE

The ways in which we communicate with each other include the ways in which we use the space around us. We all have an internal and individual definition of what is called 'personal space' which reflects:

- Our psychological and physical needs.
- Our preferences about the distances between ourselves and others.

Argyle[10] reports that this personal space approximates to a circular shape, but with the individual displaced from the centre, i.e. more frontal than rear space. The size or area of this circle appears to be influenced by personality, age, gender, status, like or dislike of the other and the nature of interaction. As noted in Chapter 7, Hall[20] writes about our use of territory and notes the existence of four main zones of physical proximity:

- *Intimate*   From contact to 18″ and in which contact takes place by the ways in which we touch, whisper to, smell and feel body heat from others. Use of this zone is usually limited to contact with those with whom we have an intimate relationship. Seeing each other in this zone is not easy.
- *Personal*   Extending from 18″ to 4′, this zone enables people to see and touch but not to feel body heat or (usually) smell each other. This zone is used for most of our two or three person conversations.
- *Social*   This zone, from 4′–12′, involves the use of higher levels of gaze and speech volume. It is in this zone that the majority of business interactions take place, with examples including meetings, interviews and presentations.
- *Public*   Extending from 12′–25′, this zone is used by high status individuals or in situations where large groups of people need to be addressed. Emphasized vocal cues, posture and gestures are needed to replace eye contact and facial expression.

Hall also notes that we will often defend what we perceive and need as our 'territory' against the intrusions of others. An example of these defensive measures is the location of a manager's office desk so that visitors sit with the desk between the manager and them, thus defending the manager's territory. Goldhaber[21] identifies a number of 'rules' associated with status and the use of personal space in organizations. These rules indicate that:

- Higher status → more and better space.
- Higher status → more and better protection of territory.
- Higher status → easier 'invasion' of the territory of lower status individuals.

While discussing interviews in Chapter 4, it was noted that Sommer[22] identified that positioning or spatial orientation was a significant factor in conversational spontaneity. People sit or stand closer to those that they like, are similar to and need approval from and further away from those that they dislike or perceive as different. The nature and characteristics of the space itself, such as style, arrangement and colour, also contribute to the communication patterns which take place. Space and associated factors, such as territoriality, are often key issues in the workplace and as such can facilitate or hinder the flow of communication.

APPEARANCE

We can change, manipulate or adjust many of the aspects of our appearance and in so doing influence how others perceive us. For example, we can change the colour and style of the clothes that we wear or the style of our hair and its colour. Badges, jewellery and other accessories can also be worn and we can change our smell with scent or aftershave or tint our skin with make-up. All of these things are done, often consciously, in order to influence the impressions or perceptions that others have of us.

These changes or adjustments may be intended to make sure that we display what we perceive to be the 'best' points of our appearance or to display our acquisition and knowledge of the latest fashion in clothing or hairstyle. They may also be intended as a statement about our self-image or our membership of a group or subculture. We may also need to dress in certain ways in order to meet the norms for a situation or a role. Examples of these are the uniforms worn by police or traffic wardens, the traditional three-piece suit of the banker and the torn jeans and ear or nose jewellery of the punk subculture. Uniforms are also often worn when we play cricket, tennis or golf.

Those who see us will use the clues that are provided by our appearance to draw conclusions about us, and will adjust their behaviour towards us in accordance with those conclusions. Status and social class are both examples of factors that are attributed to us because of the way we appear to others, and can be transmitted by elements of appearance such as the style and apparent cost of clothes and the condition of hair, skin and hands. However, appearance can also be used to tell others something about our attitudes towards them. Clothes can, for example, indicate sexual availability or unwillingess to conform to the norms and expectations of a dominant subculture. Male hair length can also be seen to be indicative of attitude, with the extremes of long hair and shaven heads having associations with non-conformity and even rebellion. Argyle[10] writes that people change aspects of their appearance in all cultures, and Morris[17] reports that in some societies or cultures these changes may be permanent, taking the form of tattoos or scars. The nature of some of the temporary changes may be subject to cycles of popularity, as with wigs, skirt lengths or the wearing of head coverings, e.g. hats or caps. Jewellery is worn in many cultures to indicate wealth and status. The nature and variety of these appearance signals will vary from culture to culture. Argyle[10] reports that, in modern Japan, almost all occupational groups wear special uniforms, whereas in the Sudan, non-Arabs wear few clothes while Arabs remain well covered. The way we dress and decorate ourselves are but two of a wide range of aspects of our appearance which send social signals to those around us. As such, the manager should be aware of these signals in the communications patterns which take place in the workplace.

PARALINGUISTICS

The study of paralanguage is concerned with the manner in which words are spoken rather than the words themselves. As such, it is concerned with aspects of speech, such as pitch, speed, volume or tone. Those who listen to our voices will draw conclusions about what emotions we are feeling, what attitudes we have and even some aspects of our personalities from the paralinguistic features of our speech.

For example, when we are angry we speak louder and faster and with clipped enunciation and a harsher but high-pitched voice quality. Those who listen to us need not understand what we are saying to know that we are angry. High levels of speech rate, duration and pitch are common with extrovert personalities while anxiety can cause and be seen to be present from speech that is stumbling and contains errors. Social class and regional accents can cause the listener to act towards the speaker in terms of the stereotype engendered by that accent, rather than the reality of the speaker's behaviour and attitudes. The pitch of our voice can, when raised, indicate to others that we are interested or excited. The manager's ability to deduce the emotional state of the speaker will depend upon a number of factors, which include:

- Ability to listen (see Chapter 3).
- Ability to hear the differences in pitch, tone and pace.
- Prior exposure to or familiarity with the vocal emotional expression involved.

The way we speak is important, not only as a medium for the message, but also as a complement to that verbal message. For example, others' perceptions of us will be influenced by the style and manner of our speech. Those who speak quietly and with frequent pauses and errors are often seen by others to be shy or lacking in confidence, while those who speak at length and loudly are often seen to be dominant and confident. The patterns of word stress in sentences can provide additional clues about attitudes and feelings. In the following simple example, the stressing of the word 'I' has a different implication from the stressing of the word 'that', i.e.:

'I *don't know about that*'   (but others do).

and

'*I don't know about* that'   (but I do know about other things)

The understanding and use of the paralingual aspects of communication can provide managers with many valuable clues about the attitudes and emotions of those with whom they work.

CONCLUSION

Managers and their staff will communicate in other ways than by the use of the written or spoken word. The use of gesture, movement, touch, dress, ornament, space and posture represent some of the elements of this extensive repertoire of non-linguistic ways of communicating. Many of these are associated with terms 'body language' or 'bodily communication', but are usually used in association with or as a complement to speech. Nevertheless, the power and capability of these other ways of communicating is considerable, and they are often credited with contributing the majority of the meaning in any interaction. The term 'bodily communication' is generally used to include:

- The ways in which we move our bodies and the postures we adopt.
- Our facial expressions and gaze.
- The when, how and why of our touching one another.
- Our use of space and distance.
- The ways in which we adjust our appearance, including our clothes, hair, jewellery, etc.
- The volume, rate, pitch, stress and duration of our speech.

Many of these involve innate behaviours, but they are, nevertheless, behaviours over which we can exercise controlled choice. They are also often used together, as when we smile, look at and touch one another. The social and physical context of these behaviours is also important and can, if ignored, lead to an incomplete or incorrect understanding of the message transmitted. The ability of managers both to understand and to use bodily communication can make a considerable difference to the effectiveness of their communications in the workplace.

EXERCISES

1. With the sound turned off, watch a film, video or TV broadcast of a speech, and see how many emblem gestures you can identify.
2. Repeat Exercise 1, but with the sound up, and see how many baton or other illustrator gestures you can identify.
3. Repeat Exercise 1, but this time for a play or drama, and see if you can correctly identify the facial expressions used.
4. In a public place observe the types of touch used and see what they tell you about the relationships between the person who touches and the touched.
5. When is touch appropriate in a mixed gender workplace?

REFERENCES

1. Lewis, P. V., *Organizational Communications: The Essence of Effective Management*, Grid, Columbus OH, 1975.
2. Mehrabian, A., *Silent Messages*, Wadsworth, Belmont CA, 1971.
3. Porter, G. W., Non-verbal communication, *Training and Development Journal*, **23**, 1969, pp. 3–8.
4. Sacks, O., *Seeing Voices*, Pan, London, 1991.
5. Stokoe, W. C., *Sign Language Structure*, Linstok Press, Silver Spring, 1960.
6. Brien, D., *Dictionary of British Sign Language/English*, Faber & Faber, London, 1992.
7. Parker, M. and MacMillan, K., Benesh: the notation of dance, in Barlow, H., Blakemore, C. and Weston-Smith, M. (eds.), *Images and Understanding*, Cambridge University Press, Cambridge, 1990.
8. Margerison, C. J., Conversational control, *Management Decision*, **27**(3), 1989.
9. Leakey, R. and Lewin, R., *The People of the Lake; Man: His Origins, Nature and Future*, Penguin, London, 1978.
10. Argyle, M., *Bodily Communication*, Routledge, London, 1988.
11. Kingman, S., How a family learnt the language of touch, *Independent on Sunday*, 12 April 1992.
12. Darwin, C., *The Expression of Emotion in Man and Animals*, John Murray, London, 1872.
13. Knapp, M. L., *Nonverbal Communication in Human Interaction*, Holt, Rinehart & Winston, New York, 1978.
14. Patterson, M. L., *Nonverbal Behaviour: A Functional Perspective*, Springer, New York, 1983.
15. Rozelle, R. M., Druckman, D. and Baxter, J. C., Nonverbal communication, in Hargie, O., (ed.), *A Handbook of Communication Skills*, Routledge, London, 1986.
16. Ekman, P. and Friesen, W. V., The repertoire of non-verbal behaviour: categories, origins, using and coding, *Semiotica*, **1**, 1969, pp. 49–67.
17. Morris, D., *Manwatching: A Field Guide to Human Behaviour*, Grafton, London, 1978.
18. Birdwhistell, R. L., *Kinesics and Context*, University of Philadelphia Press, Philadelphia, PA, 1970.
19. Ekman, P., Friesen, W. V. and Tomkins, S. S., Facial affect scoring technique: first validity study, *Semiotica*, **3**, 1971, pp. 37–58.
20. Hall, E. T., *The Hidden Dimension*, Doubleday, New York, 1966.
21. Goldhaber, G. M., *Organizational Communication*, Brown, Dubuque IA, 1974.
22. Sommer, R., Studies in personal space, *Sociometry*, **22**, 1959, pp. 247–60.

ELEVEN
STYLE AND OTHER ISSUES

'Style is the hallmark of a temperament stamped upon the material at hand.'
Andre Maurois

*'If the Great Spirit had desired me to be a white man he would have made me so in the first place.
He put in your heart certain wishes and plans, and in my heart he put other different desires.
Each man is good in His sight. It is not necessary for eagles to be crows.'*
Sitting Bull

INTRODUCTION

Style is one of the ways in which we express our individuality. As such it can exert a considerable influence upon the quality and effectiveness of our communications with others. For example, managers with a personal style which is abrupt and sceptical will do little to encourage their staff to share their difficulties or successes with them. It will also be evident that managers whose style involves a very high level of concern for their staff and their well-being will be perceived by those staff as 'good' managers. However, if that level of concern overwhelms those managers' ability to carry out those tasks which the organization requires of them, then they will not be viewed, by the organization, as effective managers. In its broadest sense, style influences what we say, how we say it and how we look when we say it. It also influences the perceptions that others have of those behaviours and actions. For example, the same sentence can be spoken in different styles. These might include the supercilious, amused, excited, sarcastic or angry styles. Each of these styles, which will include a way of speaking and a way of appearing to others, will produce a different response from the listener.

Other views of style are concerned with concepts such as fashion, manners, or elegance, but Dickson[1] identifies style, more broadly, as being 'how what is done is done'. Alternatively, Norton[2] suggests that style consists of 'an accumulation of micro behaviours' which represent a relatively stable and long-lasting pattern of individual behaviour. The typical dictionary definition also identifies style as being the 'general characteristics and manner of an individual'.

Style is a significant factor in the leadership aspects of the manager's job, and the research work on this issue is comprehensive and well documented. While the full range of this work is beyond the scope of this chapter, it and the other theories on leadership will merit examination by most managers. Handy[3] summarizes some of the major views in this area under the broad classifications of 'Authoritarian' or 'Structuring' and 'Democratic' or 'Supportive'. The Supportive style is described as being associated with higher levels of productivity. We also demonstrate our personal style by the way in which we take decisions. Kagan *et al.*,[4] when working with children, identified the Reflective–Impulsive continuum of individual decision-taking styles. The Reflective style is described as involving delays during which the relative validity of the alternative responses is considered. This style is also said to be characterized by fewer errors and persistence in undertaking difficult tasks. The Impulsive style is described as being less concerned with errors or mistakes and is faster in its decision-taking.

Entwistle[5] proposes two groupings of the above and other cognitive styles, which encompass:

- *Style A*   Impulsive: does not assume single solution to problem (Divergent), broad, multi-faceted approach (Holist).
- *Style B*   Reflective: assumes single best answer to problem (Convergent), systematic step-by-step approach (Serialist).

Other aspects of style reflect the ways in which we view the world around us. Morgan[6] describes Jung's views on how people relate to and hence express their versions of reality. Jung is said to have identified the behavioural dimensions of Reality Perception with the opposing extremes of Intuition and Sensation, and Reality Judgement with the opposing extremes of Thinking and Feeling. These dimensions can be used to identify different basic personality types and to provide some indication of the consequent styles or ways in which that personality is expressed. These basic types are as follows:

- *ST* individuals, who combine sensation and thought and can be described as logical, arriving at conclusions and judgements on the basis of what they perceive as 'hard' facts.
- *IT* individuals, who combine thought and intuition and can be described as shaping their conclusions on ideas and insight rather than facts and as being concerned with the possibilities represented by a situation.
- *IF* individuals, whose patterns of behaviour reflect a view of the world which is influenced by intuition and feeling and can be described as being more concerned with values than facts.
- *SF* individuals, who combine sensing and feeling and are primarily concerned with the evidence of their senses. They arrive at conclusions on the basis of 'gut' feelings.

Each of these different ways of viewing and making judgements about the world will also be expressed in behaviour which represents a different style or a different way of being. Kakabadse *et al.*[7] describe an application of these basic Jungian personality types in the Myers Briggs personality test.

Style is also expressed or shown in the ways that individual managers undertake their managerial tasks. Stamp,[8] after examining a number of studies of management style, uses the dimensions of Analytical–Holistic and Simple–Complex to identify four distinct management styles, which are described as follows:

- *Divergent*   A flexible, intuitive style which involves the ability to view situations from different perspectives.
- *Integrative*   A style which identifies patterns from diverse data sources and generates new concepts from ambiguity and uncertainty.
- *Convergent*   A logical, rational problem-solving style that works well within defined limits.
- *Pragmatic*   A style that adapts well to short-term situations and generates good decisions from minimal data.

Blake and Mouton developed the Blake Grid[9] as a way of describing managerial styles. The grid identifies five basic managerial styles using the dimensions of the concern for task achievement or production, and the concern for people or relationships. These basic styles are:

- *Task management style*
  A manager with this style manages in such a way as to keep human variables to a minimum. This is done by intensively planning, scheduling and organizing the work in order to achieve high levels of productivity.

- *Team management style*
  This style of management attempts to balance the human and task needs and, in so doing, to gain commitment from the team and support from the organization, together with high productivity levels.
- *Country club management style*
  Managers with this style are primarily concerned with satisfying their staff's social and relationship needs and ensuring that the workplace is always comfortable.
- *Impoverished management style*
  Distant relationships and minimum exertion of effort to achieve targets are said to describe this style.
- *Middle of the road management style*
  An adequate level of performance is achieved by trading off staff morale and needs against output.

Trist[10] describes the use of the Blake Grid as a framework for organizational change. This change is generally towards the 'optimum' position of the team management style, and is said to involve a six-phase programme taking a minimum of four years.

Different management styles can also be described in terms of personal qualities, such as age, experience or education, or traits, such as extroversion or introversion. Adcock[11] lists traits as including sociability, dominance, introversion, anxiety, nervous tension and suspiciousness, and Argyle[12] discusses the warm and friendly or affiliative style and the use of domination. Norton[2] describes how these traits can be used to generate a range of continua or spectra of communication style, and these are illustrated in Table 11.1.

It will, from these and previous descriptions, be evident that style has considerable potential for influence upon the communication process. This chapter will examine a number of views about style and its effects upon all interactions. The views examined will include:

- Transactional analysis.
- Role theory.
- Assertion.

Table 11.1   Continua of style

1. Dominant	←→	Submissive
2. Dramatic	←→	Reserved
3. Contentious	←→	Affiliative
4. Animated	←→	Inexpressive
5. Relaxed	←→	Frenetic
6. Attentive	←→	Inattentive
7. Impressive	←→	Insignificant
8. Open	←→	Closed
9. Friendly	←→	Hostile

TRANSACTIONAL ANALYSIS

Transactional analysis was pioneered and developed by Berne, who has written extensively describing its development,[13] application to group dynamics[14] and its use in analysing the social 'games' that people play.[15] It is based upon a theory about the structure of personality and the social actions by which personality expresses itself.

Transactional analysis aims to:

- Enable people to clearly describe their own and other's interactions.
- Enable people to understand these interactions and hence have more control over them.

Transactional analysis uses a number of concepts to apply its theory to the social interactions that we all experience at work and at play. Two of the key concepts are those of the transaction and the ego state, and these will now be examined.

The transaction

This term is used to describe the social interactions that occur when two or more people meet. It is described as a unit of 'social intercourse'. When one person speaks or acknowledges the presence of the other, this interaction is termed a '*transactional stimulus*'. The response, from the other person, is termed a '*transactional response*'. These transactional stimuli and responses may be as simple as exchanging 'Good morning' or, as we shall begin to see later in this chapter, as complex and as multi-levelled as the majority of our interactions.

The ego states

Transactional analysis states that each human being possesses and uses three different types of ego state. These are not acted roles or artificial constructs but 'coherent systems of thought and feeling manifested by responding patterns of behaviour'.[16] Harris[17] also describes these ego states as being produced by the 'playback of recorded events in the past involving real people, real times, real places, real decisions and real feelings'. This means that these ego states are not generalized states, but are specific to each individual and as such reflect that individual's memories or recordings of events that they experienced.

These ego states are given the names of Parent, Adult and Child and their simplified descriptions are as follows:

- *Parent*
  This ego state is derived from the person's memories of the ways in which the individual's parents or parent figures behaved during the first five or so years of his or her life. It is that part of the personality which is concerned with caring for or controlling and leading others and identifying rules and procedures. In carrying out these actions it uses the rules, admonitions or 'how to' data which were acquired from these early parental influences. This ego state may function as a powerful directing influence or as actual parental behaviour. It is not surprising to find that the parent ego state can be either nurturing or controlling.
- *Child*
  While the parent ego state is about the memories of external events, the child ego state is about the memories of internal events, i.e. emotions, feelings and responses. This ego state is childlike rather than immature or childish. It is described by Berne[16] as being either 'adapted',

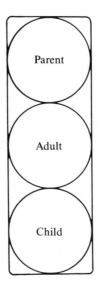

Figure 11.1   Ego state structure.
Source: Thomas A. Harris, *I'm O.K. – You're O.K.* Reproduced by permission of HarperCollins Inc.

i.e. following parental directives, or 'natural', i.e. autonomous. It is also the source of all our pleasure, excitement, curiosity, fun and sadness, and is described as being the powerhouse or core of all our personalities.

Unlike the physical state of childhood the child ego state is not grown out of but remains with us for all our lives. It is the only ego state that we are born with and is modified in the period from birth to five or so years of age.

● *Adult*
In this ego state, which is said to begin development at as early as ten months of age, the person will behave autonomously and objectively, using past experience to calculate probabilities and possibilities. The adult ego state is said to function like a computer and to draw its data from three sources:
— Parent ego state.
— Child ego state.
— Data it has acquired itself.

The role of the adult ego state is that of solving problems, making estimates, generating strategies and logically evaluating the outside world. It does this at a conscious and unconscious level by being both logical and intuitive and continually checking, validating, revalidating, filing and refiling old and new data.

These ego states are described as being integrated within the personality and are usually illustrated as shown in Fig. 11.1. Each of these ego states expresses itself in a different manner using words and gestures in different ways. Some of these are illustrated in Table 11.2.

While we all have these three structural elements of parent, adult and child, what is different and unique to each of us is:

● The experiences recorded by each of those ego states
● The working arrangement or relationship between our unique parent, adult and child.

Table 11.2 Ego state characteristics

Ego state	Words used	Gestures used
Parent	Always, never, should, ought, don't, right, wrong, insist.	Pointing finger, arms folded across chest, sighing, tongue clicking, patting another on head.
Adult	Could, possible, true, probable check, test, I think.	Listening, continual movement of face, eyes and body, eye blink every three or five seconds.
Child	Want, let's, wish, why, guess, dream, funny, magic, great, super.	Whining voice, shrugging shoulders, downcast eyes, teasing laughter, asking for permission to speak.

It is the relationship between and nature of these unique and individual ego states that influences the ways in which we interact with each other, Transactional analysis views these interactions as 'transactions' or 'units of social discourse'.[18]

TRANSACTIONS AND INTERACTIONS

Transactional analysis states that when two people encounter each other, the resultant interaction will involve all of the six ego states which these two people possess and use. One aspect or 'snapshot' of this interaction is illustrated in Fig. 11.2, which shows a typical *complementary* transaction, in this case between the parent ego state of one individual and the child ego state of another. Harris[17] defines a complementary transaction as being one in which the stimulus and response make parallel lines and states that this type of interaction 'can go on indefinitely'. Nine possible complementary transactions can occur between two individuals, and these are shown below in Table 11.3.

Table 11.3

Individual A		Individual B
P	⇄	C
P	⇄	A
P	⇄	P
A	⇄	P
A	⇄	A
A	⇄	C
C	⇄	C
C	⇄	A
C	⇄	P

A simple example of a complementary parent–child transaction might involve the following dialogue:

A (Child ego state): '*I can't cope with all these letters today.*'
B (Parent ego state): '*Oh dear – let's see if I can help.*'

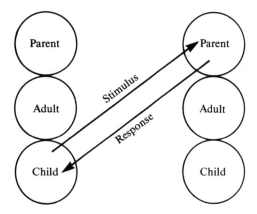

Figure 11.2 A complementary transaction.
Source: Thomas A. Harris, *I'm O.K. – You're O.K.* Reproduced by permission of HarperCollins Inc.

This transaction will continue until A decides to move out of the child ego state being used and moves into the adult ego state. In this ego state, A would wish to connect to B's adult – but B has remained in the parent ego state. The subsequent dialogue might be:

A (Adult ego state): '*Thanks for your help – I think I can manage now*'
B (Parent ego state): '*Are you sure? You've such a lot left to do.*'

What has happened is that the transaction has become *uncomplementary* or *crossed* as the stimulus and response are crossed (Fig. 11.3) and, as a result, communication stops.

Another example of a crossed transaction is:

A (Adult ego state): '*I have to finish this report today because it's needed for tomorrow's board meeting.*'
B (*Parent ego state*): '*Why do you always leave these reports so late?*'

Crossed transactions can be very common occurrences, and Berne[16] identifies that out of a total of 81 possible transactions there are 72 possible types of crossed transaction.

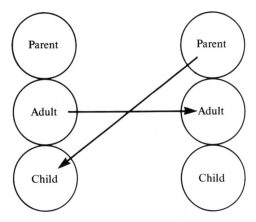

Figure 11.3 A crossed transaction.
Source: Thomas A. Harris, *I'm O.K. – You're O.K.* Reproduced by permission of HarperCollins Inc.

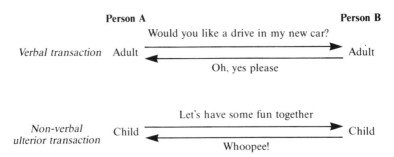

Figure 11.4   Two-level transaction.

These transactions can also take place at more than one level. The first level will consist of the spoken message and will take place at the social level. The second and unspoken transaction takes place at a psychological level and is often communicated by non-verbal means. This second message is called the *ulterior* transaction and can take place at a conscious or unconscious level. An example of these different levels of transaction is shown in Fig. 11.4.

Transactional analysis also takes the view, based on research in other fields, that we all need stimulation and recognition from our social interactions. This view is expressed by the concept of 'stroking'.

STROKING

At its most basic level, stroking is what a mother does to her child. It is that process of physical contact which gives the child the sense of being cared for. This physical process occurs less as the child grows and by the time physical adulthood is reached the adult will often limit its physical stroking to sexual partners or its own children. Transactional analysis suggests that the physical strokes of our childhood are converted into or substituted by the social strokes or recognition of adult interchanges. Stewart and Joines[18] classify these strokes as being:

● Based on use of language or bodily communication.
● Positive or negative.
● Conditional or unconditional.

As we move along the road from childhood to adulthood the range and versatility of these strokes increases. Verbal strokes, for example, might consist of any verbal interchange, from a 'Good morning' or 'Hello' greeting through to a full-blown extended conversation. These can, of course, be negative or positive, i.e. be experienced as being unpleasant and painful or as being agreeable and pleasant. Non-verbal strokes, which can also be positive or negative, consist of many of the aspects of bodily communication which were discussed in Chapter 10, and include touch, gesture, gaze, physical proximity, etc. Stewart and Joines[18] describe conditional strokes as being about 'what you do' and unconditional strokes as being about 'what you are'.

For example, a conditional positive stroke might be:

'That's a nice suit you've got on today.'

whereas an unconditional negative stroke might be:

'I don't like you.'

Another aspect of the view taken of our social interactions by transactional analysis is reflected in its view that we all have a set of basic beliefs about ourselves and others. This set of beliefs is called a life position.

LIFE POSITIONS

Transactional analysis states that each individual has a central emotional position which is established in early life and to which they return automatically during the rest of their lives.

There are said to be four of these positions, which are described by Harris[17] as being:

1. I'm not OK – you're OK.
2. I'm not OK – you're not OK.
3. I'm OK – you're not OK.
4. I'm OK – you're OK.

These basic beliefs about self and others are used to account for or interpret the ways in which we behave and the decisions that we take. The first three of these positions are arrived at or chosen as a result of what Harris[17] describes as non-verbal decisions and are said to be conclusions rather than explanations. Harris also states that for most people the 'I'm not OK – you're OK' position persists throughout life. The commonality of this position is perhaps explained by the fact that in childhood the 'I'm not OK – you're OK' position is a universal experience. This results from the physical and emotional dependence upon their parents which all children experience. These parents, and indeed all adult figures, are seen, by the child, as being superior, and the child is said to feel 'at the mercy of others'. Just as the child needs physical strokes to provide reassurance and support, an adult in this life position needs and will seek others who are seen as being OK and can provide the strokes needed. These stroke givers will typically have a strong parent ego state and the strokes are earned from them by behaviour which displays eagerness, willingness and compliance. This position is coped or dealt with by playing what are termed 'games'. Berne[15] describes these as having a 'predictable, well-defined outcome' and as being a 'series of moves' with a 'concealed motivation' and provides a detailed description of many of them. Unlike the first three positions, the fourth position of 'I'm OK – you're OK' originates from a conscious decision and is said to be based on 'why not?' whereas the first three are based on 'why?' However, the conscious choice of this position does not eliminate the old 'not OK' feelings. But it is said to enable the demands and pressures arising from the old 'not OK' position to be recognized and, if the need is strong enough, for the chain of cause and effect to be broken. It is in this ability to act to change the influence of past experiences that the value and power of transactional analysis lies. It provides a language with which a transaction can be analysed and alternatives evaluated and chosen. Berne,[14] James[19] and Jongeward[20] write about the application of the concepts of transactional analysis to the manager's role and to organizations. Transactional analysis provides an analytical framework from which managers can view and review their social interactions and the communications within them. As such, it can provide managers with a way of enhancing those interactions and communications.

ROLE THEORY

Role theory is concerned with how individuals behave in carrying out their roles and how they and others perceive they ought to behave in those roles. The role can be defined as a pattern of being or behaving which is perceived to typify a person in a certain social position. Any

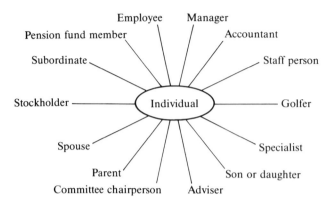

Figure 11.5   A spectrum of roles.

individual occupies a number of roles and does so in relation to a wide range of people. An example of the spectrum of roles that might be carried by an individual employee of any organization is shown in Fig. 11.5. Each of these roles represents a pattern of behaviours that others expect from any individual who occupies that role in society or in an organization. For each of those roles there can be a large number of expectations about how that role will be carried out. For example, individuals in the role of managers will occupy that role in relation to a wide range of people. These will include the staff which they supervise, their peer group of managers, the managers who supervise them, managers and staff in other departments or sections within the organization, customers, contractors, union officials and others. This group of people is often called a *role set*, and the individual, who in the above example is in the managerial role, is usually called the *focal person*. The role set for the above example is illustrated in Fig. 11.6. All of the people in that role set will have expectations of that managerial role, as

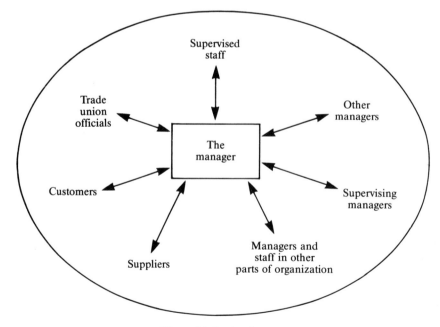

Figure 11.6   A role set.

also will the individual who is in the role. These expectations will be about patterns of behaviour, beliefs and attitudes. These will include how the individual in the role behaves, how he or she relates to others in the organization, what values the individual espouses, how the individual communicates with others and even how he or she dresses. For each role, the combination of these expectations is said to comprise a *role definition*. When a role exists within an organizational environment, for example, an operations manager or a ward sister, it can often be defined in terms of a written job description. However, this description will be generally limited to the duties involved rather than the manner or style in which those duties are carried out. Other roles are often defined in more generalized cultural terms. For example, we all have expectations about the behaviour and appearance of a pop star or a lawyer or an accountant.

One of the ways in which roles are identified is by the use of dress. The use of uniforms with attached insignia, e.g. badges or stripes, will, for example, indicate a particular and precise role definition which will give rise to expectations about behaviour patterns. Obvious examples of this are the police and the armed forces. The *role sign* of dress or, in more general terms, grooming, is used in less obvious but just as effective ways when organizations ask their employees to dress in consistent and coordinated ways in order to ensure recognition and to present a uniform and 'positive' image. Examples of this include the uniforms of airline cabin attendants, the name badges of salespeople and even the absence of beards among male UK banking hall personnel. The presence of a separate and private office with a sign on the door and a secretary to regulate access also constitute a set of role signs which, in organizational terms, provide a number of clear indications as to the occupant's status and role. As indicated in the previous chapter, gesture, gaze and posture are very effective methods of communication, and these are often used to transmit role signs.

When individuals change their role this is often noted or celebrated by rituals or special events. Examples of these include employee induction programmes, bachelor or 'hen' parties, leaving parties, engagement parties, house warming parties and even wedding ceremonies.

As individuals we all have choices about the degree to which we conform to the expectations of others about the roles that we carry out in both our working and social lives. Indeed, it is not difficult to identify from our own experience examples of individuals who chose to behave in ways which differed significantly from the expectations of others. This mismatch in expectations can give rise to difficulties for both the focal person and for the role set. In many organizations the expectations of the role set are significantly influenced by the expectations of the senior management about what the individual ought to be doing and thinking in that role. When there is uncertainty or even contradiction in expectations about the role, this is termed *role ambiguity*. Role ambiguity can lead to stress, insecurity and conflict and is said by Handy[3] to arise from lack of clarity or definition about:

- Evaluation of role output.
- Responsibilities of role.
- Others' expectations of role.

This lack of clarity or definition can arise for both the role set and the focal person. For example, a newly appointed manager might perceive, because of experience in other organizations, that his or her role is responsible for purchasing external services and raw materials. In doing so, the individual will be in conflict with the purchasing manager who had traditionally carried out these duties. Similarly, a manager with a democratic and delegative style of management will be in conflict with the expectations of staff who had become accustomed to the previous role occupant's autocratic style of management. The role of effective communication in resolving these differences and diminishing the level of role ambiguity is both obvious and crucial. It is both unreasonable and ineffective for managers to expect their staff to know and understand what is expected of their roles or how their performance will be measured without those staff having been told – and yet this often occurs.

Even when expectations of others are clear and understood there still can be difficulties. One of these is termed *role conflict*, and occurs when the individual carrying one role experiences conflicting role demands from his or her other roles. Examples of this include the manager who is asked to discipline or sack someone with whom they have a close and positive social relationship, or the manager who is asked to undertake tasks or activities which he or she feels are unethical. *Role overload* is another example of a difficulty that can arise. Mintzberg[21] identified some ten separate roles that are subsumed within the overall role of manager. It is not surprising, therefore, to find that there are occasions when individual managers find that either the workload involved is too high or the roles involved are beyond their experience or capacity. *Role underload*, however, occurs when the demands of a role are less than those which the individual perceives that he or she is capable of handling. Handy[3] states that whether this assessment is valid or not is irrelevant – the underload occurs and does so as a result of the individual's own assessment of his or her capabilities.

Many of the above difficulties lead to *role stress*. The causes, effects and costs of stress within the working environment are well documented elsewhere[22,23] and this text will limit its content to some of the comments made about role stress. Handy[3] differentiates between *role pressure*, which he states is beneficial, and *role strain*, which is described as causing harmful stress. French and Caplan[24] differentiate between quantitative role overload (= 'too much to do') and qualitative role overload (= 'too difficult to do'). The presence of stress in the workplace will give rise to reactions from managers which reflect their different and individual capabilities and psychological patterns. Some will be able to adapt and cope while others will be less able to do so.

The role of communication in reducing the stress levels generated by these difficulties is significant. Cooper and Davidson,[25] in examining the changes which can reduce stress in the workplace, cite the need to create an organizational climate in which openness, trust and communication are encouraged. The skills and abilities which will enable the manager to contribute to the creation of that climate include the choice and use of a relevant style and the use of the skills of listening (Chapter 3) and counselling (Chapter 4).

ASSERTION

The typical dictionary defines the meaning of the verb to assert as 'to declare to be true' and defines the act of asserting oneself as that of 'insisting upon one's claims' or 'pushing oneself forward aggressively'. This definition displays the common confusion which exists between aggression and the form of behaviour which is now known as assertion. The behaviour that we now call assertion is not new, and has been the subject of considerable interest and research over the last twenty years. One of the common strands throughout that work has been the view that assertion lies within a spectrum of behaviours whose extremes are represented by aggressive behaviour and passive (or submissive) behaviour. This spectrum, which displays some similarity with the first of Norton's nine continua of style (Table 11.1), locates assertion at its mid-point and is illustrated in Fig. 11.7.

Nevertheless, assertion is often associated with conflictual or contentious behaviour and even with aggressive behaviour or aggression. This association is to some extent supported by the vocabulary used in some of the guides to the use of assertion. For example, a definition given by Back *et al.*[26] identifies assertion as being behaviour which involves 'standing up' for one's own

Figure 11.7 Behaviour spectrum.

rights without 'violating' another's rights. However, Rakos[27] comments, from a broader point of view, that assertion:

- Is a social skill.
- Is situation-specific, i.e. its use depends upon the situation and the interaction involved.
- Involves both verbal and non-verbal communication.
- Is risk-taking in that it may not produce the desired outcome.

The non-conflictual or 'positive' side of assertion is further identified in a literature review by Shroeder *et al.*[28] which identifies seven different classes of assertive response. Four of these involved 'positive' responses and are said to involve compliments, articulating positive feelings, admitting personal limitations and faults and beginning interactions. The three 'negative' assertive responses are said to include communicating opinions which are unpopular or non-conformist, asking people to behave in different ways and refusing or rejecting others requests. However, despite the existence of 'positive' assertion, the majority of popular literature and skill training associated with assertiveness focuses on its use in 'negative' or conflict situations.

The differences between aggression, passive or submissive behaviour and assertion can be outlined as follows:

- *Aggression*
  The popular dictionary definition for aggressive behaviour includes comment on 'unprovoked attacks', 'eagerness to quarrel' and 'threatening'. Kakabadse *et al.*[7] describe aggressive people as wishing to 'overpower' others. Back *et al.*[22] identify aggressive behaviour as that behaviour which assumes that the aggressor's needs, views and rights are paramount and that those of others are insignificant or non-existent. Examples of aggressive responses are shown in Table 11.4.
- *Passive or submissive behaviour*
  This type of behaviour is the antithesis of aggression and assumes that the needs, views and rights of others are paramount and that those of the person are unimportant or insignificant. Kakabadse *et al.*[7] suggest that it can be seen to be 'dishonest' behaviour. It is also said[24] to be designed to 'avoid conflict' and described as 'non-assertive' behaviour. Examples of this behaviour are shown in Table 11.4.
- *Assertion*
  This behavioural style is generally described as lying midway between the extremes of aggression and submission and as such displays contributions from both extremes. For example, assertion involves:
  — Expressing one's needs and wants, but doing so without exerting undue pressure.
  — Being aware of one's own rights, but not diminishing or neglecting another's rights.
  — Expressing oneself in honest and direct ways, but doing so in a manner appropriate to the situation and the listener.

  Back *et al.*[26] state that assertive behaviour has the objective of ensuring that all involved have their needs and wants answered.

Table 11.4 Response choices

Situation	Responses		
	Passive	Assertive	Aggressive
1. Someone lights up a cigarette in a no-smoking section of a train.	Say nothing and do nothing. Suffer in silence.	Point to the no-smoking sign and ask the smoker to stop.	Get angry and threaten to call guard.
2. Your boss asks you to attend an after hours meeting on the evening of your wedding anniversary celebration.	Say that you'll attend but without saying anything about your celebration.	Tell him of your celebration and that normally you'd like to help out – but not tonight.	Respond with anger, saying that he always picks on you and you have had enough.
3. One of your staff is openly and unfairly critical of you in a meeting with an important client.	Say nothing and allow the client to think that the criticism is valid.	Tell the person that you are surprised by the comments and would like to discuss their feelings at a more appropriate time.	Tell the person that they don't know what they are talking about and should shut up.
4. Your secretary has produced an unsatisfactory letter with spelling mistakes and omissions	'I wonder if you could spare the time to change a few things?'	'I'd like you to do this letter again. I have marked the mistakes that you made.'	'Why is it that you can't type a decent letter?'

This spectrum of behaviour and its implied choices for the style of managers' interactions with their staff, bosses, customers and others has a considerable influence upon the quality of managers' communications.

CONCLUSION

The style of a communication can be said to be the way or manner in which that communication is conducted. As such, it can significantly influence the outcome and the effectiveness of that communication. The range of potential individual styles for the communication process is wide, with Norton's nine continua of style representing the most comprehensive description. The variety of styles that can be adopted by the manager in the workplace has attracted considerable attention and have been described by the use of a number of dimensions, which include:

- Analytical – holistic.
- Simple – complex.
- Concern for people.
- Concern for task.

Transactional analysis, role theory and assertion are all views about the style and nature of interactions within the workplace and as such all have a contribution to make to the effectiveness and quality of the manager's communications.

EXERCISES

1. Working in threes, with two talking and one observing, briefly interact using the following complementary transactions:

   (a) Parent–child.
   (b) Child–child.
   (c) Adult–adult.

2. Choose one of the roles that you carry out and write down the members of your role set for that role.
3. Working in twos, with one talking and the other observing, briefly explore in turn, using the styles of passive, aggressive and assertive, the following situations:

   (a) A smoker lights a cigarette in a room which does not contain no-smoking signs – you suffer from asthma.
   (b) Your manager has asked you to (as applicable):

      ● Shave off your recently grown moustache.
      ● Stop wearing long decorative earrings.

4. Examine the value and potential use of transactional analysis in your organization.
5. What sorts of organization would benefit from the provision of assertion training for their staff.

REFERENCES

1. Dickson, D., Reflecting, in Hargie, O. (ed.), *A Handbook of Communication Skills*, Routledge, London, 1986.
2. Norton, R., *Communicator Style: Theory, Application and Measures*, Sage, Beverley Hills, 1983.
3. Handy, C. B., *Understanding Organisations*, Penguin, London, 1985.
4. Kagan, J., Rosman, B. L., Day, D., Albert, J. and Phillips, W., Information processing in the child: significance of analytical and reflective attitudes, *Psychological Monographs*, **78**(1), 1964.
5. Entwistle, N. J., *Styles of Learning and Teaching*, Wiley, Chichester, 1981.
6. Morgan, G., *Images of Organisation*, Sage, London, 1986.
7. Kakabadse, A., Ludlow, R. and Vinnicombe, S., *Working in Organisations*, Penguin, London, 1988.
8. Stamp, G., Management Styles, *Management Decision*, **27**(4), 1989, pp. 23–9.
9. Blake, R. R. and Mouton, J. S., *The Managerial Grid*, Gulf, Houston, 1964.
10. Trist, E., The professional facilitation of planned change in organisations, in Vroom, V. R. and Deci, E. L. (eds.), *Management and Motivation*, Penguin, London, 1968.
11. Adcock, C. J., *Fundamentals of Psychology*, Penguin, London, 1964.
12. Argyle, M., *The Psychology of Interpersonal Behaviour*, Penguin, London, 1967.
13. Berne, E., *Transactional Analysis in Psychotherapy*, Grove Press, New York, 1961.
14. Berne, E., *The Structure and Dynamics of Organisations and Groups*, Grove Press, New York, 1966.
15. Berne, E., *Games People Play*, Grove Press, New York, 1964.
16. Berne, E., *What Do You Say After You Say Hello?*, Corgi, London, 1975.

17. Harris, T. A., *I'm O.K. – You're O.K.*, Pan Books, London, 1973.
18. Stewart, E. and Joines, V., *TA Today: A New Introduction to Transactional Analysis*, Lifespace, Nottingham, 1987.
19. James, M., *The OK boss*, Addison-Wesley, Reading MA, 1976.
20. Jongeward, D., *Everybody Wins: TA Applied to Organisations*, Addison-Wesley, Reading MA, 1973.
21. Mintzberg, H., *The Nature of Managerial Work*, Harper & Row, New York, 1973.
22. Marshal, J. and Cooper, C. L., *Executives Under Pressure*, Macmillan, London, 1979.
23. Cooper, C. L. and Payne, R. L., *Stress at Work*, Wiley, New York, 1978.
24. French, J. R. P. and Caplan, R. D., Psychosocial factors in coronary heart disease, *Industrial Medicine*, **39**, 1970, pp. 383–97.
25. Cooper, C. L. and Davidson, M., *High Pressure: Working Lives of Women Managers*, Fontana, London, 1982.
26. Back, K., Back K. and Bates, T., *Assertiveness at Work*, McGraw-Hill, London, 1991.
27. Rakos, R. F., Asserting and confronting, in Hargie, O. (ed.), *A Handbook of Communication Skills*, Routledge, London, 1986.
28. Schroeder, H. E., Rakos, R. and Moe, J., The social perception of assertive behaviour as a function of response class and gender, *Behaviour Therapy*, **14**, 1983, pp. 534–44.

TWELVE

IMAGES, ICONS AND INFORMATION

'We look and, behold, we see.'
Francis Crick

'In analysing the distinct attributes of images, the brain invents a visual world'
Semir Zeki

INTRODUCTION

The act of seeing is that process by which we perceive the world around us and in so doing receive the majority of the information about that world. We also instruct, direct, persuade, inform and influence others by appealing to and exploiting their ability to see. Others will strive to influence and inform us by transmitting information in visual form as advertisements, letters, reports, gestures, smiles, scowls and frowns. Our children, when very young and before they have acquired a basic understanding of language, are dependent upon what they see and how they interpret those visual messages for their understanding of the world. Those managers with visually impaired staff or personal experience of visual impairment will be aware of how much the ability to see is taken for granted in the ways in which we communicate.

The apparently everyday nature of this process of seeing is deceptive, as it is, in fact, a process of considerable complexity. For example, when we look at objects the information that we receive will very often consist of a flux of constantly changing and complex data. The composition of the light reflected by an object changes as the illumination of that object, or our position relative to it, changes. If the object moves we are able, from what we see and without conscious effort, to reach conclusions about that object's direction and speed. We are also able to recognize shapes and decide, for example, whether the object is a car or a cup. This process of seeing also enables us to make judgements about other attributes, such as how far the object is from us, what colour or how big the object is, and even to arrive at conclusions about the texture or nature of its surface.

The role of the brain in this process is crucial and is described by Zeki[1] as that of extracting the 'constant, invariant features' of the object seen from the 'perpetually changing flood' of information received. However, before we explore that role further it is worthwhile examining, albeit briefly, the nature of the exterior process of seeing.

The nature of the eye and its capability are widely reported in many texts on human biology. These report that the light which the human eye sees is restricted to that between the wavelengths (distance between peaks) of 400 nm and 700 nm (1 nm = 10^{-9} m). The eye can receive light which is emitted by a source, i.e. a lamp bulb, and light which is reflected by ourselves and the objects around us. The eye can also see light of different colours, which comes about because of the colour of the light source or the light absorption characteristics of the object viewed. The eye also has the ability to receive light from a considerable proportion of the environment which surrounds it. It is capable of seeing objects in the far distance and as close as 15 cm and its field of view is said to extend to just over 200° in the horizontal plane and to 120° in the vertical plane.

The quality and level of information contained in the image received by the eye is influenced

Figure 12.1   The blind spot.

by the light level, colour, contrast and shape of the seen object. The eye can see in different levels of light because of specialized cells in its retina. These specialized cells or receptors also display different sensitivities to colours, and as a result blue–green objects appear brighter under low light conditions than in daylight, while green–yellow objects appear brighter in daylight than in low light. The eye is also able to adapt quickly from light to dark conditions. This process, which is called dark adaption, enables the eye to reach its maximum sensitivity in the dark after some 30 minutes.

However, this complex seeing mechanism, the eye, also has its limitations, and one of these is the 'blind spot'. This can be illustrated, using Fig. 12.1, as follows:

Holding the book at arm's length, cover or close the left eye and look at the cross with the right eye. Move the book slowly towards your eye. At some point the dot in the picture will disappear. This is caused by the blind spot.

This blind spot exists in both eyes and is caused by a receptor-free spot on the retina where the nerves and arteries leave the eye. Another limitation is that the binocular vision that we find so essential for distance judgement is limited to an arc of some 100° in front of us.

So how does the brain handle, analyse and process this 'perpetually changing flood' of information? Views about the way in which this is done have changed over the years. Barlow[2] describes these changes, starting with the late 1920s and the view that the brain acts as a store for acquired visual information. However, by the mid-1940s the brain was seen as interpreting that visual information to make working models. By the mid-1980s, this view had changed to one in which the brain was seen as using the stored information and models to reconstruct objects. This view of the way in which the brain uses visual information has continued into the early 1990s, with Zeki[1] writing that the brain does not just analyse the visual information that the eye presents, but uses that information to construct an internal 'visual world'. The brain, which undertakes this amazingly complex task, weighs, on average, about three pounds (1.4 kg) and contains some one hundred billion nerve cells or neurons. The area of the brain concerned with the processing and analysis of visual information is called the visual cortex, and is located towards the back of the brain. In order for the messages, which represent what we see, to reach this area of the brain they have to follow a complex pathway starting with the transformation of light into a nerve signal by specialized cells (rod and cone cells) in the retina of the eye. These cells send signals to a 'sorting office' in the mid-brain area (lateral geniculate nucleus) and this area retransmits the signal to specific and specialized cells in the visual cortex area.

As we saw earlier, views on how the brain analyses this information have changed. The introduction of positron emission tomography (PET) has enabled changes in blood flow within specific areas of the brain to be identified and measured while people are actually performing specific tasks. The power of PET as a research tool has enabled increasingly sophisticated and detailed views to be developed about the ways in which the brain processes visual information. For example, Zeki[1] expresses a view of these processes that includes the presence of four specialized processing systems which operate in parallel. These systems are said to decode and

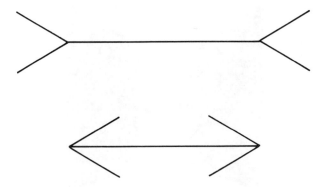

Figure 12.2   The Müller–Lyer illusion.
Source: N. J. Wade and M. Swanston, *Visual Perception*, Routledge. Reproduced by permission of Routledge, London.

analyse the information received from the retina and to be concerned with different character-istics of the visual information received. Two of these specialized systems are said to be concerned with form, one with motion and the fourth with colour. However, the level of integration or cross linkage between these systems is said to be considerable because they each contribute to the 'seen' or perceived image. The sophistication and power of these and other visual systems within the brain are considerable, with measured data handling capabilities of up to 500 data 'pulses' per second. Nevertheless, it is still possible for us to 'see' non-existent or illusory features of the seen objects. Examples of these illusions, which continue to be seen even when we know that they are false, are shown in Figs. 12.2, 12.3 and 12.4. The Müller–Lyer illusion (Fig. 12.2) consists of two parallel lines of equal length which appear to have different lengths because of the relative positions or orientation of the oblique lines or fins. The Kanizsa

Figure 12.3   Kanizsa triangle.
Source: H. Barlow and C. Blackmore (eds.), *Images and Understanding*, Chapter 20 (R. Gregory), Cambridge University Press. Reproduced by permission of Cambridge University Press, Cambridge.

Figure 12.4   Rubin's vase.
Source: H. Barlow and C. Blackmore (eds.), *Images and Understanding*, Chapter 20 (R. Gregory),
Cambridge University Press. Reproduced by permission of Cambridge University Press, Cambridge.

Triangle (Fig. 12.3) appears to have an upright triangle embedded within it, even though the interconnecting lines are missing. The object ambiguity of Rubin's vase (Fig. 12.4) leads us to see two facing human profiles – or a vase – and to be able to switch from one to the other by choice. Some of these illusions can be partially explained by the processes that the brain follows when handling the information provided by the retina of the eye. Gregory[3] suggests that these illusions are created by the brain in order to fit a 'model' that it creates from the information available. Coren[4] suggests that some of these illusions result from depth cues, while Gregory[5] notes that other illusions, which are generally those involving figures with gaps in them, occur when:

- The gaps are unlikely.
- The gaps form a likely object shape.

Whatever the future holds for the understanding of the role of the brain in the seeing process, it is evident that this process represents a key factor in the way we communicate. The following sections will look at the use of images in the communication process and examine what these images can contribute to the ways in which the manager communicates.

PICTOGRAPHS, PETROGLYPHS AND PICTOGRAMS

The use of images or representations of objects and people is a core aspect of the communication process. The first of these images was probably produced by the use of natural pigments on the surface of cave walls, and recorded aspects of the world in which the painter lived, such as animals and birds. The cave paintings at Lascaux in France, which were painted some 22 000 years ago, are examples of these initial efforts to communicate. The need to communicate by visual images appears to have been universal, and examples of rock paintings have also survived in North America and Australia. Nor were these images limited to the use of natural pigment. Petroglyphs, which were scratched or pecked into the rock surfaces of Arizona and Utah, show how much labour primitive people were prepared to invest in creating these images.

However, the use of images has not always been limited to representations of real animals or objects. By 4000 BC, i.e. some 6000 years ago, these images had changed into more stylized

Figure 12.5   Representational pictograms.

representations of objects, or pictographs, and had begun the process of change into what we now call written language. Around that time, the Sumerians were using some 2000 pictographs in their clay tablet writing, with each of these representing an object or person. The next step in the evolution of written language was taken when the shapes used began to represent the sounds of the spoken language rather than the shape of characteristics of an actual person or object. This cuneiform writing went on to develop an alphabet and to be used not only to record the sounds of the spoken language, but also to be used as an alternative medium for communication. However, some languages retained the use of petrographs. For example, Jean[6] states that the hieroglyphic language of the ancient Egyptians used:

- Pictographs to represent objects or people.
- Combinations of pictographs to represent ideas.
- Signs to represent sounds.
- Signs to represent class, rank or categories of objects or people.

The pictograph is also said to be still found in modern Chinese writing.

The use of images to instruct, influence or inform has also continued in other areas. Wildbur[7] uses the word 'pictogram' to describe the modern use of graphic images or emblems for information purposes in signs. Other examples of this include the use of 'icons' on computer screens associated with the use of a graphical user interface (GUI). All of these graphic images are designed to inform others and to do so without the use of language. They are generally most effective when they are used to represent the object depicted, as shown by the train, car and ship of Fig. 12.5.

However, not all pictograms are as clear and unambiguous as these examples. The greater the separation between what Wildbur terms the 'direct visual equivalence', or the conventional use of the object portrayed and the intended message, the more the risk of visual ambiguity or misinterpretation. This spectrum of this separation begins by the graphical image being used to represent the location in which the objects portrayed are used. Figure 12.6 shows the pictograms

Figure 12.6   Pictograms with low direct visual equivalence.

for a bar, barber shop and restaurant by showing the beer glass, comb and scissors, and knife, fork and plate, respectively.

The greater the separation of the pictogram from its 'direct visual equivalence', the greater the assumptions about the viewer's level of knowledge and, sometimes, even their culture. One example of this is the generally accepted use in Western society of the outlines of a man or a woman to denote the presence of single-sex toilet facilities in public places. This graphical image does little, by itself, to indicate what objects or service are to be obtained at that location, but the image is commonly accepted and understood in many public places. The image has, therefore, become symbolic of the service rather than portraying the service. These symbols may not be uniformly interpreted. These symbols, to be effective, require viewers to have been exposed to Western culture to the extent that they are capable through experience or guidance of interpreting the sign. However, the symbolism may be universal, as with the 'dove of peace' or the 'skull and crossbones', representing danger or poison. The context in which these symbols are used is also important. One example of this is the use of the wineglass symbol. On packaging this will indicate fragile contents and 'which way up' for the box or container. However, in an airport or in a public place this symbol is often used to indicate the presence of a wine bar.

The visual power of these pictograms is such that they are, as a way of communicating without the use of language, in very common use in our offices, factories, streets, airports and railway stations. In fact, they are used in any place where people congregate. Wildbur[7] states that these pictograms are often designed as a group or system of signs in order to ensure continuity in size, scale, colour and style. Examples of these sign systems would include the road signs in use on UK or mainland European roads or the signs used in American airports.

The use of graphic symbols is not, however, limited to these situations. Many organizations use visual symbols as trademarks or logos to ensure organizational visibility or to achieve increased levels of product recognition by customers. While some of these symbols have their roots in the histories of the organizations, others are increasingly abstract and symbolic and associated with what the organization perceives to be an acceptable or fashionable public image for itself. Familiar examples of these uses of graphic symbols will include the 'black horse' symbol associated with one of the major UK banks, the 'shell' symbol associated with a major oil company and the 'apple' symbol of a major US computer company. These corporate logos and symbols are often developed after considerable research and expenditure and used in and on the organization's letterheads, vehicles, buildings, products and advertisements: in short, at every point of contact between the organization and its customers.

NUMERICAL INFORMATION

Computer technology has made it possible for managers to have access to vast amounts of information from a considerable variety of sources. This technology has also enabled the creation of computer communication systems which exchange information at rates as high as several thousand binary digits per second. These networks can be global in their extent and will, in the future, be capable of handling information at rates in excess of one thousand, million binary digits per second. This continuing tidal wave of change is often referred to as the 'information revolution' or the 'information explosion', and its implications for the manager are considerable. However, many of the key managerial issues and challenges associated with the introduction and management of this information and its associated technology are beyond the scope of this book. Nevertheless, whatever the information technology or information system the manager uses, it will inevitably be characterized by an outpouring of numbers. This 'numbers

(a)

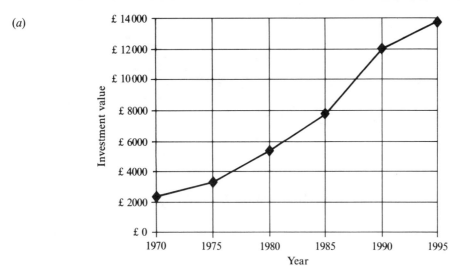

(b)

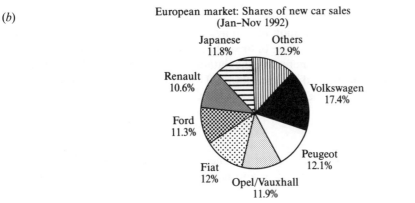

(c)

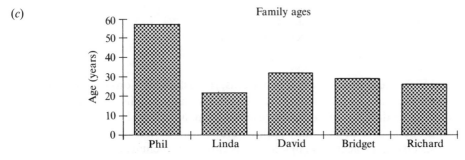

Figure 12.7   (a) Graph or time series diagram; (b) pie chart; (c) bar chart.
Source: (b) data taken from *Sunday Times*, 20 December 1992.

explosion' will consist of data which are often, though not always, the key to the manager's role. These data can be explained, displayed and made useful by the use of diagrams.

Tufte[8] reports that these diagrams had their beginnings in the work of mathematicians and economists in the late 18th century. These early examples of the diagrammatic representation of data included:

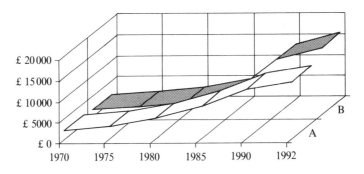

Figure 12.8   Three-dimensional graphs.

- Times series diagrams (graphs).
- Bar charts.
- Pie charts.

and these types of diagram remain in common use today (Fig. 12.7).

These diagrams are intended to make sense of or simplify complex tables or lists of numbers. They do so by displaying the patterns inherent in the data in a simple and visual form which is more easily recognized and remembered by the viewer. The specific characteristics and main types of these diagrams are described below.

Graphs (Figs. 12.7(a) and 12.8)

The graph is a form of diagram that we all learn to generate and use at school. It shows how changes in one aspect of the data are related to another aspect. The usual conventions about graphs are:

- The graph progresses from left to right and from base to top.
- The horizontal axis is used for the independent variable.

Graphs should enable the viewer to identify any patterns, trends, fluctuations or discontinuities in the displayed data. They can be used to compare sets of data and can also be shown, though with limitations in data readability, in three-dimensional form, as in Fig. 12.8.

Straightforward and simple as they may appear, graphs can be misread and also used to distort or misrepresent data. Typical ways in which this can occur include:

- *Omission of zero on the vertical scale*   With the *y*-axis scale starting at just below the lowest value, this can lead to ambiguity and uncertainty about the real magnitude of the changes represented.
- *Extension of vertical axis scale relative to horizontal axis scale*, which makes the peaks and troughs more obvious.
- *Use of non-linear or logarithmic scale without adequate annotation*, which will compress the graph but also mislead the viewer.
- *Use of different scales on right- and left-hand sides of graph in double line graph*, which will

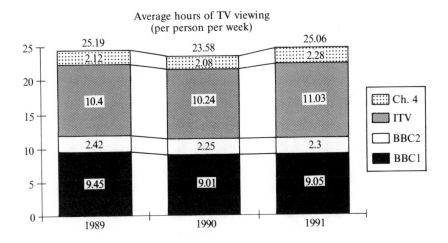

Figure 12.9   Bar chart.
Source: data taken from BFI Film and Television Handbook, 1993.

overcome the need for two separate graphs but which, even with careful annotation, can be misread by the viewer.

Bar charts (Figs. 12.7(c) and 12.9)

Bar charts consist of vertical or horizontal bars whose height or length corresponds to the value of the data represented. These bars are separated from each other, but each bar can be built up from a number of different data elements which add up to the total represented. These bars can also be transposed into a shape or shapes which reflect the nature or identity of the data represented as, for example, with the use of bars consisting of railway engines in a bar chart comparing the passenger miles for separate regions of British Rail. The bar chart can also be used in a three-dimensional form or to provide comparisons between data sets.

It is generally agreed that, in visual terms, the format of the bar chart has more flexibility than that of the graph.

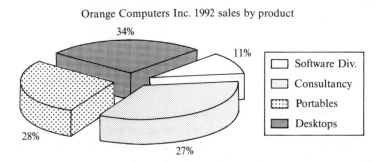

Figure 12.10   3D pie chart.

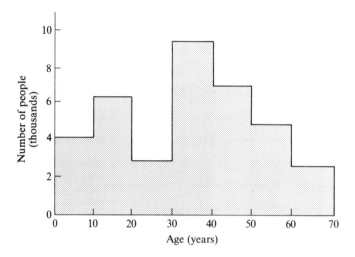

Figure 12.11   Histogram.

Pie charts (Figs. 12.7(b) and 12.10)

These charts are usually used to show the breakdown of a total for specified data. They are produced as subdivisions of a circle and can be shown in two or three dimensions. The calculations involved in their production, which involve conversion of original data into percentages and then into degrees, usually inhibit their use. However, the use of computer software often overcomes this limitation, and can also aid the creation of the pie chart diagram itself. The usual convention is to use percentages for each segment and to locate the annotation or legend within the segment. With small segments this can sometimes create difficulties, due to limited space for this annotation, but this can usually be overcome by location of the annotation outside the pie. A three-dimensional pie chart is shown in Fig. 12.10.

Histograms (Fig. 12.11)

Histograms are used to show frequency distributions and consist of vertical bars or columns whose area (rather than just the height) reflects the frequency of the variable. Unlike the bar chart, the columns of a histogram are not separated from each other, but form a continuous area representing the continuous variation of the factor represented on the horizontal or x-axis. Figure 12.11 shows a histogram for a population age distribution.

Stem and leaf plots

A stem and leaf plot does not convert the original data into representative shapes, lines or areas but arranges the data itself in such a way as to provide an indication of a pattern, or more generally, a distribution. This is illustrated, for the data shown in Table 12.1, by Fig. 12.12. One of the advantages of stem and leaf plots is that it preserves a significant part of the original data while providing a visual indication of the distribution pattern. The visual impact of these plots compares favourably with that provided by the histogram.

   The characteristics of these diagram types can be summarized as shown in Fig. 12.13.

Table 12.1 Staff salaries (data in tens of thousands)

J. Field	1.56	R. Walker	1.05	S. Smith	2.34
P. Preston	3.62	F. Gamble	2.34	J. MacCullough	5.28
D. Stenning	0.36	K. Watson	1.76	L. Hill	0.85
I. Williams	4.59	S. Thorpe	0.35	A. Woods	4.23

Tens of thousands

0	0.35	0.36	0.85
1	5.6	0.5	7.6
2	3.4	3.4	
3	6.2		
4	2.3	5.9	
5	2.8		

Figure 12.12 Staff salary stem and leaf plot.

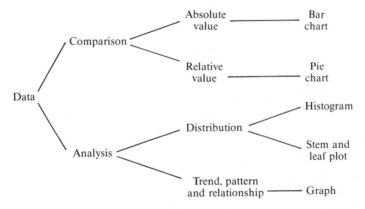

Figure 12.13 Diagram characteristics.

EXPLANATORY INFORMATION

Information that explains and informs plays an increasingly important role in all our lives, whether at work or at play. The effectiveness of the ways in which this type of information is communicated can be considerably enhanced by the use of visual images. The instruction cards for emergency procedures that many of us don't bother to read at the beginning of our aircraft flights and the DIY manuals which make it appear so easy to undertake the most complex of tasks are two common and successful examples of the use of visual images to explain and support the written word. However, there are many examples of sources of explanatory information which are less successful. These might include the speaker or lecturer who tries to explain a complex subject or concept with words alone or the user manual for the typical video recorder.

In the workplace, the speed and effectiveness with which managers train, inform, instruct and make presentations to their staff can make a considerable difference not only to the effectiveness of the staff but also to the business unit or team as a whole. So how can visual images help in these processes of training, informing and instructing?

In answering this question we shall need to look separately at the use of visual images to enhance communication via the medium of, firstly, the written word and secondly, the spoken word.

Written explanatory information

Part 3 of this book is concerned with how written language is used. This section will look at how written language can be reinforced and supplemented by the use of visual images. This does not come about by a random and indiscriminate use of these images, as, for example, occurs when procedure manuals or even company reports are littered with glossy colour photographs. The power and impact of these visual images will only become evident as a result of a careful and thoughtful integration of text and images. The result will be a document which the reader can quickly and fully understand. But that integration will only come about when the design and contents of the documentation reflect:

- *The use.*
  The intended purpose of the documentation can vary considerably, as can the actual usage. For example, is it intended as a reference manual or a 'how to' guide or a 'what to do if something goes wrong' guide, and do these intentions meet the *real* need of the user?
- *The user*
  The assumed and actual levels of user's skills and abilities should be, but often are not, at the same level. For example, the use of technical jargon can mislead or intimidate the user who has a limited technical background. Typical word processor users do not, for example, need to know that their equipment has a CPU, 2 Mbyte of RAM and the MS-DOS operating system. Yet many of the operating manuals for these systems assume that the user does need to know, with a resulting reduction in value to the user of the manual. Apart from these and other subtleties in the use of the English language, there may be more basic issues, such as whether the user is fluent in the use of this language or could be communicated with more effectively by the use of documentation in another language.
- *The environment of use*
  The documentation should also reflect the need and demands of the environment in which it will be used. For example, use in dirty or outdoor environments will dictate that the documentation is waterproof and can be wiped clean. Other work environments will require documents that are small enough to be carried in a pocket, capable of standing up without support on the top of a machine or a shelf or capable of being read in poor light conditions.

Failure to recognize and take account of any of the above can severely erode the effectiveness and usability of the explanatory documentation. However, let us assume that the manager has thought through these issues and is quite clear about for whom, for what purpose and in what environment the documentation is to be used. These decisions will influence the page size (A4, B3 or A3?), the material used (paper, card, laminated?), the number of pages (single or double-sided, printed card or multi-page book?) and the construction (loose-leaf, ring binder or bound?) of this documentation. They will also influence the type of visual images that you use. However, whatever the type of the images, they should only be present if they ensure that the

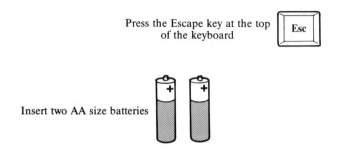

Figure 12.14   Text and diagrams.

reader's ability to understand the document is enhanced. This can be done by:

● Amplifying, confirming and supporting the written text.
● Taking the place of text to illustrate complex actions or ideas.

Examples of how to amplify, confirm and support the written text are shown in Fig. 12.14.

A well-known and familiar example of the substitution of image for text is contained on the familiar airline emergency procedure instruction cards, which contain diagrams of people exiting the cabin, putting on life-jackets and getting into inflatable boats, all in a clear diagrammatic form which presumes little about the reader's ability to understand a particular language.

The sources of visual images for written documentation include:

● *Photographs*
These will often need to be taken with the end usage in mind in order to provide clear informative images. They can be rendered or tonally adjusted in order to ensure that attention is focused on the relevant portion of the image. It is also possible to scan photographs into the computer in which the document is being word processed and to adjust and manipulate that image before its insertion into the final document.
● *Line drawings*
These are generally easy to produce. They can also be accessed, for computer produced documents, from libraries of 'clip art'. As they do not contain tones or light and shade they are easier to produce and print than photographs and can be as detailed as required. For example, the use of 'exploded' views for assemblies can show the components involved as well as how they fit together. The process of designing line drawing visual material to support written text in an international news magazine is described and illustrated by Holmes.[9]

Spoken explanatory information

The use of visual material to supplement and support the spoken word generally occurs during that flexible and effective communication process which is called presenting. The process of presenting is examined in some detail in Chapter 7, and this section will examine how visual images can be used to enhance that process. There are very few presentations that cannot be improved – even transformed – by the use of visual aids. These visual images can, if designed, produced and used well, portray, quickly and effectively, concepts and information that are difficult, if not impossible, to portray verbally. Visual images also save time, add interest and create impact. But most importantly, visual images are remembered by the audience far longer than they remember words. The design, creation and use of these images, which can be in colour or monochrome, is not, however, an 'add-on' or optional extra. The images used need to be chosen or created as an integral part of the process of preparing the presentation. As indicated in Chapter 7, the purposes of these visual aids can include:

- Illustrating a point.
- Showing a complex diagram or graph.
- Explaining a complex process or sequence.
- Linking presentation sections.
- Posing a question.
- Summarizing points and proposals.
- Saving words.

These visual aids should be created in such a way as to ensure that they:

- Consist of text or images that can be read or seen at the limits of the audience.
- Do not contain too many words or too much information.
- Are comprehensible.
- Gain the audience's attention, i.e. they have impact.

The equipment involved in the use of visual aids is readily available, very versatile and easy to use. The types of generally available equipment are:

- Overhead projectors.
- Slide projectors.
- Flip chart boards.
- Videos and films.

However, the use of more than two of these types in any one presentation will serve only to confuse the audience and make the presenter's job more difficult. The core of the presentation material should be presented using either an overhead projector, a slide projector or flip charts. These can be supplemented by video or film source material. However, film and video can often require the room to be darkened and shift the audience's attention away from the presenter. Consequently, the presenter will, at the end of the film or video, need to reclaim the attention of

Table 12.2   Simple rules for overhead projector transparencies

- Maximum lines per transparency = 6–7.
- Maximum words per line = 5–6.
- Minimum clear edge margin = 1″ (2.5 cm).
- Minimum letter height = 0.25″ (7 mm).
- Justify text and images but be consistent.
- Be consistent in text font and format.
- Use landscape layout.
- Use top 70 per cent of transparency area.
- Use darker colours for impact.

the audience and to remind them of the primary purpose of the presentation. All of this takes time and is generally only justifiable when:

- The material in the video or film is required to illustrate some particularly complex information.
- The moving image adds significantly to the audience's understanding.

Simple rules for the design and format of overhead projector transparencies are given in Table 12.2, and Jay[10] writes about the design and use of slides. The creation and design of both of these media can be considerably facilitated by the use of computer software. Figure 12.15 shows part of a 'storyboard' generated by the use of a typical presentation software package. This contains size-reduced copies of the slides or overhead projector transparencies in the numbered sequence of presentation and, apart from facilitating the design of the sequence of the presentation, can also serve as a post presentation handout. The use of flip charts as a presentation medium is common and inexpensive. However, the skill demands placed upon the presenter, during preparation, can be considerable. The information presented, in either visual or textual format, will almost always have to be created by hand. Consequently, unless the manager is trained as a graphic artist or prepared to hire one, he or she and the audience must be prepared to accept limits to the quality of the presentation material and particularly the visual images.

The key issues in the use of visual aids in presentations are described by a number of writers, including Jay,[11] Janner[12] and Zimmer,[13] as being those related to their simplicity and impact.

There should be little doubt that the use of visual aids can make a significant contribution to the quality and effectiveness of presentations, which are such an important aspect of the manager's role.

CONCLUSION

The use of images to represent people, objects or animals is a process which has been in use since the earliest days of human history, and began the process of written communication. The ability of the eye to see objects is considerable, and provides most of the information that we receive from our environment. These visual images can be used to:

- Represent objects and services in the form of pictograms.
- Represent numerical information in the form of graphs, pie and bar charts, histograms and stem and leaf plots.
- Amplify, confirm and support written language.
- Take the place of written language.
- Illustrate, explain, link, summarize and take the place of spoken language.

EXERCISES

1. Look around your own workplace and see how many pictograms you can identify.
2. Working in groups and using the same numerical data, design and create as many different diagrams as you can to illustrate, make sense of or simplify that data.
3. Identify two examples of complex and/or unclear written communication and then show how these could have been improved or supported by the use of visual images.
4. Prepare a storyboard about the contents of this chapter using not more than 10 OHTs or slides.

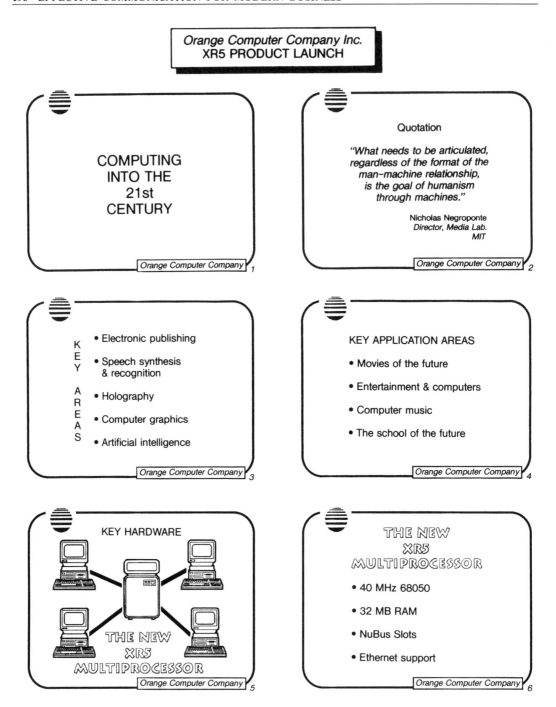

Figure 12.15 Presentation storyboard.

REFERENCES

1. Zeki, S., The visual image in mind and brain, *Scientific American*, **267**(3), September 1992.
2. Barlow, H., What does the brain see? How does it understand?, in Barlow, H., Blakemore, C. and Weston-Smith, M. (eds.), *Images and Understanding*, Cambridge University Press, Cambridge, 1990.
3. Gregory, R. L., Cognitive contours, *Nature*, **238**, 1972, pp. 51–2.
4. Coren, S., Subjective contours and apparent depth, *Psychological Review*, **79**(4), 1972, pp. 359–67.
5. Gregory, R. L., How do we interpret images?, in Barlow, H., Blakemore, C. and Weston-Smith, M. (eds.), *Images and Understanding*, Cambridge University Press, Cambridge, 1990.
6. Jean G., *Writing: The Story of Alphabets and Scripts*, Thames & Hudson, London, 1992.
7. Wildbur, P., *Information Graphics*, Trefoil Publications, London, 1989.
8. Tufte, E. R., *The Visual Display of Quantitative Information*, Graphics Press, Cheshire CT, 1983.
9. Holmes, N., *Designing Pictorial Symbols*, Watson-Guptill Publications, New York, 1990.
10. Jay, A., *Slide Rules*, Video Arts, London, 1988.
11. Jay, A., *Making Your Case*, Video Arts, London, 1982.
12. Janner, G., *Janner on Presentation*, Century Hutchinson, London, 1989.
13. Zimmer, M., *Effective Presentations*, Sphere, London, 1987.

SUGGESTED FURTHER READING

'Some books are to be tasted, others to be swallowed, and some to be chewed and digested.'
Francis Bacon

Argyle, M., *Bodily Communication*, Routledge, London, 1988.

Back, K., Back, K. and Bates, T., *Assertiveness at Work*, McGraw-Hill, London, 1991.

Belbin, M. R., *Management Teams: Why They Succeed or Fail*, Butterworth-Heinemann, Oxford, 1981.

Berne, E., *What Do You Say After You Say Hello?*, Corgi, London, 1975.

Cooper, B. M., *Writing Technical Reports*, Penguin, London, 1964.

Crystal, D., *Linguistics*, Penguin Books, London, 1985.

Egan, G., *The Skilled Helper: A Systematic Approach to Effective Helping*, Brooks/Cole, Belmont CA, 1990.

Gowers, Sir E., Greenbaum, S. and Whitcut, J., *The Complete Plain Words*, Penguin, London, 1986.

Handy, C. B., *Understanding Organisations*, Penguin, London, 1985.

Hargie, O. (ed.), *A Handbook of Communication Skills*, Routledge, London, 1986.

Harris, T. A., *I'm OK – You're OK*, Pan, London, 1973.

Hodgson, P. and Hodgson, J., *Effective Meetings*, Century, London, 1992.

Janner, G., *Janner on Presentation*, Century Hutchinson, London, 1989.

Jenkins, S. (ed.), *The Times Guide to English Style and Usage*, Times Books, London, 1992.

Kakabadse, A., Ludlow, R. and Vinnicombe, S., *Working in Organisations*, Penguin, London, 1988.

Leech, G., *Semantics: The Study of Meaning*, Penguin, London, 1981.

Millar, R., Crute, V. and Hargie, O., *Professional Interviewing*, Routledge, London, 1992.

Morgan, G., *Images of Organization*, Sage, London, 1986.

Morris, D., *ManWatching: A Field Guide to Human Behaviour*, Grafton Books, London, 1978.

Pedler, M., Burgoyne, J. and Boydell, T., *The Learning Company: A Strategy for Sustainable Development*, McGraw-Hill, London, 1991.

Sacks, O., *Seeing Voices: A Journey into the World of the Deaf*, Pan, London, 1991.

Senge, P., *The Fifth Dimension*, Century, London, 1992.

Tannen, D., *That's Not What I Meant!*, Virago, London, 1992.

Tannen, D., *You Just Don't Understand: Men and Women in Conversation*, Virago, London, 1992.

Trudgill, P., *Sociolinguistics: An Introduction to Language and Society*, Penguin, London, 1983.

Wildbur, P., *Information Graphics: A Survey of Typographic, Diagrammatic and Cartographic Communication*, Trefoil Publications, London, 1989.

3M Meeting Management Team, *How to Run Better Business Meetings*, McGraw-Hill, London, 1987.

INDEX